Lying Wonders, Strangest Things

Michael Harold Brown

Spirit Daily Publishing
www.spiritdaily.com
11 Walter Place
Palm Coast, Florida 32164

The publisher recognizes and accepts that the final authority regarding the apparitions in the Catholic Church rests with the Holy See of Rome, to whose judgment we willingly submit.

—*The Publisher*

For additional copies, write:
Spirit Daily Publishing
11 Walter Place
Palm Coast, Florida 32164

or contact: www.spiritdaily.com

ISBN 978-0-578-49804-1

Printed in the United States of America   First Edition

To Chris, who shared my fascination with the arcane.

Acknowledgements

I'd like to thank my wife Lisa for her tremendous help in this and all my books. Her advice, encouragement, and very sharp eye were essential. My love always! Crucial, too, was the exceptional work of Judy Berlinski. No one could have a more competent, thorough editor. I'd also like to acknowledge Steven Katona for the striking cover.

Table of Contents

contents

contents

Preface

We live at a time of unprecedented supernatural mani-festations or more correctly put, spiritual invasion. A full-scale assault is at hand, and it takes many forms. Some of it is subtle; some is beyond belief (literally); much is part of a massive deception. For unloosed from what Scripture refers to as the netherworld, Hades, or sheol (*Psalms*: 88:3) are legions of spirits—demonic entities—that take surprising, astounding forms, so prevalent that occasionally it finds its way onto the news, television, movie screens, and social media.

Some of the enigmas, the phenomena, the mysteries, are widely known—though, for the most part, the ultimate ones have fallen by the wayside, buried, if present at all, in the deeper recesses of the internet. They've been rejected or obscured by a scientism (and skeptical theology) that excludes anything outside current (and let me emphasize, *current*) understanding. As soon as scientists, priests, and ministers can't explain something, they too often set it aside so as not to upset notions they hold dear.

Yet many such phenomena have profound spiritual implications and must be confronted by vigilant Christians as such. Fascinating they are. But in many ways—as you will see, bizarre and deceptive ways—they can be a threat. I'll let you make the discernment.

Sometimes they are mere oddities, truly, the "strangest" of things. Sometimes they're glimpses of pitched spiritual warfare. Mostly they demonstrate a powerful spiritual dynamic around us all. There are "hauntings." There are curses. There are miracles, prophecy. There are "coincidences" that indicate beyond any question that the supernatural overarches all things physical, even if we can't touch or see it—*normally* can't see it, for in the stories that follow are cases where the paranormal certainly does make itself seen. In the real "twilight zone," in the real "x-files," is everything from apparitions to unexplained lights in the sky, from strange creatures to people who have disappeared—actual, witnessed vanishings. Half a century ago a broadcaster penned a massive bestseller called *Stranger Than Science*. He had a secular take on such curiosities. I update that work, but with yet stranger accounts, and from a Christian perspective.

To many—even, in some cases, to exorcists—such topics have been relegated to the dustbin of superstition: Nothing is accepted that academics can't study in a microscope, telescope, or bell jar. This goes to our need to feel in control, when in fact humans are anything *but* in control when it comes to life's greatest mysteries. The incidents you are about to encounter prove out a philosopher named J. D. S. Haldane, who famously said the "universe is not only stranger than we imagine, but stranger than we *can* imagine."

While there is certainly skullduggery (especially with photographs, in the time of Photoshop, as well as internet dupery, in this era of "fake news"), I know after fifty years of studying and investigating such mysteries as a journalist, for the past couple decades as a Christian journalist, and having spoken at hundreds of churches (meeting tens of thousands of faithful) that fantastic oddities exist in great and sometimes startling abundance, and are proliferating. In the accounts that follow are examples of how the supernatural can manifest in the strangest and sometimes most deceptive ways (as wonders of Creation, on the one hand, but too often as "lying wonders"—*2 Thessalonians* 2:9).

I leave it to you to connect the dots. We live in a time that is upside-down, a time of great deception, a time when what had been invisible—including the netherworld—is becoming manifest, a time in which we must be cautious about where our curiosity leads, a time in which the veil thins. Many such instances are included in the following pages—"legends" that may be more than legends, and more precarious. Can the devil haunt and taunt an entire area? Are certain locales like portals for the "shades"? How is sighting a "bigfoot" or remnant dinosaur (such as the one alleged at Loch Ness) similar to a UFO—and spirits at a séance? Might the enemy even be behind certain "new" and very strange ailments? Could it be that there are links—dark ones—between phenomena that for centuries, even millennia, have been treated as unrelated? Let us be deceived and perplexed no longer.

What I have collected are the most astonishing examples of people and things and circumstances, preternatural or natural, mundane and supernormal—not all menacing (some simply amazing, and giving God glory), but too many exactly that. It is truly a volatile time. I don't pretend to have heard *every* unusual account; every time I hear of a new case of possession, it seems more powerful than the last. Schoolgirls in Africa who are suddenly attacked by evil forces? A Bible in the United States exuding oil? Strange objects that fall from the sky? Secret prophecies? Mysterious strangers?

Coincidence that *can't* be mere . . . coincidence?

You have seen examples of some of the above—but perhaps not the ultimate examples.

What follows are the most striking cases of various phenomena, a new one in each chapter. Call this a compilation of oddities, mysteries, phenomena, and extremes that sail beyond what we can fathom, beyond our reality, our understanding, if we are not with Jesus. Call this, therefore, a warning (and as such, a spur to prayer). Call what follows vignettes from the edge of what we call reality.

Michael H. Brown
Palm Coast, Florida
May 9, 2019

1

Into Thin Air

Every now and then are reports of folks who suddenly—inexplicably—disappear. This isn't about Jimmy Hoffa, or Amelia Earhart. Amelia probably crashed. Hoffa may be in a landfill. When hikers or hunters go missing, there are rational explanations.

One speaks here of supernatural absence: cases where folks seem to have strutted off the face of our planet, whether for a few minutes . . . or for good.

In Transylvania, Romania, is a small forest called Hoia Baciu that some think transgresses time, known too for unusual lights, a strange black fog, and eerily curved trees. Just a square-mile in size, it's named for a shepherd who entered and, along with his entire flock (two hundred strong), was never seen again.

The same fate, it is alleged, has befallen others—including a five-year-old girl who emerged from the woods *years* after getting lost, wearing the same unsullied clothes—and with no recall of what happened.

Some believe "UFOs" are to blame. Others theorize the existence of time warps. Is it demonic, a portal to unseen "elsewheres," or just plain urban legend?

No fiction is what happened to a Filipino named Cornelio Closa Jr. in 1952.

Thirteen at the time, Cornelio was walking with a friend named Rudolfo Carmine across a large field on the way home from school in Manila when he suddenly started to point toward a spot in front of a brick wall.

Cornelio had stopped in his tracks. His eyes were "almost bulging out of their sockets," said the friend. He said he saw a girl in a long white dress, beckoning him. He said she was gorgeous. "I looked," said Rudolfo. "I looked several times. As he approached the wall I saw him put out his hand and as he did I swear I saw Cornelio disappear from sight."

That was a temporary disappearance, but immediately after, Cornelio became what can be most charitably called a problem child. Once amiable, he was now sullen, antagonistic, and angry, fighting with his parents, pushing away food, and snarling, said his father, "like an animal." With each passing day, young Cornelio became less manageable. "I was losing control," his mother said. He sat in a corner of the room, brooding and staring into space. He refused to study. His parents were at a complete loss. "I was getting used to this kind of behavior," said his mother, "until one evening when he looked particularly flushed and sick and with the doors and windows in the house locked, he vanished into thin air in front of my eyes. I was horrified."

The boy kept appearing and disappearing. No one wanted to be near him. He hid objects from his parents and stole money from them. He leapt at his father in a wild, uncontrolled manner, smashing dishes. Doctors at a national mental center had no answers, and in desperation Cornelio Sr. brought his son to a juvenile correction facility—but so disruptive was the boy that he was tied to his bed and finally sent back home, where his parents resigned themselves to living with a "monster."

There were disturbances at school—including fisticuffs, which, again, were totally out of character. He had been a "quiet boy," said his teacher. Now he was such "a nuisance" that she wished he didn't attend her class. He battled with others at the slightest provocation. "The strange thing about these fights was that Cornelio, as small as he was, would take on three or four boys larger than him and together the larger boys could not hold him down," the teacher, a Mrs. Agospi, told a film crew. "He had superhuman strength."

A few days after the fight—when the boy was called to the front of his class to give a presentation—"he went to the blackboard," testified his teacher, "stood there for a few moments, and then simply . . . evaporated."

He was there and then he was not—solid and then transparent and invisible.

In front of an entire classroom.

The teacher immediately resigned.

The events caused Cornelio to "laugh and laugh," she recalled, "a hideous kind of laughter. It didn't belong to a boy. In fact it didn't belong to a human being." Sleep became impossible. He said it felt as if his clothes were burning. When he opened his eyes, he would see the girl, enticing him to come. Touching her hand, he felt like he was floating in the air. "Many times [she and I] would go to the movies," claimed the boy, "and I knew no one could see us. Other times we would go to a restaurant, and when the time came to pay, we would conveniently disappear."

If it was just one witness, one would hurriedly brush it off—blame it on too much fiction (or too much *something*). But that wasn't the case.

"He was tormented by an alien entity for more than a year," said a well-known evangelical missionary, Dr. Lester Sumrall, who personally talked to the teacher and visited Cornelio's home. "This spirit would cause him to disappear from a classroom at school or from his home. Because of his disappearing from the classroom, the boy's schoolteacher had a nervous breakdown and never recuperated sufficiently to teach again. Cornelio's father would nail the doors and windows shut, but Cornelio did not need natural openings to get in and out of the house. The story of the invisible boy is true. It is a story to which I was intimately related. I hired people to check out the validity of this story, including policemen who took signed affidavits about it. We investigated the whole matter very carefully. We didn't want the slightest possibility of falsehood or misrepresentation in it. It is surely one of the most well-documented cases in our files and interesting to note that a religious leader, Reverend H. A. Baker, traveled from the United States to the Philippines to verify the facts of this case. They were unbelievable to him. But after talking to all of those involved and establishing the facts, he wrote me and said: 'Unbeknown to you, I visited the Philippines. I contacted Cornelio, the schoolteacher, the parents, and their neighbors. I discovered that it is absolutely true . . .'

"This went on for one entire year, with the situation becoming worse and worse," Sumrall added. "The parents told me that the whole family would be in the front of their home and their children would be down on the floor playing. Suddenly, with everybody looking, Cornelio would just disappear. The other children would start coughing and vomiting because of the stench he would leave behind. When he disappeared, he might be gone for two days or more. Then he might just appear again in bed, asleep. He would come in the house without using windows or doors. He would just suddenly *be* there."

A Methodist preacher who tried to help told Sumrall that the child once "disappeared right out of my hands."

But prayed over by Sumrall at a service—"Lord Jesus, we plead Thy holy blood; be free in Jesus Christ's Name!"—it came, we are told, to a screeching halt. The entity morphed into an angry, ugly being. But no more missing Cornelio, ever again.

It was the beautiful "girl" who disappeared.

2

Lights in a Woodland

Was it an extraterrestrial landing site?

A veil between dimensions?

Or just plain spiritual deception?

One speaks here of Rendlesham Forest in England: Around the witching hour of three a.m. the day after Christmas in 1980, a security patrol from the nearby U.S. Bentwater-Woodbridge air base saw a light descending into the woodland—one illuminating trees with brilliant white light, as well as a red light on top and several on its side or bottom. The two security guards summoned superiors who sent three officials to investigate, men who in their turn reported something with colored lights indeed had landed—had been there—in the nearby woods. Two of the three took to their feet, approaching what they described as a metallic craft nine feet wide and six feet high, with a surface smooth as glass. While wildlife amid the broadleaf trees and conifers were in nothing less than a tizzy—clearly, a cacophony of discomfort—it quieted as they drew within fifty and then twenty meters of the object, a prickly static pervading the air as they lost radio contact with the third investigator. The object was shiny, black, and shaped like a triangle—one of three lights that had been spotted. No seams, no rivets. No sign of propulsion. Approaching yet closer, and gliding his hand over the exterior, Sergeant Jim Penniston felt several raised symbols he described as resembling hieroglyphics. That led the craft to turn all the brighter, frightening Penniston and causing him to assume a defensive crouch. The object lifted a few feet, negotiated between the vegetation, rose to treetop level, and was gone, he recounted, in a blink. When they got back to the base, they were debriefed and told to forget about it. But forget they could not—returning to the spot and finding three indentations punched into the heath as if by a large tripod. There was a forty-five-minute span of time missing—that Penniston could not account for.

Soon after Deputy Base Commander Charles Halt went to the scene carrying an AN/PDR-27 radiation meter and saw it himself flashing lights across a field, lights that seemed to wink at him. The most brilliant hovered for more than two hours.

"I see it too . . . it's back again . . . it's coming this way . . . there's no doubt about it . . . this is weird . . . it looks like an eye winking at you . . . it almost burns your eyes . . . he's coming toward us now . . . now we're observing what appears to be a beam coming down to the ground . . . one object still hovering over Woodbridge base . . . beaming down," said a transcript of Deputy Commander Halt's recording. *"I have confirmation that (radar operators) saw the object go across their sixty-mile scope in two or three seconds, thousands of miles an hour, he came back across their scope again, stopped near the water tower, they watched it and observed it go into the forest where we were.*

"Whatever was there was clearly under intelligent control."

As his men scrambled about, his recorder logged him saying, *"Pieces of [the light] are shooting off . . . This is unreal."*

As the *Telegraph* in London noted, "Things were about to get even stranger, though. This red light suddenly exploded and a craft appeared on the forest floor," as if teleported. It moved "in a downward arc, so fast. [It] stopped and hovered about twenty feet off the ground," said another witness, soldier Larry Warren. "It was the size of a basketball, [an] American basketball. [It was] self-illuminated, not quite red, yet that's the closest I can describe it." According to Warren, it had "no windows, no markings, no flag or country of origin. Nothing. You could hardly look at it head on, and if you looked at it through the side of your peripheral vision you'd get a shape of it . . . there it was, clear as a bell." Obviously, a number of various . . . devices.

Radioing back, Warren and another sergeant, Adrian Bustinza, were asked to retreat by a senior official. Witnesses claim when Wing Commander Gordon Williams approached the craft, he encountered an alien being that had "what looked like eyes, facial features, bright clothing, and some other device." Rather than communication, there was a "silent stand-off."

Then, a flash. It all but blinded him—hurt his eyes. His skin was prickly, like there was an electrical charge. He claimed a light emanated from the "craft" like a bubble and split into three lights, each with the form of a three-foot entity inside.

At one point he was within five feet of the "object," taking radiological readings.

Electrical equipment (especially spotlights known as "light alls") blinked on and off. There was static on radios. No protocol for how to handle this!

Right off, the commander made it clear that the matter should be kept quiet. Personnel from the Office of Naval Intelligence arrived, likewise debriefed the men (in all, from what I can tell, *sixty* had seen strange lights) and once more made it clear they were to say . . . nothing.

Lest we immediately dismiss so extravagant an assertion, it helps to know that the Supreme Commander of the U.S. Air Force in Europe, Lieutenant General Charles A. Gabriel, soon arrived, and that details of the incident itself came to us when United Kingdom military files were released in 2015.

At the eastern edge of the forest had been concrete bunkers that once housed nuclear weapons. A serious place. A serious mystery. Halt said a craft had hovered over bunkers and beamed a light into them. He felt they were time travelers from the future.

Traumatized, one serviceman later committed suicide . . .

The enigma only deepens when one takes stock of the forest itself. For strange things, it seems—occult happenings—were hardly new to it. In decades and centuries past, those same conifers and heath wood and leaf mold had entertained witches and druids performing coven rituals under cover of night, and at Bentwaters was the legend of the ghostly "Lady Without a Face."

There were the wraiths. There were creatures—dogs with incendiary eyes. There was what they called the "shug monkey" ("shug" old English for *scucca* . . . which translates as "demon").

It was said that "hairy wild men" roamed the turf—sort of a British yeti.

Those had been recorded as far back in the 1100s—by an abbot from Coggershall who wrote in what is known as *Chronicon Anglicanum* about the remarkable capture in nearby Orford of a primitive caveman-like entity. In 1983, it was reported a couple was walking in the area when they came upon a phantom, dog-like creature, though with the movements of a cat, plus a mournful, uncanny expression: a creature that soon lost physical form, turning translucent.

And so, what went on—what goes on—here?

We are not likely to ever know.

There were strange owls, ghostly monks, showers of stones. The devil can take many forms.

And the dogs: when they disappeared, it was like UFOs—instantly, into nothingness, but leaving behind the odor of brimstone.

3

The No-Tell Hotel

What *is* it about the Hotel Cecil in Los Angeles?

Suicides, murders, and just plain strangeness.

An aura of darkness.

There are secrets.

Take the case of Elisa Lam, a 21-year-old from Vancouver, British Columbia, who "accidentally" drowned in the hotel's rooftop water tank in February of 2013 with no one able to explain how.

She was found when hotel guests reported a drop in water pressure and tap water that bore a foul taste and was dark—almost black.

Elisa, whose Cantonese name was Lam Yo Yi, had a history, no question, of mental distress: bipolar disorder . . . had even taken medication for it. And though she was in a cheerful mood shortly before the incident, she had been observed acting oddly in days leading up to it.

But there seemed no way she could have found her way into that tank herself. The lid would have been all but impossible to lift and close from inside. There wasn't even a ladder for Elisa to have climbed up. And her clothes were found floating in the dark watery grave . . .

A "very, very strange incident," remarked Sergeant Rudy Lopez of the L.A.P.D., employing understatement.

When police picked apart video from an elevator security camera, it only deepened the enigma, for it showed Elisa doing unusual things, behaving very oddly, at one point pressing all the buttons and waiting somewhat urgently for the door to shut. Her behavior was especially odd—and desperate—when, after an inexplicably long delay, the door remained open, and all but panicked, she stabbed at the buttons again, furtively peering out of the elevator into the hall, as if afraid someone or something might be pursuing her. She seemed alternately to be hiding from, looking for, possessed by, and fleeing from something. Stepped out, stepped back in, peered again around a corner—seemed to be speaking and gesturing to someone. Yet, there was nothing and no one in the hall.

To her great agitation, the elevator still wouldn't move. It was as if it refused to budge while she was in it. At one point, it looked like she was practicing martial arts against an unseen opponent. She bowed forward, in a stance. Her arms flailed. It wasn't until three minutes into the video that the door finally closed, and by then, Elisa had exited and was out of view in the hall as the elevator doors mysteriously opened again, and then closed, now with no passenger, just a vaporous black blotch near the buttons.

Foul play?

Psychomancy?

Well on its way to decomposition, Elisa's body was discovered two weeks later.

Was the macabre nature of the hotel *itself* to blame? Were spirits attached to it?

Constructed near L.A.'s skid row in the Roaring Twenties, the Cecil had been designed for opulence (a marble lobby), but then came the Depression, which turned it into a fleabag. "Low daily, weekly rates, 700 rooms," a sign painted on one side of the Beaux Arts structure soon said. Eventually, the 14-story hotel became known as "The Suicide." At least eleven took their lives there. A place of pills, leaps from windows, and ransacked rooms. There were also rapes and murders. In fact, the Cecil had drawn guests like Richard Ramirez, the infamous "nightstalker," who was said to have disposed bloody clothes in the hotel dumpster, and another serial killer, Jack Unterweger. Guests regularly reported dark figures in their rooms, or waking to the sensation of someone or something tugging at the sheets. A photograph taken by a local resident showed what appeared to be a spectral figure outside a window on the fourth floor. Did they have Gideon bibles in this place?

The Cecil had an "evil twin" in London, a hotel of the same name with a built-in Masonic hall, said to have been a favorite place for those worshiping Lucifer. It was at this hotel that the most famous and perhaps most diabolic occultist in modern history, Aleister Crowley, later credited with founding the Church of Satan, stayed. But was that really in any way related?

Strangest of all, the Lam case bore eerie similarities to a murder movie called *Dark Water*, about a woman named Dahlia whose daughter—Cecilia!—talks to an imaginary friend named Natasha . . . in an elevator. Though set in New York, the movie has a scene whereby water is dripping from the ceiling and then pouring from the taps—blackened water that led Dahlia to the roof, where she finds the body of a real woman named Natasha . . . in the apartment building's water tank.

Natasha was wearing a red hoodie.

The movie was released in 2006—seven years before Elisa's death.

Elisa had likewise worn a red hoodie.

A second movie, *Black Dahlia* (note the name Dahlia), also bears mention. It was based on L.A.'s most famous unsolved homicide, the sensational, gruesome, and perhaps ritualistic murder in 1947 of an aspiring actress named Elizabeth Short in Los Angeles, a woman who was cut in half, bled dry, and cleansed with chlorine. More than seven hundred investigators combed the city to solve the extraordinary case. All failed. It remains an open case, and also macabre: Noted a review in *The New York Times*, "one fantastic cinematic shot moves up from street level to peer over the roof of a building . . . where some crows are ominously cawing" . . .

Who was Short? What was she doing, at the tender age of 24?

And the Cecil: unusual it seemed, the folks who took overdoses at the hotel, committed crimes, or leapt from its windows, one bouncing off the marquee, another landing on (and killing) a pedestrian.

Some believe that Elizabeth Short—Black Dahlia—had frequented and stopped for a drink at or at least was seen near the Cecil, which was seven miles away . . . back in 1947 . . . in the days or hours before her body was found. But the greatest mystery: What evil originally occurred, what was it about this building or land, or part of L.A., that caused this place to become . . . a magnet for evil?

4

The Israeli Who Flew Through Time and Space

In 2018, a fellow with a strange device that measures electrical signals found, using a cable, that a spot near Las Vegas indicated what he perceived as a sudden micro-change in the rate of time. He had never seen this before. With no little bravado, he went over national airwaves to proclaim the spot, not far from the Nevada military installation known as Area 51, a "time warp."

Whether there is any credibility to such a claim, there are other strange—and perhaps aberrant—places.

In Massachusetts is the "Bridgewater Triangle": like Rendlesham, a hotbed of UFOs, ghosts, and creature reports—along with vanishings.

I don't recommend visiting; when it comes to the occult, curiosity can kill the cat. It is good to know it exists and where it is and then . . . move on.

There are also the opposite: strange *appearances.*

A fellow from New Zealand shows up, for example, in Manhattan—with no idea how he got there, and no financial means of having done so!

In Germany, two youngsters simply appeared one day in a small town, acting baffled by our world, which . . . seemed entirely new to them.

Tall tales?

There are Himalayan gurus who supposedly teleport among the mountains and Islamic holy men who while praying in one place were transferred to a distant city like Mecca or Medina, according to Islamic and Jewish legend.

There was a clairvoyant named Nicholas Williams. Through no physical means he could put his arm—it was insisted—into a wall and pull it out, arm and wall intact.

Was the process governed by information fields in some way, or a new type of quantum wave field limits?

Two Italian boys named Pansini (plagued by poltergeist activity) vanished from their home in 1901 and were found a half an hour later in a Capuchin convent thirty miles away (this before cars). After another disappearance, the boys were located miles out to sea on a fishing boat. One of them, Alfredo, fell into a trance and suddenly could speak Latin, French, and Greek.

Does it reflect back to a prophecy given to a Christian at LaSalette in France in 1846 that, warning of coming times, said, *"People will be transported from one place to another by evil spirits . . ."*

On perhaps the good side: one can cite Ken Peters, a "born-again" Christian who was awakened in the middle of the night at a parsonage when a bright light came into the room—so brilliant he thought it was sunrise. "The bright light shined in the room and I began to look and I said who's there and the light peeled back and there was Jesus with this light around Him and He began to speak to me," claimed Peters, "and the next thing I know, I'm standing on a mountain in what seemed a South American country. At the top of this mountain was a huge statue of Jesus with His arms stretched out."

When Peters later saw a clip on television of the famous "Christ the Redeemer" statue in Rio de Janeiro, he identified that as exactly where he had "been"—somehow been transported from the U.S. to Brazil! Or so it seemed . . .

In this regard, nothing is stranger than what happened to former Israeli paratrooper Uri Geller—the famous "psychic" who's largely viewed as a fraud but who, to the contrary, according to a CIA document declassified in 2017, "has demonstrated his paranormal perceptual ability in a convincing and unambiguous manner." That document referred to secret government experiments during the 1970s—research that led to meetings between Geller and government luminaries like Israeli Prime Minister Benjamin Netanyahu, U.S. President Jimmy Carter, and later Secretary of State, Henry Kissinger (all of whom were photographed with the psychic during this period of time) . . .

At the Naval Surface Weapons Center, in Silver Spring, Maryland, a physicist named Dr. Eldon Byrd said he had attended one briefing on the phenomena "in the most secure briefing room in the Pentagon. You had to have seven levels of badges to get down there. Every time you go through a level, [the guards] have this list. They check you off, they touch the badge, they look at your face and compare it to the picture on the badge. This room was swept everyday for bugs. It was the 12th floor down underground) . . ." Dr. Byrd was there to present experimental results that showed Geller—known to contort spoons, forks, and other metal objects, by simply rubbing or focusing on them—had caused unexplained effects on a metal alloy called nitinol, which always bends back to original shape when heated . . . except after the psychic touched it.

Whether or not, under pressure to perform, Geller had occasionally resorted to legerdemain, there were situations where cheating was precluded by stringent laboratory protocols—happenings no magician could replicate. At Kent State University a physicist named Dr. Wilbur Franklin documented microscopic effects on a platinum wedding band. He told me the ring had split as Geller held his hand over it during government-funded testing at Stanford Research Institute. The fracture surface showed what looked like incipient metallic melting *and*—next to it, on the same surface!—a freezing effect, as if at absolute zero: effects that could not be reproduced in the most sophisticated laser laboratory. Dr. Franklin called it a "teleneural influence."

Was it from UFOs—as Geller perceived—or a source that was deceiving him (and the scientists who studied him)?

A witness recalled that a strange blue aerial light had followed Geller as a schoolboy, and when tape recorders were set near him, bizarre mechanical voices boomed forth, claiming to be computers from another place and time— light years in the future.

What baffled dozens of scientists most were the instantaneous appearances or disappearances of objects around Geller—a nail clipper, a glass tumbler, a magnifying glass— something I personally witnessed when I met with him in his Manhattan apartment on East 57th Street in New York in 1976. During our interview a loud bang issued from across the room. It turned out to be a porous rock, perhaps volcanic, or a small meteorite, that somehow had winged into the far corner of the living room . . . from nowhere . . . hitting an expensive wood chessboard. "You see!" shouted Geller, as we stood there, entranced. "People don't believe me! But things like this happen all the time!" (I politely searched the apartment, including a closet, finding no accomplice and wondering, if it was a hoax, why Geller, who was world-famous, would damage an expensive chessboard to impress a 24-year-old Upstate New York newspaper reporter.)

All of the above paled in comparison to what a medical doctor from Ossining, New York, Andrija Puharich, had recorded on a freezing early Friday evening three years before in November 1973.

This time it wasn't an object around Uri.

This time it was Uri himself.

He had left a friend's apartment, walked toward Bloomingdale's in the bracing air to purchase a pair of binoculars before heading to his own place. The walk should have taken ten minutes in each direction. But Geller never made it. As he approached the canopy at the front of his building, the psychic said he suddenly felt a pull "backwards and up" and, glancing down, caught a fleeting glimpse of the ground as if he was swept several inches above it. "The next thing I can remember is like someone had cut out a split second piece of my life, like a piece of film taken out with scissors," he later told a British journalist. "I remember the lifting off, then I recollect there being a porch screen in front of me, and putting my arms up to protect my face, as my instinct told me I was about to crash into something."

That "something" turned out to be the mesh on a sunroom at the home of Dr. Puharich, who had been studying Geller.

Puharich—who held dozens of medical patents—lived *thirty-four miles from midtown Manhattan.*

By car, that was at least fifty-five minutes of driving—not the flash of time it took Geller that frigid evening. It was rush hour on a Friday. No vehicle known to man could have gotten him there.

In shock, Geller called the friends who'd seen him just before he left for Bloomingdale's. The call, they testified, occurred twenty-five minutes after he had set out from their apartment.

There is no way, even by helicopter, for the Israeli to have made it to Ossining, never mind find himself gently forced into the screened room, where the psychic described landing on a round glass table (which was shattered) before falling onto the floor.

One moment in Manhattan, the next in Upstate New York, miles north of the stately towers on that caisson span once known as the Tappan Zee Bridge . . .

5

Did Giants Once Roam America?

And what about giants?

Or this question: might humans have coexisted with the dinosaurs, but a larger *version* of humans?

Was everything bigger in the centuries of the unimaginable past?

Here, legend and recent reports, some insistent, meld into a conundrum.

At the headwaters of the Tennessee River, as one researcher pointed out, remarkable footprints were imprinted in what's now solid rock. The tracks included the ball of a human heel that measured thirteen inches wide. That's giant-sized.

In November 1926, miners discovered two human molars of such size that only a giant could have owned them.

Giants are throughout the Bible—29 references. How tall was Samson? One intrepid interpreter estimates six-foot-nine inches ("four cubits and a span").

That's hardly outlandish—when one considers that the height of the average player in the National Basketball Association is six-feet-four. The tallest man on record, Robert Pershing Wadlow of Alton, Illinois, towered at eight feet and eleven inches (and was still growing!) when he died. He made Wilt Chamberlain look like a point guard!

And he is two feet taller than was—supposedly—Goliath . . .

Unless Goliath was, as others estimate, well over nine feet . . .

In various mythologies from Europe to India, gigantic people are featured as primeval creatures associated with chaos and the wild nature, frequently in conflict with the gods.

How about *Jack and the Beanstalk*? Or Jonathan Swift?

In the Bible were the "nephilim"—giants said to have been the product of fallen angels . . . or aliens.

Did giants build the pyramids, or are we back to aliens again?

In the late 1800s, it is claimed, excavation of burial mounds near Lake Delavan in Wisconsin revealed skeletons of statures between seven-and-a-half and ten-feet. More frightening was their smile. The teeth in the front were like molars. There was a double row of them. They had six fingers and six toes. Their skulls were elongated.

Reporting from Maple City in that state, *The New York Times*, in May of 1912, said, "One of the three recently discovered mounds in this town has been opened. In it was found the skeleton of a man of gigantic size. The bones measured from head to foot over nine feet and were in a fair state of preservation. The skull was as large as a half-bushel measure. Some finely tempered rods of copper and other relics were lying near the bones." One can imagine the quizzical looks that skewed the faces of newspaper readers that spring morning! Some said the bones were sent to the Smithsonian, where they were placed in sealed vaults, accessible to a select few. Officials denied it . . .

A couple short decades later, but much farther west, the newspaper followed up with a headline that said "Giant Skeletons Found," explaining that "owing to the discovery of the remains of a race of giants in Guadalupe, New Mexico, antiquarians and archaeologists are preparing an expedition further to explore the region. This determination is based on the excitement that exists among the people of a scope of country near Mesa Rico, about two hundred miles southwest of Las Vegas, where an old burial ground has been discovered that has yielded skeletons of enormous size." A rancher there found two stones with most curious inscriptions, and beneath them: bones that belonged to someone no less than . . . twelve feet in length.

Was it a simple mistake in reassembly?

The men who opened the grave insisted that one forearm was four feet long and that a well-preserved jaw contained lower teeth ranging from the size of a hickory nut to that of a large walnut. The chest was said to be seven feet in circumference . . .

American Indians insist that in the annals are accounts of ancestors who encountered twelve-foot-tall beings and even procured some of their bones.

If so, one is excused for asking: where are the bits and pieces of skeleton now? Why no bones left? Were they spirited away? (Some go so far as to blame extraterrestrials for removing them—believing they are the remains of "alien-human hybrids" . . .)

At least one eight-footer was found in New Jersey (near Pleasantville).

Not to be left out, Virginia, in 1871, reported the finding of bones belonging, said *The Times,* to a body that was "as great as eight or nine feet."

Teeth as large as those of an equine.

The San Antonio *Express* reported the same in Texas.

Some of these cases were investigated by staid Ivy Leaguers.

A retired Ohio doctor discovered relics from a tribe of giants in caverns that stretched across an area of nearly two hundred miles, through Death Valley, California, across the Colorado River into Arizona. He figured them to be 80,000 years old—and to have used caverns as ritual halls, with markings similar to those used in our time by the Masonic order!

Some, in places like Pennsylvania, seemed much more recent: seven centuries old and nearly twelve feet tall, according to a fellow named McAllister who himself was six-four and lay down beside the bones, comparing them to his own legs—before the bones, exposed to air, began turning to dust.

The largest may have been one investigated by a researcher from the University of Texas in Victoria County. The verdict: well, the skull was about twice that of the average human.

Just a freak?

Or a lost race that once roamed across North America?

Or as the Bible (*Numbers* 13) says:

"There we saw the giants (the descendants of Anak came from the giants); and we were like grasshoppers in our own sight, and so we were in their sight."

6

The Woman Who Predicted 9/11

What are the most amazing predictions of all time? You could never come up with a list.

In 1783, a fellow named Ezra Stiles—president of Yale—predicted that America's population would reach three hundred million in two centuries. A little over two hundred years later . . . it did precisely that.

In 1840, Alexis de Tocqueville foresaw that there would be "two great nations in the world—Russians and Anglo-Americans—that would be set against each other": a direct precognitive anticipation of the Cold War more than a hundred years later.

In 1900 a civil engineer named John Elfreth Watkins Jr. foresaw that "man will see around the world. Persons and things of all kinds will be brought within focus of cameras connected electrically with screens at opposite ends of circuits." No need to explain what that came to be!

In 1914: a bishop in Hungary, Joseph Lanyi, was startled from slumber when he saw a letter from Archduke Franz Ferdinand in a dream. "Dear Doctor Lanyi," said the note, "I wish to let you know that today I will perish with my wife, due to a political assassination. We recommend ourselves to Godly prayers and Holy Masses of Your Lordship and ask you to remain as loving and devoted to our poor orphaned children as you have been before. With the most cordial greetings, I am yours, Archduke Franz, Sarajevo, June 28 1914. 3:30 a.m." There was even a picture of the shooter.

Later that day Bishop Lanyi was informed that the archduke and his wife indeed had been . . . assassinated.

Like other science fiction authors, Robert Heinlein hit the bull's-eye a number of times. In 1940 he foresaw the United States as a nuclear power (before such weapons were created) and predicted the waterbed (which came to objective reality in 1971). Fellow writer Arthur C. Clarke foresaw the internet tablet, and pentecostalist Glenda Jackson claimed to have foreseen the shooting, but survival, of Ronald Reagan (and fall of the Berlin Wall). A woman from Vancouver, Rebecca Hoffner, awoke from a dream April 18, 1966, and heard a voice say, *"Three months from today."* Precisely three months later, on July 18, a beautiful angel appeared to her, wings folded like those of a dove—and shortly after, around three p.m., her husband died . . .

In 2013, an Italian dreamt that Pope Benedict would resign and a man named Francesco would replace him.

That occurred two weeks later.

In his book *Witness*, Christian mystic Josyp Terelya of Ukraine related a vision in which he "saw" eight men plotting to overthrow the leader of the Soviet Union, and days after the book came out, a group of eight in Russia led a coup against Mikhail Gorbachev (causing the book to bolt to bestseller status).

Many were those who foresaw September 11. I spoke to one woman whose husband, Thomas Burnett, became so obsessed with the idea that he would soon die that he increased his life insurance, certain he'd be involved somehow in saving the White House.

How could this be, his wife wondered—he was a businessman! But it did: Burnett was one of those who rushed the cockpit on Flight 93 . . . causing it to crash onto farmland in Pennsylvania instead of hitting a target . . . in Washington, D.C.

There was an artist in Canada who years before had sketched the World Trade Center with smoke coming out, in a way quite exact to what was later photographed.

But the most startling prediction was that of mystic Maria Esperanza.

During the early 1990s she told a group of pilgrims that she'd had a vision of two tall buildings falling in New York. She saw smoke. She envisioned collapse.

And in December of 2000, she said that "enemies" were on "American soil" and planning to strike.

"World-known mystic Maria Esperanza warns U.S. of foreign danger, sees world 'saddened' in a short while, is concerned with the Mid-East, the Pope, and two nations," was a headline across our online newspaper.

She repeated this warning to me while staying in New Jersey that following March (2001).

It would be something, she was certain, that would "shake the world."

On August 25, 2001, at 9:35 p.m., her family sent me a fax warning that the proscribed event was about to occur— in "three weeks or three months" (she wasn't quite sure of time, only the "three").

It happened 17 days later . . .

And on September 11, the Catholic mystic happened to be in Manhattan—crossing the George Washington Bridge back to New Jersey, when terror struck by way of those three planes.

Right after September 11, when everyone was trying to figure out what terrorist group might be involved (Al Qaeda wasn't even known to the public at that point, as eyes turned toward Hamas), I called Maria and asked who *she* thought was behind it.

Her laconic reply: "a roaring lion."

Weeks later, my wife was at a website of etymology and searched for "Osama." That name, according to the site, was associated with "a lion that roars . . ."

7

Prophecy of a President

Unnerving it is when a book foresees the future. The Bible is one thing—filled with prophecy. But secular books? Do they occasionally stumble on the future by accident? Jules Verne saw a giant "space cannon" shooting something in Florida. *Was it on that stretch of shore later called Cape Canaveral,* site of the Kennedy Space Center? Sci-fi king Arthur C. Clarke foresaw virtual reality. A book called *Futility* about an "unsinkable" ocean liner called *Titan,* largest in the world, was published fourteen years before the tragedy of the *Titanic.* Like the real-life, ill-fated ship, it lacked lifeboats and hit an iceberg—the same 400 nautical miles from Newfoundland—in the same month of April.

But none are more startling than the precognitive hand-iwork of writer and lawyer, named Ingersoll Lockwood who wrote a series of novels in the late 1900s. The titles of two, written for children: *Travels and Adventures of Little Baron Trump and His Wonderful Dog Bulger* (1889) and *Baron Trump's Marvelous Underground Journey* (1893). You read that name correctly.

The "baron" here was a title—not a first name, and thus is short an "r"—but the point remains and grows with each detail. The fictional Trump, archetype for a future president (remember, this is the nineteenth century!)—is a rich kid bored with his lavish lifestyle and fixated with foreign women—"distracted" by them—as well as the size of his brain, of which he often brags—even suing a tutor for learning more from him than he did from the tutor. He travels to Russia in a life-changing journey during which he meets a "master of masters" named "Don."

Possessed of a biting tongue, young Baron Trump has a personalized insult for everyone he meets ("Little Man Lump," "Little Man All Head," "Flip-Flop," and "Sir Pendulum Legs," in case this brings to mind "Little Marco" and "Crooked Hillary"). His own full name is actually Wilhelm Heinrich Sebastian Von Troomp—German, as the future president is part German—and constantly finding himself in quandaries that he must then escape. Like the 45th future president, "Baron Trump" preferred familiar comfort food over exotic cuisine (McDonald's, anyone?).

And where, you might wonder, in Longwood's novels, did Baron Trump live?

"Castle Trump" on Fifth Avenue.

A century later, Donald J. Trump, of Trump Tower (on Fifth Avenue) would build a casino in Atlantic City named—"Trump's Castle."

So close are the parallels that some have come to the conclusion—rather wildly—that President Trump was a time-traveler. Conspiracists and delusionists alike wonder, if Trump inherited a travel machine, perhaps one designed by the inventor-genius-eccentric Nikola Tesla, with whom President Trump's uncle, an MIT graduate, was an acquaintance.

Lockwood was from Ossining, New York (where Geller landed during that supposed teleportation) and was the son of Munson Ingersoll, who founded a bank and was an intimate friend of Henry Clay.

Ingersoll followed in dad's footsteps, at one point appointed Consul to the Kingdom of Hanover by Abraham Lincoln. On his return he established a legal practice in New York City, dying in 1918 at the ripe old age (by nineteenth-century standards) of seventy-seven, after writing *Alice in Wonderland*-type tales.

Uncanniest of all: Lockwood's final novel was published in 1896. It was about an election and describes a "state of uproar" in New York City over an outsider winning the U.S. presidency. The name "Trump" is not in this Lockwood work, but the links are both clear and mystifying— focused on street protests in front of "Castle Trump" following the stunning victory of a populist candidate. "Mobs of vast size are organizing under the lead of anarchists and socialists, and threaten to plunder and despoil the houses of the rich who have wronged and oppressed them for so many years," Lockwood wrote.

"The Fifth Avenue Hotel will be the first to feel the fury of the mob," wrote Ingersoll. The chant: "Death to the rich man."

A "terrible night for the great City of New York," said the novel, which asked, "Would the troops be in time to save it?"

The president in Lockwood's novella is paranoid over the gold standard and fears—with good cause—a civil war. The downfall of America is at hand.

A few months after the disturbances, the president appoints a man to his cabinet . . . named "Pence."

Oh, the shouts on the street: in November of 2016, you will recall, they were heard in various cities, including New York at Trump Tower. The title of this last Lockwood book: *1900, or The Last President.*

8

The Electric People

Call them "the electric people," because that's what they are. High voltage seems to course through their veins. A phenomenon of nature or a manifestation of dark spiritual forces? After all, Satan fell "like lightning" (*Luke* 10:18).

This is not to speak about someone who, to use a term, is *magnetic*: Charisma has nothing to do with it. Instead one is addressing actual electrons that seem to move through or around humans as if they're conductors, capacitors, even generators.

One woman named Leanna Murphy walks into the parking lot of a Home Depot and all the lights—and then the huge store sign—blink off. Another in Illinois causes street lamps to darken or flicker as she passes by in her low-slung Mitsubishi. The whole block. There are those who burn out wedding bands, earrings—anything conductive—or jewelry turns their skin black. An estimated one percent of the population has unusual electrical potential, with those who, at the extreme, affect street lamps classified under "street-light interference syndrome (SLI)," or simply labeled "sliders" or "HVP," for high-voltage people.

Is it simply that they strip electrons from the air (we breathe about 25,000 times a day)? And store far more static than the average person? Or might it be that an undiscovered virus alters the lungs enough to super-charge a person?

More than thirty prisoners held at Dannemora, New York, in 1920 found that watches went haywire around

31

them, compasses swung madly, and they could deflect small metal objects. It all began with an outbreak of botulinum poisoning.

Botulism causes dry sky and static favors that.

It also disrupts the body's electro-chemical process . . .

Now, we all produce an electrical current. It powers the nervous system. It's what keeps our hearts beating. As a kid, you rubbed a balloon on the top of your head, charging it enough to pin it to the wall. Or perhaps you dragged your slippers on the carpet in a dark room on a cold dry night and watched a discharge from fingertip to metal. Or combed your hair to ignited sparks. Nothing supernormal here. Electrons are no more alien to the flow of human life than oxygen . . .

But some people go beyond normal static—affecting televisions, house lights (the husband of one such "slider" keeps thinking it's the dimmer), and crashing ATMs—no doubt unwelcome near slot machines (not to mention the cockpit of a transatlantic plane) . . .

Cell phones crash; computers are known to freeze. A woman named Mary Weigant who lives along the Colorado River in Arizona told me she was doing dishes once "and when I put my hands in the water, I saw like lightning coming from the fingers on both hands." Another had trouble in courtship: when she kissed her husband, there were sparks between them, all right—they both felt it! "Light bulbs?" complained a woman named Lisa Veillaesque in Mississippi. "Please, I should buy stock in them. I can't seem to keep up with the bulbs going out."

"While vacationing at Epcot in Florida, I touched the computer screen at a display and brought down the server," testifies another. "It took about twenty minutes for them to bring it back up. I also disrupt credit card machines where you have to sign your name with an electronic pen. The machine goes haywire and makes all kinds of squiggles and stray marks where the person is supposed to be signing. My mother makes me stand about five feet away from her when we're shopping and she wants to pay by credit card!"

Batteries don't last. Neither do clocks. One woman caused a television station in Wichita, Kansas, to go off the air! Nuclear silos have no need for anyone with such a proclivity. Nor are they needed in the massage business . . . The problem with this is that those in deliverance ministry will tell you a first sign of a preternatural influence is often . . . a power fluctuation.

Said Aimee from Tampa, "Every time I go to the grocery store I get shocked mercilessly from static. It doesn't matter what footwear I have on. Most of the time I wear 'Chuck Taylors,' so its not that I'm not wearing rubber soles. My mom has the same problem—only I actually throw tiny lightning bolts off of my fingertips to the shelves when I'm reaching for something."

Heavy metals? Dry skin? Do *those* cause a build-up of electrons?

Or is it something more mysterious?

"I too explode light bulbs, crash computers, cash registers at stores, etcetera," says a slider woman in Arizona. "And if that isn't weird enough I have dreams that come true."

Adds a woman from Albuquerque, "Walking down aisles in grocery stores and canned good-bottles jumping out and breaking on the floor. Both of my grandsons are also electric people. I made sure that the cart was in the middle of the wide aisle and the grandsons held onto the cart."

Does one call in an electrician—or exorcist?

There are those who say they have encountered "UFOs" and henceforth cause streetlights to blink, illuminated highway signs to go dark, computers to show "lethal errors," and radios to crackle . . . and hiss.

Perhaps most poignant was the case of Jacquelyn Priestman of Manchester, England. She was living with her first husband, Ron, when she discovered it. It started with a nasty argument.

As Ron headed off on his scooter in the middle of it, Jacquelyn shouted, "I hope you break your neck!"

Later that day Ron was involved in an accident that caused fractures in his spine and neck—dying from complications a month later.

Bathing one evening and in deep remorse, Jacquelyn says the light bulb above her exploded, showering her with glass and cutting her arm badly—a faulty bulb, she surmised. Within days, though, her vacuum cleaner inexplicably burned out; more bulbs burst; and more vacuum cleaners died, along with five irons and two washing machines. Was it her powerful emotions powering the happenings?

A stove burned out. The television went off of its own accord, or switched channels. So did her radio.

Of all things, her second husband—a witness to later events—was an electrical fitter. He noticed that the discharges were particularly intense if indeed Jacqueline was having her period or upset at something. For example, when a reporter suggested it was just fraud, Jacquelyn got so angry a new vacuum clear burst into flames. (She was asked by local stores to stay clear.)

Such cases have been tallied at least going back to 1837.

Concluding that it was a build up of surface electricity, a local professor, Roy Gough, deduced an alkali-acid imbalance and suggested a change in her diet (more veggies). Her husband decided that Jacquelyn might carry around onions to disperse the excess static, causing it to go into the vegetable. It worked—although Jacquelyn had difficulty dismissing the notion that Ron was behind it, for when she went near his clothes, a light bulb had detonated . . . and while hospitalized he had joked that if he died, he'd come back to haunt her.

9

Can a Car Be Cursed?

One is open to a "curse" only when one strays from the faith—is disobedient, in rebellion, says Scripture (*Ephesians* 4:27). Christians cannot be cursed if they are walking where God wants them to walk. Look at Balaam: he tried to curse the Israelites but could not (*Numbers* 22). His "curse" was turned into a blessing!

Can a car be cursed?

Seems that way. Take the Porsche 550 Spyder owned by legendary actor James Dean. He bought it with proceeds from his first hit film, *East of Eden*, and it was trouble right off. There was just something *about* it. When Dean met up with actor Alec Guinness outside a restaurant, on September 23, 1955, Guinness took one look at it and told Dean it had a "sinister" appearance. "If you get in that car, you will be found dead in it by this time next week," the fellow actor had told Dean!

The number "130" was painted on the hood and two red stripes over the rear tires, for Dean raced it.

Oh, and the name Dean gave it: *"Little Bastard"* . . .

That year, Dean had appeared in a car safety television spot, warning youth not to speed because "the life you save might be mine" . . . And so it was no small irony that at 5:45 p.m. on September 30, 1955—seven days after the Guinness warning—the Hollywood idol was motoring near Cholame, California, when he smashed into a Ford Tudor driven by a college student in this sleepy ranch town and famously died in the collision.

News spread on radio and television.

America mourned. The star of *Rebel Without A Cause* was dead.

Hundreds attended his funeral.

It had been a head-on crash and instantaneous death, the Spyder doing cartwheels and landing in a gully.

That was only the beginning. Trouble seemed welded into the car's frame. Dean's companion, a German mechanic who survived that crash, died in a second very similar accident soon after. Meanwhile, when a man named George Barris bought the Spyder, it immediately slipped off a trailer and broke a mechanic's leg.

Not long after, parts from the car—the engine, drive train—were sold . . . neither boding well. One man who was in a vehicle powered by the Spyder engine lost control during a race and hit a tree, killed instantly. A second man bought that drive train—and was in the same race—was injured severely when his car suddenly locked up and rolled over. Two tires from Dean's car blew out—simultaneously. If that wasn't enough, thieves who tried to strip the car were injured as they attempted it!

Spooked, Barris hid the car until the California Highway Patrol prevailed upon him to lend it for use in a highway safety exhibit.

And: the first exhibit failed due to a fire that burned the garage housing Dean's car to the ground—though mysteriously sparing the Porsche itself. The next exhibition, at a local high school, was canceled when the car fell off its display and broke a student's hip.

It also fell off transport trucks . . .

Perhaps "Christine" (as in the Stephen King movie) would have been a better appellation than *Little Bastard*.

Finally, the car vanished—no one seeming to know where it has been taken . . .

Astoundingly, Dean's automobile is not the best example of an automotive hex.

Here, "history" is the word.

For, arguably, that standing goes to a brilliant red touring car on loan to Austrian Archduke Franz Ferdinand and wife Sophie, the Dutchess of Hohenburg, for a state visit to Sarajevo. Date: June 28, 1914.

These were tense times, with Serbians upset their territory had been annexed by Austria. A bomb was thrown at the car, striking the side, bouncing off, and injuring four members of their staff.

Soon after, their driver inexplicably drove off the scheduled course and to a dead-end street, where a young man shouting and waving a pistol fired point-blank, killing the archduke and his spouse.

This was the spark that ignited World War One.

But the "curse" would live on far past that—at least according to folklorists. For if they are to be believed, the car—a Gräf and Stift double phaeton—fell into the hands of a "General Potiorek" of the Fifth Austrian Corps, who nearly immediately after suffered a crushing military defeat and eventually lost his mind, living his final days in an almshouse.

Another Austrian assumed ownership and struck two Croatian peasants—fatally—and then swerved into a tree that ended his own life.

Time of possession: nine days.

Following the war, the ill-fated Archduke's roadster landed in the hands of the Governor of Yugoslavia, who found himself involved in not one but four accidents . . . in four months (losing an arm). He ordered it destroyed, but a doctor, chuckling at his superstition, purchased it for a pittance. He was later found beside the auto, likewise deceased—the Gräf and Stift double phaeton upside-down but just slightly damaged.

A jeweler bought it from the widow and loved it (and its weird history) until, or so it is said, he committed suicide.

Now, whether these details could ever be substantiated, a writer for *Smithsonian Magazine* reported "an even more astounding coincidence concerning Franz Ferdinand's death limo—one that is considerably better evidenced than the cursed-car nonsense. This tiny piece of history went completely unnoted on for the best part of a century, until a British visitor named Brian Presland called at Vienna's Heeresgeschichtliches Museum, where the vehicle is now on display. It was Presland who seems to have first drawn the staff's attention to the remarkable detail contained in the Gräf & Stift's license plate, which reads AIII 118. That number, Presland pointed out, is capable of a quite astonishing interpretation. It can be taken to read A (for Armistice) 11-11-18—which means that the death car has always carried with it a prediction—not of the dreadful day of Sarajevo that in a real sense marked the beginning of the First World War—but of November 11, 1918: Armistice Day, the day that the war ended."

Is it true that a Swiss race driver ended up with the Archduke's car and was killed when it overturned at a sharp bend? And finally, that five were killed when the car was driven by a garage owner and crashed while he was passing another driver?

Sixteen dead, not to mention the war . . . which, if there really was a link, would tally to millions.

10

The Strange Number Eleven

The number eleven seems everywhere, and not just in 9/11. For years now, many have claimed to constantly see 11:11 when they glance at a clock—too often for coincidence. I have received dozens if not hundreds of e-mails to this effect.

Is it a sign of coming change? The first citation of this number is in *Genesis* 32:22, where Jacob takes his wife and eleven sons on that return to the land of his inheritance. That sounds like "11" means good news! Or does it signify (*Matthew* 20: 6-7) an "eleventh hour"—the last possible moment?

If you want, you can rationalize this way: "11:11" are the only numerals on a clock that are repeated twice a day, and this, it takes no actuary to realize, doubles the chances of seeing it.

Just New Age bunk? Perhaps. But some of it seems like more than that. "My dear sweet husband passed December 19," a woman named Nancy said. "A speeding car hit him at his work site. He was a lineman and was ready to retire. That day on the clock I saw 11:11 a.m. That evening is when it happened. The day before I saw 11:11, too. This number was always showing and he and I both noticed it."

"I see it everywhere and I mean *everywhere*," wrote another. "It started with 11:11 on the car clock back in the mid-1980s and hasn't stopped. I constantly see 111 or 1:11 or 11:11. It makes me think of the ominous 'eleventh hour'—

denotes urgency. It's eerie, the feeling of 'time is short.' I don't like seeing it."

When we look for something, don't we notice it more?

"Today my hairdresser told me that she had a 'groundhog-day' kind of dream," wrote Jean LoGiudice. "She was at work and it was three o'clock and person after person got in her chair and it was still three o'clock. She couldn't get off 'three o'clock.' I asked her if she ever sees 11:11. Her eyes widened and she told me the week before when she got in her car the time was 11:11 for just an instant before it turned to 11:12 and that night when she looked at her alarm clock, it said 11:11, but only for an instant again, before it went to 11:12. She wanted to know why I asked that! I always book my next appointment when I leave, and it's always six weeks out. She handed me my appointment card and it said 'Nov. 11.' I asked her if she noticed that was . . . 11/11!"

Gremlins?

Superstition?

Is it not the simple repetition of the same number that makes it stand out?

- The day of the terrorist attack on New York: 11
- The Date of the Attack, September 11 or 9/11 = 9 + 1 + 1 = 11
- 911 is emergency number = 9 + 1 + 1 = 11
- September 11th is the 254th day of the year: 2 + 5 + 4 = 11
- After September 11th we have 111 remaining for the end of the year
- The first plane to hit one of the buildings was Flight 11
- The State of New York was the 11th State to join the Union
- New York City = 11 letters

- Afghanistan = 11 letters
- The Pentagon = 11 letters
- Flight 11 had 92 passengers, 9 + 2 = 11
- Flight 77 had 65 passengers, 6 + 5 = 11
- Twin Towers look like an 11
- Twin Towers had 110 floors . . .

Is this stretching it?

In Switzerland is a town named Solothurn that's obsessed with the number eleven—and has been for centuries. It was established twenty centuries ago and has eleven museums, eleven fountains, eleven churches, eleven chapels, and eleven towers, not far from St. Ursus Cathedral which: took eleven years to build, has a couple of fountains, each with eleven taps; possesses eleven doors, eleven altars (consisting of eleven types of marble), and eleven bells in its tower; and is divided into three parts, each eleven meters in height. "To dig further back into history," notes a writer, "the guilds elected 11 members to the town's council in 1252, followed by Solothurn becoming the 11th canton of the Swiss Confederation in 1481, and then it was divided into 11 protectorates in the sixteenth century. Why the fascination with the number 11? Legend has it that magical elves were sent to the town from nearby Weissenstein Mountain to bolster the morale of the hard-working locals.

"Oddly enough," notes the writer, "the number eleven in German translates to 'elf.'"

Elves we'll stay clear of. Another theory is that it "has significant meaning in the Bible and therefore holy number"—although let's add that it is considered to be the most intuitive of all numbers according to numerology, which is likewise avoided by those with no taste for superstition or the occult!

Some believe there is a biblical basis for believing that "eleven" signifies the "last hour" or "judgment." Others say strange things occur at three a.m.—that they wake up precisely then and see the clock hands settled precisely on that time, or encounter various spirits, including ungodly ones. It can be argued that you can find associations with any set of numerals.

"There are two clear meanings associated with the number eleven," noted a website, "one meaning of the number 'eleven' is urgent, the last chance, or something is about to happen. This meaning is expressed in the 'eleventh hour.' The Lord Jesus Christ speaks of the number 'eleven' only twice, both times in *Matthew* 20, in the phrase 'the eleventh hour.' The eleventh hour is urgency, the last chance before something happens."

Again: "perhaps."

"The first 'judgment' executed upon mankind after the fall of man, resulted from Cain killing his brother Abel. The judgment was executed in *Genesis* chapter four, verse 'eleven.' The second judgment was Noah's Flood, *Genesis* 7:11. The 'curse of Canaan' was executed upon the 'eleven" sons of Canaan.'" The chastisement associated with the Tower of Babel? That judgment on Nimrod "occurred in *Genesis* chapter 'eleven' verse seven.

And Sodom?

Genesis 19:11.

The judgments on Egypt? There were eleven of those . . . including in *Exodus* 9:11!

11

The Inn of No Return

"Don't mess with the Bender family."

That would have made more sense—at the door of their general store—than a mat saying "Welcome."

Or perhaps better yet, a "welcome" mat saying: *"Abandon all hope, ye who enter."*

For there have been serial killers who murdered more— in South America, one was thought to have slain up to six hundred!—and several just as frightening, such as the Charles Manson clan. At one point, during the trial of that "family," prosecutor Vincent Bugliosi said he happened to check the time and noticed that—oddly—his wristwatch had just stopped . . .

Looking back up, he glanced across the courtroom to the defense table and saw Manson staring at him with a smirk . . .

That's spooky. But perhaps even more so were the Benders of Labette County in Kansas.

Immigrants from Germany or the Netherlands (no one is quite sure which), the father, John, had such a thick, gurgling accent that strangers couldn't make out what he was trying to say. He was in his mid-sixties, a frowzy, even grossly disheveled man, of mien a bit wolverine, and didn't seem to want much to do with anyone. The Benders built a cabin that was then partitioned with canvas from a covered wagon—this just after the Civil War—so that there were two rooms: one a living quarters, and the other a combination inn and general store, where dry goods could be purchased by those passing on the Great Osage Trail (now known as the Santa Fe) on the way to the promised West.

Travelers could also opt for a meal there, or an overnight stay.

None of the above, it turns out, were highly recommended . . .

For strange as it sounds, the cabin was designed for robbery and thrill-seeking homicide, perhaps mixed with an unspoken (and unspeakable) occult ritual. Part of a small spiritualist community, the mother, known as Almira or Elvira (or simply "Ma"), was said to hold séances, and if that went unproven, it was clear that daughter Kate, in her early twenties, had a mystical streak, advertising herself on posters as able to heal the mute, cure the blind, and resolve seizures. A real altruist! She had an alluring attractiveness that proved as much a selling point with men as her alleged psychic gifts, and rumors floated that she sometimes moonlighted as a prostitute. Along with brother (some said husband) John Junior, the two offspring spoke English capably and were more adept at greeting potential customers of whatever sort—unknowing sojourners on this trail of the macabre.

The problem with the Benders, and their store, was that too few returned from it. In less than a couple years, a dozen and perhaps more than twenty met their ends there. Most bizarre was . . . *how.* If someone was having dinner with them, the standard protocol was for Kate or her mother to seat a stranger against that canvas partition, behind which stood John or John Junior (or both)—with upraised hammers.

As soon as a visitor's head was close enough to the canvas, or even leaning into it, one of the Bender men would crush the visitor's skull with either a sledge, claw, or shoe hammer (all of which were later found in the house), usually on the right side of the skull, indicating that they reached around the corner of the curtain to deliver most blows.

Once thusly dispatched, bodies were dropped through a trap door under the table, plopping into a small cellar where throats were slit ear-to-ear for good measure.

By light of a lantern, and perhaps after rituals, bodies were buried in shallow graves under the family's orchard.

The first two deaths directly attributed to the Benders were a man and his infant daughter. The daughter showed no signs of bludgeoning or knife wounds (unlike her father), but rather asphyxiation, leading authorities to believe she had either been suffocated or buried alive, under the body of her dad.

But they were not necessarily the first.

In 1871, the corpse of a man identified only as "Jones" was discovered in nearby Drum Creek (skull crushed, throat slashed), and the following February, two bodies of men with the same injuries were located nearby.

The disappearance of that father and daughter—George Newton Longcor and little Mary Ann—led William Henry York, a doctor who knew them, to investigate, but neither did *he* return home—prompting his two brothers, one a colonel, the other a state senator, to take up the cause.

When the community began to notice that too many were disappearing from the Great Osage Trail, a public meeting was organized; townsfolk decided to search every cabin in the county.

But that night, as it turns out, a peculiar storm swept in, postponing the investigation for several days. And when the weather cleared, the Benders . . . were gone; how or where, no one could say.

Folks knew only that a search of the property—soon dubbed "Hell's Acre"—yielded nine suspected graves, along with body parts and the body of Dr. York, his feet barely buried below the surface.

A priest who had visited, Father Paul Ponziglione, fled just before he met his demise—suspicious when he saw the Bender men concealing a hammer (an observation he attributed to Divine inspiration), as were two visitors who incurred Kate's wrath when they refused to sit against the canvas. Soon, the Benders themselves fled.

Groups of vigilantes searched for the outlaws, rumored to have headed for St. Louis or a no-man's outlaw community between the Texas and the U.S. border. Some claimed a posse shot the family members south of a town called Thayer, tracking them by their wagon's distinctive wheel imprints. At least, that's the favorite theory of a local history buff, Don Richardson, with whom I spoke.

Others said they were lynched.

No one has provided definitive documentation.

In 1884, a man matching Pa Bender's description was arrested in Montana for murder. No positive identification was achieved and the prisoner died after amputating his own foot to break free of leg irons! Others believed that Ma—never of the gentlest disposition—killed him (over some stolen goods). She was also suspected of murdering previous husbands—and several of her children!

A murderous clan this was.

A "Mrs. Almira Monroe," *aka* "Almira Griffith," *aka* possibly Elvira Bender, and someone going by the name "Sarah Eliza Davis" were apprehended in Niles, Michigan—on October 31, 1889, Halloween—for larceny along with the Kansas homicides.

That came about when the daughter of another victim tracked them down (after a dream about her father). While some witnesses swore it was the Bender women, evidence was lacking and the women were eventually set free, with no one sure it was the Benders and leaving us, to this day—

with no idea where these four mysterious relatives ended up. "Their fate remains one of the great unsolved mysteries of the Old West," says a historical marker on U.S.-169.

It was one thing for a single person to become homicidal, quite another for an entire family to do that, particularly when, in some cases, robbery did not seem to be the main motive.

Now a lonesome wheat field, those who ventured to the ruins of the house, which soon was reduced to a hole in the earth, were said to be scared off by glowing apparitions, and a moaning, keening sound that came from the prairie darkness . . .

12

The Oddest of Odds

Do you believe in "coincidence"—that is, that certain astounding circumstances whirl into our reality through mere chance?

That concept stretches the imagination. *Is* there really anything by happenstance?

Einstein himself—not exactly a preacher—famously said that "God does not throw dice."

Case in point: Irving Kupcinet, a famous newspaper columnist and television talk-show host in Chicago. I did his show back in the 1980s. Many years before, when he was a reporter, Irv took a trip to London, covering the coronation of Queen Elizabeth II. He was staying at the Savoy, a luxurious hotel, when, in the bedside table, he found several items, all with the name *"Harry Hannin"* emblazoned on them.

That was strange enough: Kupcinet knew a Harry Hannin. He was a basketball player who starred with the Harlem Globetrotters. Was it the same one? Irv called him. Had he stayed at the Savoy, he asked Hannin? Yes. But before Kupcinet could tell the athlete about the items he'd found, Hannin interrupted, and with excitement: for, as he quickly explained to Irv, it was quite a coincidence that he was calling: Hannin had been at Le Meurice, another hotel, in Paris, two days before, and had found a tie in his room. The name embroidered on it: *"Irv Kupcinet."* Seems Irv had stayed there too and was likewise forgetful.

In Detroit was the baby that fell and miraculously hit a fellow, Joseph Figlock, passing by. That broke the fall and saved the child—who, however, fell a second time a year later and was caught by the same man—passing by, again, at that exact right moment. Some call them "Godincidents."

There was Mark Twain . . . born the year of Halley's Comet and dying the year of its return (and predicting this!).

There were John Adams and Thomas Jefferson, two signers of the Declaration of Independence—both dying on July Fourth (of the same year).

On December 5, 1664, a ship went down in the Menai Strait off the coast of Wales. The only survivor was a fellow named Hugh Williams. Precisely 121 years later, on December 5, 1785, another ship disappeared below the waves of Menai Strait, and once more, all perished but for a passenger named . . . Hugh Williams. Nearly a century *later*, on December 5, 1860, yet a third ship, this one carrying twenty-five passengers, was swallowed by the Menai Strait, the sole survivor a fortunate gentleman who like his predecessors was named Hugh Williams . . .

There were the twins, separated at birth, yet each named James by adoptive parents, each with a keen interest in law enforcement, each marrying a woman named Linda, each having a son named James Alan (one of them spelled it with two l's in "Allan"); both divorcing and remarrying women named Betty.

If that's not enough to impress the actuary (as was found out when, eventually, the men were reunited), both of their new wives had dogs named "Toy."

There was Anthony Hopkins . . . When this British actor was chosen to play the lead in a movie based on the novel, *The Girl from Petrovka,* by George Feifer, he tried a number of bookstores in search of a copy. He could find none. In

London's Leicester Square, waiting for a ride home, he noticed a book someone had left on a bench. Remarkably, it was—*The Girl from Petrovka.*

If that wasn't enough, two years later, filming in Vienna, and meeting with Feifer, the author lamented that he had no copy of his own book: he had lent the last one, with notes scribbled in the margins, to a friend in London who had lost it—whereupon Hopkins, with real-life drama, produced the book he had found . . . annotations and all!

What cosmic force puts these things together? They call it "synchronicity," but that impressive scientific appellation tells us little . . . Perhaps a better answer is "the Lord" (and His angels).

There was the account of Ken Gaub of Yakima, Washington, who at the time of his "miracle" was traveling in a music ministry and going through a crisis. He wasn't sure which direction his life should take. Should he continue to do what he was doing? Should he continue to minister? Or should he find a regular job?

The answer came when he was out of state and a thousand miles from home and walking out for a Pepsi. There was a phone booth near a gas station, and suddenly, as he walked past, he heard it ringing. Hesitating at first, he finally picked it up. "I said 'hello' and the operator said 'person-to-person call for Ken Gaub,'" he recounted. "I yelled out, 'You're crazy.' I thought it was *Candid Camera* or something."

But he finally acknowledged that he was indeed Ken Gaub—there in a strange town, on a strange street, picking up a payphone!—and found himself speaking to a woman who was ready to commit suicide (a woman who had once seen him and had been inspired and now said she got the number she had just called in a vision.) "She just saw a little collection of numbers in her mind and called an operator to place the call," says Gaub. "What are the odds of that—*one in a billion?*" Probably higher.

The woman didn't commit suicide and Gaub didn't leave the ministry.

Amazing, too, was one I personally heard from a Christian woman who owned a beauty salon on the Gulf Coast in Florida. Her world had been falling apart. She and her husband were doing well financially—all kinds of clothes, the accoutrements of wealth, many "toys"—but there were deep personal issues and a straying from the faith . . .

Then came the "event."

It was July . . . the sweltering summer of 2003. "That day we were out on our jet skies and I got stuck in the mud," she told me. "When I got back, I realized that I had lost my watch." Her valued timepiece was somewhere in the water, amid the muck and stone crabs.

The following January, she and her husband were staying at a bed-and-breakfast when she felt a peculiar presence around her. Shaking it off, they went to relax on the sultry Gulf of Mexico. "We had gotten a brand new boat, put it in water, and headed out to this island, but the presence never left me," she said. "Suddenly I turned right with the boat. I didn't know why. I had been beelining for the island and suddenly took a right and I thought, 'Why am I doing this? What is going on? What—does God want me here?'

"I was zig-zagging in and out of mangroves and I hit this sandbar and my boat stopped. And I saw a reflection, like a jewel."

There, on the exposed sand, was her TAG Heuer designer watch—four miles from where she had lost it and nine months later. Obviously, the tide had taken it out. Something—or Someone—unseen had returned it. The event figured into her conversion. It set her on fire for the Lord. "The watch still worked," she exclaimed, "and the date was correct. The message was time. I don't like to say end of the world, but I feel something very significant in my spirit. There is no time for sinning. There were all these magazines at the salon and they were falling all over the place and I had them brought out and that's when I noticed that every one of them was *Time* Magazine."

13

Scientists Meet a Phantom

Strangest of all, when it came to psychics, was what happened to scientists—this time including one from the CIA. Take the instance of a physicist named Don Curtis at Lawrence Livermore Laboratories in California.

Dr. Curtis and his wife were relaxing one Saturday afternoon during the Uri Geller investigation when an apparition or hologram—*something*—materialized before their eyes. It was in the middle of their living room and can only be described as macabre: the hologram or apparition of an artificial arm draped by a black suit sleeve. It rotated as if on a spit. Instead of a hand, there was a hook at the end of it.

Very bizarre.

Too much so?

Could something from the subconscious have manifested in a collective way? Or was it plain and simple a visitor from the netherworld?

Neither the physicist nor his wife had ever reported hallucinations. Nor was either on medication. So unnerved was Curtis that word got back to Dr. Kit Green, the CIA caseworker overseeing the research.

ESP was one thing. That, they believed, was an undiscovered mental skill. This was something else.

Dr. Green immediately demanded a meeting with the two researchers from Stanford Research Institute, Dr. Hal Puthoff and Dr. Russell Targ, who, under government contract, were spearheading the testing. The caseworker was angry. An arm? A hologram? *What on earth was everyone talking about?*

They met in Dr. Green's motel room, where, calling it "bizarre nonsense," he demanded to know all that the Curtises were saying. It was not a casual conversation. It's called a debriefing. At the moment the grilling began, there was a bang on the door: no polite rap or even insistent knock—but like someone was trying to barge in!

Now it was their turn to be petrified.

Psychics were one thing. Robbers another.

Green opened the door and with no greeting a short middle-aged man—in a dark gray suit—strode in (a "man-in-black"?). He bore an ashen complexion—to match the suit—and despite the bangs on the door, he moved now gently . . . his gait slow, deliberate; he muttered a few words—nothing of much significance (at least, no words were recorded)—and left as strangely and quickly as he had entered.

While he did, the scientist and CIA official noticed that one of his suit sleeves was pinned up.

He was missing an arm . . .

The sleeve was empty.

This was no ghost, but a corporeal human with no explanation to proffer—and certainly nothing physics, nor any exercise of logic, could comprehend, "as real as it gets," recalled Puthoff.

Immediately they rushed out after the strange intruder, fanning out in three directions—two circling the floor, another clamoring down the stairwell.

But no one was around.

Not a sign of him whatsoever, just a sudden aura of inexplicability . . . and the hint of danger.

14

Living Water

What about communicating with *non*-living things—say, water? Can sounds and noise and, yes, music affect them?

We've all heard about the "living waters," in the Bible: "He who believes in Me, as the Scripture said, 'From his innermost being will flow rivers of living water'" (*John* 7:37-39) or "Then he showed me a river of the water of life, clear as crystal, coming from the throne of God and of the Lamb" (*Revelation* 22:1-2).

But a preposterous question, on the surface, nonetheless—except for a Japanese researcher named Dr. Masura Emoto.

He wondered if, at the moment of freezing, just as water forms crystals, the spiritual ambience influenced formation of intricate crystal structures. For years, as a sidelight, Dr. Emoto, an expert in alternative medicine, took microphotographs, finding, much to his incredulity, that the answer was "yes": water seemed to react to music and even the mood created by *words* (such as prayers). Yell out something mean and you get ugly ice microphotographs!

Fringe science or a legitimate avenue of study?

Claiming astounding results, he displayed microphotographs of crystals that formed beautifully in the presence of classical music, alongside ones that were malformed or unformed altogether when tension was expressed in the room in which they were frozen or when what he was playing there was hard rock music. "Crystals emerge for only twenty or thirty seconds as the temperature rises and the ice starts to melt," Dr. Emoto explained. "This short window of time gives us a glimpse into a world that is indeed magical."

Was it really proof that words, vibrations, and thoughts affect the inanimate around us? Wasn't this *pagan*?

"I put fifty different types of water in fifty different Petri dishes," explained Emoto. "I then freeze the dishes at minus-four Fahrenheit for three hours in a freezer. The result is that surface tensions form drops of ice in the dishes about one millimeter across. The crystal appears when you shine a light on the crown of the drop of ice."

And therein came the alleged results.

Emoto—who acknowledged the experiments as "off-the-wall"—said that playing Mozart resulted in beautiful, well-formed crystals, while rock-and-roll jangled water as much as it jangles some ears. All matter, he argued, is energy vibrating at the atomic level. And it's at that threshold, he posited, that there's an almost mystical dimension.

Meanwhile, physical factors such as pollution affected the water adversely—dramatically so. Unformed or misshapen structures were noted in experiments with water exposed to cell phones, television, certain computer screens, and microwaves. Malformations were especially prominent in water that contained dioxin, a toxic compound made famous at Love Canal. The researcher said even small amounts of chlorine threw a wrench into the delicate process of formation, while H_2O from pristine mountain streams led to beautifully formed geometric designs.

"The water of Tokyo was a disaster—not a single complete crystal was formed," huffed Emoto. "However, within natural water, no matter where it came from—natural springs, underground rivers, glaciers, and the upper reaches of rivers—complete crystals formed.

"Learning about water is like an exploration to discover how the cosmos works, and the crystals revealed through water are like the portal of another dimension. And the more you understand water, the more difficult you will find it to deny the existence of a God," he almost preached.

Picture a gorgeous snowflake. It's also what he got with water from Lourdes in France. Nice ones also crystallized as Gospel music was played. Was Dr. Emoto a religious fanatic? Hardly. In fact, no religion was attributed to him. "As a result, people who have been made ill by the vibrations of hate can be miraculously healed by drinking this holy water," he said, in reference to samples from France.

When water was exposed to words relating negativity—such as *"You fool!"* or *"You make me sick"*—the results were equally dramatic—and negative. When the name "Satan" was uttered, it produced a malformed crystal that looked like . . . the eye of a reptile.

Yet, introduce the word "angel" and the result was a vibrant and well-formed crystal . . .

Prayer and praise.

Water from the Fujiwara Dam in Japan was blob-like and disfigured before offering a prayer, he reports . . . and beautiful after. "If you have one person praying with a deep sense of clarity and purity, the crystalline structure will be clear and pure," the researcher asserted. "Even if you have a large group of people, if their intention as a group is not cohesive, you end up with an incohesive structure in the water. However, if everyone is united together, you will find a clear, beautiful crystal." When people acted out of greed, it turned out, they emitted an energy that "serves to destroy the harmony within nature," Emoto further insisted.

Distance, said the Japanese scientist, was "irrelevant."

Everything is linked, he concluded. And if nothing else, we think of the living waters. "This same principle also applies to objects and locations," reported this most unconventional researcher. "For example, there are locations where accidents frequently happen, locations where businesses succeed, and locations that create happiness."

"The Old Testament states, 'In the beginning there was the Word.' This would mean that before the creation of the universe, there existed 'the Word.' My interpretation of this is that 'the Word' created human beings, and human beings then learned words from nature."

"This principle is what I think makes swearing and slang words destructive," he believed. "These words are not in accordance with the laws of nature. For example, I think you would find higher rates of violent crime in areas where a lot of negative is being used. Just as the Bible says, first there was the Word, and God created all of Creation from the Word."

While some may say it is an interconnected "energy," others would argue that it is all . . . coincidence.

"The vibration of good words has a positive effect on our world, whereas the vibration from negative words has the power to destroy," argued back the scientist.

The most potent words: those of love, in combination with gratitude, said Emoto. Most powerful were, *"Thank you."*

Enter, once more, classical music. Beethoven made for beautiful structures . . . but heavy metal?

Forget about it.

15

Faces on a Floor

They call it pareidolia.

Is it always the case?

That's when you see what you expect or want to see on or in something.

Once, in Minnesota, traveling the Mississippi (for an article in *Science Digest*), I watched roiling thunderheads form over the river's modest headwaters at Lake Itasca, where there were tornado warnings. A local man told me to head for cover if there was any hint of green in the sky.

I not only saw that hue, but for a moment—perhaps too long a moment—there appeared what seemed, in a towering cumulonimbus, like the shape of a skull.

Years later, about seven miles south of Buchach, in Ukraine, I was shown an image, on a window pane, of what looked like a bearded man with a halo—apostle-like—the glass wrapped in blankets as a priceless relic they hid under beds in various homes, fearful, though freedom had dawned, of lingering Communists. It was neither etched, nor painted, nor penciled—just *there.* It had materialized to a Catholic villager who was window-cleaning on Sunday, May 21, 1987, and took it as a sign not to work on the Sabbath!

How about Maria Gomez Pereira of Bélmez, Spain?

In August of 1971, the housewife spotted a "stain" on a tile on her kitchen floor. When she went to scrub it, no amount of elbow grease, nor detergent, could remove it.

The stain grew, shifted, and evolved into what looked like a man's face.

That evoked considerable terror, and summoned, Maria's husband, Juan, and son, Miguel, saw it too; shared her fright; and under her orders, aimed an axe at the floor, and re-cemented it.

All for naught. In quick order the image not only reassembled but was joined by a cluster of other visages, some of which disappeared and morphed into new ones, some so detailed one could discern facial wrinkles. There were detailed profiles of men, women, and children—worthy of a gallery. They bore expressions that seemed to change, eyes and mouth widening, the predominate emotions: fear and despair. Demons do things like this. So do the earthbound deceased—lingering "unclean spirits." By their fruits . . .

So desperate were the Pereiras that they welcomed help from the city council, whose mayor, on seeing for himself, decided not only to have the new floor torn up, but to excavate the ground underneath. He had a tile cut out for study.

So it went, and so, during that excavation, ten feet down, did workmen come upon a slew of bones.

Skeletons.

Some were decapitated.

Dated to seven hundred years, there were men, women . . . and children.

Executed?

Slain during Muslim invasions?

Many are those who believe souls can become "earthbound" through over-attachments and sin—or to send a message (such as "pray for me"). The caution: evil spirits are only too happy to masquerade as spirits of the dead.

In this case it was a gravesite used, it turned out, by Romans, Spanish Muslims, and medieval Christians.

Off to a Christian cemetery went the remains.

But that didn't end it. When another floor was poured, images stubbornly formed again, about a dozen. Bring in experts. The floor was photographed in sections, tested for dyes, pigments, and paint (negative), and the cement covered, by the *Instituto de Ceremica y Vidrio*, with plastic that was sealed at the edges, as were the door and windows. Recorders were set up, and then everyone was shooed away, the vault-like kitchen certifiably left alone for three months.

When it was unsealed, the faces were not only there but found to have moved.

One would manifest—only to dissolve into another.

In fact, more faces than ever were appearing—some resembling ancient portraits, others bearing ghoulish resemblance to a decaying skull. "Sometimes," noted an official report, "this regeneration would happen over the course of mere hours." On the recordings were vaguely detected wails and moans. At times, the facial expressions—more sketch-like than photographic—seemed to mimic Mrs. Pereira's emotions.

Was Maria behind it?

The cynical notion was dispelled when the beleaguered Mrs. Pereira died in 2004 and the Bélmez faces continued to manifest.

Some say they do so to the current day.

"Hoax," cried a number of observers, predictably.

"Thoughtography," said paranormalists (thoughts causing physical impressions).

"Bring in a deliverance ministry," some might also declare.

Without one, they were lost.

The final word from the city?

"If the council had done anything for the Pereiras," said the report, "it actually made things worse for them"!

16

Etched in Time

Lightning is a peculiar thing. Not only, as I said, did Satan fall as a bolt of it, but there's also the famous photo of lightning hitting the Vatican the day a pope, Benedict XVI, shocked the world on February 11, 2013, by resigning.

Head on I-4 to Tampa and you can see hundreds of flashes during a good thunderstorm. Go west near Orlando and a place named Cassadaga, a camp for psychics, same thing: constant flashes during a humid summer night, as storms sweep over inland lakes.

It's the lightning capital of the U.S., Florida—though not of the world. That particular distinction goes to Lake Maracaibo in Venezuela, which registers 1.2 million lightning strikes each year. There's also a mountain town called Kifuka in the Congo which during a storm records several lightning strikes a minute. In central Africa an entire soccer team was killed by a single bolt (blaming it on voodoo, for the score was tied)!

In native lore, there are "lightning shamans," people who seem to attract frenetic atmospheric energy. The official record-holder: Roy Cleveland Sullivan, who died in 1983—but not from lightning, though he was struck seven times. In this case, the explanation was easy: Sullivan was always among trees as a United States Park Ranger in Virginia's Shenandoah National Park.

Mysterious is "ball lighting." Associated with thunderstorms, it's been reported for centuries around the world, listed as a dangerous unexplained atmospheric discharge. Some have observed it outside, others watch as it floats into homes—luminous spheres of throbbing plasma, gaining entrance (and sometimes polite exits) through doors or windows, a mind of its own; sometimes through walls.

Usually, ball lightning, never fully explained by science, dissolves without harm; at times it explodes. Lasting but a second, it has been known to cause injuries, even fatalities, and sometimes leaves the odor of sulfur. An estimated five percent of people have reported it—whatever "it" is. In 1726, British newspapers printed excerpts of a letter from John Howell of the sloop "Catherine and Mary" in which he testified that *as we were coming thro' the Gulf of Florida on 29th of August, a large ball of fire fell from the Element and split our mast in Ten Thousand Pieces, if it were possible; split our Main Beam, also Three Planks of the Side, Under Water, and Three of the Deck; killed one man, another had his Hand carried off, and had it not been for the violent rains, our Sails would have been of a Blast of Fire . . . "*

Suspiciously, ball lightning was recorded by occultist Aleister Crowley (who lived at Loch Ness).

(And that sulfur! . . .)

There's also chain-lightning: From space it's claimed that astronauts have witnessed bolts of electricity that start on the East Coast and follow in links clear to the Pacific, like an electrical necklace.

Spookiest?

The award for that is bequeathed a courthouse in Carrollton, Alabama, which sports a ghoulish likeness that could be seen night or day—the face of a former slave-turned-criminal who peered from one of its windows as a lynch mob rushed the building and, shouting down to them, vowed that if he was slain, "I am going to haunt you for the rest of your lives!"

Michael Harold Brown

Just then, it's said, a bolt of lightning struck nearby, flashing against the window and revealing Wells' face, contorted with fear, to the crowd below.

And so it is—according to local historians—that his image, with that fear etched all over it, was seen for years on the garret window. On one occasion, every pane in the courthouse was smashed in a raucous hailstorm—every pane, that is, except the one sporting Wells' face.

There are other instances in which lightning has been said to have impressed images on glass objects. In fact, there's even a name for it: keraunography. No less than Benjamin Franklin, who knew a thing or two about lightning, reported the case of a man who had been standing opposite a tree struck by lightning and afterward bore an image of the tree—an inverse image—on his chest. In August of 1853, a young girl was standing at a window in front of a small maple tree when the plant was struck by a bolt that in like manner left the image of a tree on the girl's flesh. Two years later the same was reported with a boy who had climbed a tree during a strike and henceforth carried a keraunograph not only of the tree but a bird's nest he had been planning to rob of its eggs!

Divine retribution? "He covers His hands with the lightning," says *Job* 36:30-33, "and commands it to strike the mark."

According to the Utica *Dispatch*, a man named Abbott Parker was hit by lightning on August 5, 1904, in his bedroom in Morristown, New Jersey. It was a case that was thoroughly investigated by scientists and doctors and made headlines nationally, including in *The New York Times*. For taken to All Souls' Hospital, those who tended to him were shocked when first stripes, and then the shape of a cross—with a man on it—formed with intricate detail on Parker's burned back, down to nails and a crown of thorns precisely that mimicked a Crucifix over his bed . . .

Can skin, sensitized by lightning, serve as a photographic plate?

In rare severe cases, lightning has been known to split men in half, as if by axe.

A boy from Utah was sitting in a car with his family when, during a storm, he wished their car would be struck and immediately after the odd request, a bolt of lightning struck the vehicle's antenna. Three tires burst, all electrical gauges shut down, and the family—probably none too happy with the boy—was stranded until a passer-by stopped and called for help.

Not to be superstitious, but: at the Lowestoft Seafront Air Festival, in the east of England, at precisely 13:13 (international time) on Friday, August 13, 2010, a British teenager was hit by lightning.

Perhaps no account surpasses the summer of 1869, when a doctor in Vienna boarded a train and, when he arrived at his destination, noticed his monogrammed, tortoise-shell purse was missing.

Someone had stolen it.

Soon after, and back at work, the physician was called to treat a man who'd been struck by lightning and upon examining the patient's thigh, was shocked to see his monogram, which was made with steel, imprinted on this injured man's skin!

His surprise can be imagined. The lightning, it seemed, had been attracted by that steel.

Once his shock wore off, the physician told those present his stolen purse must be on the stricken man—and so it proved to be.

They had the thief.

However strange, there was "photographic" evidence.

17

Rock Stars and UFOs

When it comes to famous folks who've seen strange things in the sky, would it surprise anyone to know that rock musicians are prominent among them?

While we can immediately guffaw—associating such folks with hallucinogens—the sheer number of musical superstars who insist they have witnessed "UFOs" is staggering—in fact, it's almost odd to hear of a famous Sixties rocker who *didn't* report such an experience!

Let's write a lot of it off to the strange cigarettes everyone was puffing, and pills washed down with copious quantities of tequila.

It's *still* strange.

John Lennon? He claimed that at nine p.m. on August 23, 1974, he and a girlfriend (at the time he was separated from Yoko) witnessed a large, circular object about thirty yards from an apartment balcony on East Fifty-Second Street in Manhattan. It was cone-shaped, with a large red light on top.

Lennon was not only known for use of LSD but was also immersed, at least at one point during his life, with the occult. It was John who famously had the vision as a teen of a man surrounded by "flames" who told him the group of musicians he formed in Liverpool should be called "The Beatles."

It's one thing—seeing a strange airborne object or light. Lennon's experiences went much further: He also felt he had been abducted by extraterrestrials as a child. This most do not know. Nor his most extravagant claim: that one night (less than a year before his assassination), now back at the Dakota, he was semi-asleep when suddenly he noticed a blazing light pouring through the keyhole and edges of the door in his bedroom. Was someone out there with search-lights—and if so, who, why? *Was the apartment on fire?* When the superstar went to check (no doubt with trepidation), he insisted there had been "these four little people out there" with insect mouths and bug-like eyes. He also insisted he had not been on drugs.

"When I took a step towards them, they kind of pushed me back," the singer told a good friend, psychic Uri Geller (who claimed his own such ferly experiences).

"I mean, they didn't touch me. It was like they just *willed* me—pushed me back with willpower and telepathy."

When he awoke, claimed Lennon, he was holding "this egg-shaped thing in my hand"—a strange, cold, inexplicable object he later gave Geller.

And others?

Jimi Hendrix and his crew said they spotted a disc come from the clear-blue sky in 1970 while making a concert film.

Drugs? Plenty of them at rock concerts! (And drugs open strange spiritual doors . . .)

Mick Jagger claimed he saw a coruscant, cigar-shaped craft larger than a football field. That was while camping at Glastonbury Tor, believed by mystics to be a gateway to fairies . . . or the dead.

Keith Richards saw one near his estate in Sussex in 1968.

The following year, amid chaos during a notorious, violent Stones concert, at Altamont Speedway in California, a UFO appeared above, captured on film by a crew making a documentary.

It was at that concert, as the Stones sang "Sympathy for the Devil," that trouble began, escalating a few songs later into the murder of a man by members of Hell's Angels.

Any number of folks claimed to have seen UFOs over Woodstock, New York (scene of the famous free concert).

Hallucination?

Curious, at any rate.

There were certainly plenty of things that stretched the brain back then—or perhaps "contorted" would be the better term!

But, when it came to drug use, many of the cases were "off-hours," so to speak.

A guitarist for the Kinks saw crystal computers aboard a craft. (Alas, his "abduction" was "telepathic.")

Add Olivia Newton-John to the list. She saw a shape-shifting one in 1974—first fairly small and of brilliant silver but instantly growing . . . as if from another dimension.

The list is not a short one. Was Cat Stevens really "sucked up" by aliens?

Jerry Garcia, of Grateful Dead renown, made the most extravagant claim: that large insect-like beings abducted him for two days in a futuristic spaceship.

Insects? I recall those who have seen huge insect-like things as ritual places. As for UFO witnesses, an expert on the paranormal named John Keel once observed, "Many suffered certain medical symptoms such as temporary amnesia, severe headaches, muscular spasms, excessive thirst, and other effects, all of which have been observed throughout history in religious miracles, demonology, occult phenomena, and contacts with fairies. All of these manifestations clearly share a common source." He added, "One hundred years from now the phenomenon may be playing some new game with us. The whole interplanetary bag may be forgotten."

How many know that when Elvis Presley was born—at 3:30 a.m., on January 8, in 1935—a blue light was reported above his family's modest house? (His father referred to it—and often—as rock's own "star of Bethlehem.")

Or was it a hoodoo star?

"As I looked around, I noticed something strange," he reportedly said. "The whole area around the house was lit up with a blue light. It seemed to surround the house. And just at that moment, the wind stopped blowing. It was so still you could hear a pin drop."

Perhaps it was no happenstance that for the rest of his life, Elvis had a predilection toward blue (recording songs such as "Blue Moon of Kentucky," "Indescribably Blue," and "Blue Suede Shoes . . .").

He was also obsessed with the occult. A friend named Wanda June Hill insisted he could make a heavy green glass ashtray move from one side of a cocktail table to another . . . without touching it.

In the 1950s, testified Lamar Fike, his burly bodyguard, he and Elvis watched what looked like a cigar-shaped "mother ship."

Take it all . . . under advisement.

Elvis told confidantes he had been in contact with cosmogenic intelligences since age five and that the entities wrote music for him; spoke of his home planet; and showed him a man under stage lights dressed in white . . . which is precisely how Elvis dressed, spacesuit-style, in his latter years.

After the "King's" death, in 1978, more than a dozen "UFOs" were sighted by fans at his final resting place in Graceland, some as low as twenty feet above the tomb and hovering as if in final homage.

18

Whispers in Space

If the astronaut Edgar Mitchell of Apollo 14 had involved himself in strange matters once he returned from the moon —founding a group dedicated to studying various phenomena—this was due to a mystical feeling that overcame him on the way back to earth. Suddenly, from up there, he explained, our planet seemed like far more than the inanimate ball of water and rock science depicted it to be. As the capsule rotated, he said, a 360-degree panorama of the heavens—earth, moon, sun—unfolded, said the astronaut, showing that everything linked, in transcendent ways, with the heavens. It was an epiphany, a spiritual "high," a new way of viewing existence; Mitchell labeled it a *samadhi.* Call it what you may. "Amazing" is probably simple enough . . .

Strange sights, *in*sights, and sounds up there!

Or at least: *seen* from up there. During his space mission Soviet cosmonaut Vladimir Lyakhov said he had looked down upon earth and at one point witnessed two gigantic waves rise from the Indian Ocean and then collide with each other—forming an evanescent mass of water that vanished . . . in an instant.

What was *that*?

Cosmonaut Vladimir Kovalyonok reported a highly similar pillar of water in the Timor Sea, which he estimated as sixty miles in height.

Delusions due to the great vacuity, the endless supernal vistas, of space? We know there are rogue waves out there—giant ones that scientists now say occur much more frequently than previously thought. In fact for decades, researchers ensconced in our Ivy Towers scoffed at such as mere seafaring fables.

Now we know better: freak waves of over a hundred feet and perhaps approaching *two* hundred, have been documented, tearing the bows off oil tankers and often causing large ships to sink like granite. We're talking about vessels that can be as long as several football fields, 186,000 tons of bulk abruptly vanishing. In one seven-year period, ninety-nine bulk carrier ships were lost—many without a trace and absent from the news. I knew a fellow named David McTaggart who piloted a yacht through the Southern Pacific from New Zealand to a remote island called Mururoa and encountered swells that were "literally the size of small mountain ranges. From the top of one to the top of another was the distance of at least two miles. Coming up over the top, we had such a vantage point that I was quite sure I could see for a hundred miles." There is no question that landslides and the great ocean gyres have caused waves up to a mile high. But *sixty*? And anyway: how did the cosmonaut estimate it? . . .

No doubt—the senses can play tricks in space, or anywhere. Some cosmonauts believe they've heard a "cosmic whisper"—so common among Russian space travelers that during training they're prepared psychologically for it. There is also unexplained music ("not of this earth," said cosmonaut Yuri Gagarin). Whispered to another, as if from a relative, were the words: *"You arrived here too early, and you did it in a wrong fashion. Trust me, for I am your ancestor on the maternal side. Do you remember, she told you: back when you were a child, about your great-grandfather, who had founded the D-s factory in the Urals?"* (Here a private detail, later confirmed. And surprising final words: *"Sonny, you*

*should not be here, go back to earth, do not violate the Laws
of the Creator . . . Sonny, you must return, return, return . . . ")*

Both cosmonauts and astronauts have seen lights and
objects for which they have no explanation, including from
the moon. "Neil Armstrong relayed the message to Mission
Control that two large, mysterious objects were watching
them after having landed near the moon module, but this
message was never heard by the public—because NASA
censored it," Dr. Vladimir Azhazha, a former Russian naval
officer, told a reporter.

This is frequently alleged: that the government is allergic
to unusual reports, and has cut live feeds of the space station
when unusual lights, shadows, small exploding objects, or
solid-looking intact ones have materialized. In 1979 a man
identified as a former chief of NASA Communications
Systems (by others as an engineer) confirmed that Armstrong
had reported two unknown objects on the rim of a crater
during that historic first step on the lunar landscape. "The
encounter was common knowledge in NASA, but nobody
has talked about it until now," asserted Maurice Chatelain.
"All Apollo and Gemini flights were followed, both at a
distance and sometimes also quite closely, by space vehicles
of extraterrestrial origin—flying saucers, or UFOs, if you
want to call them by that name. Every time it occurred, the
astronauts informed Mission Control, who then ordered
absolute silence. I think that Walter Schirra aboard Mercury
8 was the first of the astronauts to use the code name 'Santa
Claus' to indicate the presence of flying saucers next to space
capsules. However, his announcements were barely noticed
by the general public. It was a little different when James
Lovell on board the Apollo 8 command module came out
from behind the moon and said for everybody to hear:
'PLEASE BE INFORMED THAT THERE IS A SANTA
CLAUS.' Even though this happened on Christmas Day 1968,
many people sensed a hidden meaning in those words."

On August 15, 1978, cosmonaut Vladimir Kovalyonok spotted a strange object that repeatedly approached and then drew back from the *Salyut-6* space station. Two years later, aboard the same vehicle, Valery Ryumin and Leonid Popo observed a school of "white glowing dots" that took off in the area of Moscow and flew off into the space above them, reporting this to ground control. And ten years later, on September 28, Gennady Strekalov recorded a sphere over Newfoundland of the space station MIR, according to a news outlet, *Rabochaya Tribuna*. The roundish object was beautiful and shifted colors like a kaleidoscope, visible for perhaps ten seconds, and then . . . gone.

Optical illusions? Space debris? Urban legend?

Fanciful it can be. And there *has* been fakery.

But by all renderings, strange things do transpire, none more so than what was reported by the six men aboard the Soviet Salyut-7 space station who were conducting routine laboratory experimentation in 1985 when a bizarre orange "gas" suddenly enveloped the station. That was accompanied by a brilliant flash that all but blinded the crew, which first startled, then stunned Leonid Kizim, Oleg Atkov, Vladimir Solovyov, Svetlana Savitskaya, Igor Volk, and Vladimir Jannibekov. For, claimed the official Russian newspaper, *Pravda*:

"As soon as they could see again, the cosmonauts saw silhouettes of seven figures outside the station. The aliens looked like humans, but were of higher stature.

"They also had large wings behind their backs and luminous halos above their heads.

"The creatures looked like angels. The crew reported the bizarre sight to the earth. The document was immediately classified as "top secret."

"All members of the crew were subsequently subjected to psychological and medical tests" (which found no abnormalities).

On day 167—it's rumored—the crew was joined by three cosmonauts from the Soyuz T-12 spacecraft. Shortly after, *Salyut 7* was bathed once again "in a warm orange light," reported one source. "Then, like clockwork, they immediately looked out the portholes—and once again, were joined by angelic beings. They were reportedly the size of an 'airliner.' This incident was deemed top secret by the old Soviet Union and the crew was cautioned not to speak of the event publicly."

It went all the way up to the Politburo, we're told—which, like NASA, ordered strict silence.

"UFOs, angels and other supernatural phenomena, which people may encounter in their lives, can only be a result of hallucinations, NASA specialists said," as *Pravda* put it (in 2011). "However, stories about such encounters, told by pilots, cosmonauts and astronauts, become classified immediately."

Is there more to space than we think—perhaps not so empty after all? Is it "heaven" or a part of heaven or the "outer darkness" (*Matthew* 22:13)? "For we wrestle not against flesh and blood, but against principalities, against powers, against the rulers of the darkness of this world, against spiritual wickedness in high places," adds *Ephesians* (6:12).

As Apollo 10 sailed around the moon's dark side, two astronauts heard an eerie music-like echo and like their counterparts in Russia, a "whisper." When such sights are seen and sounds heard, the first recourse of explanation is the biological effect of spacesuit pressure, zero gravity, temperature shifts, changes in brain oxygen levels, and simple solitude.

It's a funny thing, though—when more than one space explorer has the same "hallucination."

19

Whispers from Beneath

There are other mysteries, and whispers, below . . .

Few realize how much a puzzle the subterranean world is. The tendency is to think every inch of our planet has been probed, plotted, scanned, portioned, sampled, mapped, and neatly tucked between notebook binders for geology confabs to ponder or displayed, with finality, and also hubris, in museum dioramas.

Facts belie such certainty. In fact we know more about the surface of Pluto than what's at the center or core of our own planet!

That's because it's four thousand miles down, greater than the distance between New York and Los Angeles.

The deepest hole drilled by humans?

Eight miles, by Russians in Siberia. It's called the "Kola Peninsula Superdeep Borehole," and it sparks a lot of lore. Most say the drilling stopped when the drill bit hit hot rock that was more borsch than stone. Others like to say what the bit hit was hell. "The last discovery was nevertheless the most shocking to our ears, so much so that the scientists are afraid to continue the project," one Russian geologist, identified as a "Dr. Azzacov"—but never verified as an actual scientist—has been quoted as saying.

"We tried to listen to the earth's movements at certain intervals with supersensitive microphones, which were let down through the hole. What we heard turned those logically thinking scientists into a trembling ruins. It was a sometimes weak but high-pitched sound which we thought to be coming from our own equipment. After some adjustments we comprehended that indeed the sound came from the earth's interior. We could hardly believe our own ears. We heard a human voice, screaming in pain. Even though one voice was discernible, we could hear thousands, perhaps millions, in the background, of suffering souls screaming. After this ghastly discovery, about half of the scientists quit because of fear. Hopefully, that which is down there will stay there!"

Legends also accompany a series of disconnected tunnels that spot landscapes from Scotland to the Adriatic.

No one knows who actually constructed them (German legend says gnomes and elves), how extensive the network is (we do know it reaches all the way to Turkey), nor the purpose. The narrowest passageways, linking upper to lower levels, are a mere sixteen inches in width—"strange winding passages," some five thousand years old, through which "one can only force oneself like a worm," said a priest who, guided only by candlelight, investigated four hundred of them.

Entryways have been found in the kitchens of archaic farmhouses, in proximity to churches and cemeteries, but also in the middle of forests. Speculation on their role: escape routes from castles, spiritual spots for those goblins, and even . . . use as toilets.

Near Oaxaca, Mexico, are "pygmy tunnels" that at points are no more than a foot high, although we have a clue as to the purpose; burials; a skeleton at the end of each one.

Are there also natural tunnels, large ones that network and connect deep lakes—and lochs—with oceans?

If so, might this be the avenue for . . . lake monsters?

And below those, could the planet be composed of a subterranean ocean: massive reserves of hidden water that, bursting forth, from below the mantle, account for what happened to Noah . . . ?

A maverick geologist, Dr. Andrew A. Snelling, says, "All available evidence points to a recent catastrophic origin for the world's vast oil deposits, from plant and other organic debris, consistent with the biblical view of earth history. Vast forests grew on land surfaces in the pre-Flood world, and the oceans teemed with diatoms and other tiny organisms. Then during the global Flood cataclysm, the forests were uprooted and swept away. Huge masses of plant debris were rapidly buried in what thus became coal beds, and organic matter generally was dispersed throughout the many catastrophically deposited sedimentary rock layers."

Is it the darkness that makes it all fertile ground for fabulation?

Under the city of Toronto are various networks of caves and tunnels and in 1978, a fifty-one-year-old man who wandered into one of them in search of a lost kitten claimed to have instead found a creature that looked like a monkey and was about three feet tall—with unsettling eyes that peered from dark sockets. Slanted. Bright orange. "I got out of there as fast as I could," he told the Toronto *Sun* with a straight face. "I was shaking with fear. I saw a living night-mare that I'll never forget. It said, *'Go away, go away'* in a hissing voice."

In the United States, legend has it that a vast complex of tunnels underlie Death Valley, caverns where—incongru-ously—Masonic symbols are claimed along with the remains of prehistoric animals like the mammoth, while the Grand Canyon was the setting for an astonishing discovery on April 5, 1909, when a man named G.E. Kinkaid found a massive chamber 1,480 feet below and radiating passages that are like the spokes of a wheel—therein found copper implements, ancient Native American weapons, a crypt of mummies (wrapped in a bark fabric), and a shrine with a

Buddha-like idol sitting cross-legged with a lotus flower in each hand and stone tablets bearing carvings that resemble . . . Egyptian hieroglyphics.

"Discoveries almost conclusively prove that the race which inhabited this mysterious cavern, hewn in solid rock by human hands, was of oriental origin, possibly from Egypt, tracing back to Ramses," reported a newspaper a hundred years ago. "If their theories are borne out by the translation of the tablets engraved with hieroglyphics, the mystery of the prehistoric peoples of North America, their ancient arts, who they were and whence they came, will be solved. Egypt and the Nile, and Arizona and Colorado, will be linked by a historical chain running back to ages which staggers the wildest fancy of the fictionist."

One tour company not far from a subterranean burial site near the Grand Canyon says, "The bodies have been removed, but the whispering sounds of the Indians can often be heard in the caverns when one listens according to reports. Overnight guests in the caverns have also reported seeing what appear to be shadows of Indian figures moving in a dance formation.

"And at night in the darkness of the caverns, you do hear things," he insists, "that are not supposed to be heard."

20

When an Animal Speaks (and Thinks)

What if you could see out of the eyes—and cogitate from the brain—of animals? What would you see?

What would you hear?

More to the point, how *smart* would those brains turn out to be?

The answer: more intelligent than the vast majority of *homo sapiens* give them credit for being.

Take a "dumb," ugly, feared creature like the American alligator (*alligator mississippiensis*). I kayak the creeks and lakes of Florida, often encountering this animal and talking with those who've been observing such reptiles all their lives.

Some of what you hear is hard to fathom.

In the Everglades an airboat guide told me gators can distinguish between the *colors* of pickup trucks that pull up along a waterway. He observed that they stay low in the water and out of sight if it's the color of a truck they associate with someone who hunts them. When the same hunter drives up in a differently colored vehicle, the animal lingers—until it knows better . . .

Alligators also know where hunting occurs and where it doesn't: At Midway Airboats in Christmas, Florida, the owner, a hunter himself, told me old, wise gators migrate south of a bridge on the St. Johns River at dusk, because dusk is when hunters arrive and south of the bridge is off-limits for hunting. He said the gators do this *only during hunting season.* Meanwhile, the director of the Alligator Farm in St. Augustine, who is a scientist, says gators there know their names, lifting their appreciable, jaw-dominated, scaly heads when their names are called. All this with a brain the size of a quarter!

When a psychologist named Dr. Irene Pepperberg, of Harvard, wandered into a specialty pet store in 1977, science had no idea that birds could communicate with man beyond mimicking their voices. Dr. Pepperberg had simply asked the store owner to pick out an African Grey for her, which he did, choosing one from a cage of eight; flipping it on its back; clipping its wings (you don't want a $1,400 bird winging out the door); and popping it into a small box.

Soon, she told me, the parrot, which she named "Alex," not only learned motions but also words associated with objects, able to discern the color of a sheet of paper or pick up the right plastic alphabet letters. If Alex desired a grape (*"Wanna grape"*), but was given a banana, he'd toss it back and with insistence say, *"Want a grape!"* He looked down his beak at less able parrots: When another wasn't responding clearly to Dr. Pepperberg's cues, Alex would tell the bird, *"Say better."* Once, when the scientist shrieked at the bird for chewing up a grant application, he cowered and said, *"I'm sorry . . . I'm sorry."* When a toy bird was introduced into the cage, Alex said, *"You tickle,"* and when the toy obviously did not respond, the irate parrot said, *"You turkey!"* The last words of Alex to Dr. Pepperberg before he died at age thirty-one: *"You be good . . . I love you . . ."*

Wasn't Balaam's donkey able to talk (*Numbers 22:28*) . . .?

Many parrots can repeat an entire sentence after hearing it once, and laugh at appropriate times. How many words can a parrot say in proper sequence? In one case: two hundred and fifty—comparable to reciting an entire page from a book, verbatim. So far the grey is the only animal tested that grasps the concept of "zero." In one countdown on animal intelligence, it placed third—just behind chimps and dolphins. Yet we use the pejorative, "bird brain . . ."

Crows? Like parrots they have been known to fashion sticks as tools, and to fly down from their perch on utility lines with nuts they can't crack, nudge them under the tires of cars stopped at intersections, and then fly back up to the power lines, where they wait for the light to turn green, and descend when the automobiles have done the cracking for them! This has been documented from Upstate New York to Sendai in Japan.

At Assisi in Italy is a statue of Saint Francis in the garden of Santa Maria degli Angeli; doves roost in a basket held by the statue's hands. I saw this for myself: wild doves. Francis was known as a bird lover!

Might animals also have ESP?

We've all heard of pets that somehow find their way back to their owners even if they were lost hundreds of miles away. *How?* Or—and here we go a bit beyond regular intelligence—canines sometimes know when an owner dies, howling uncannily even if that owner is miles away. Some refuse to leave graveyards where their masters are interred.

Many are those who believe that animals pick up their emotions and thoughts, or that seem to see into the spiritual—things we cannot. There are those who have clinical death experiences and claim they saw their deceased pets on the other side. Wishful thinking? Billy Graham once said, "It may be that God's purpose for animals is fulfilled on this earth. However, if animals would make us happier in heaven, surely there will be a place for them there . . ." Why would God have bothered to have Noah save them all, if they, or at least some, were worthless? In *Isaiah* 11:6 is the prophecy of a new reality that includes the wolf and lamb, a leopard and calf, a young lion lying with a calf. Pope Paul VI added, "One day we will again see our animals in the eternity of Christ"—although the Catholic Church does not teach this directly (and steps back from it).

Some believe they have seen apparitions of their pets. This includes a soldier named Joseph who, returning home after World War Two, in Virginia's Shenandoah Valley, was walking toward a river and had a choice of two bridges, one old, one new. Naturally he chose the shortest way but as he was upon the bridge he was met by "Shep," his old family dog. Joseph greeted the pet, playing joyfully with it before going back toward the bridge.

Suddenly Shep tugged on his pant leg, barking in agitation . . . obviously opposed to what Joe was doing. It was strange, but intuition led the veteran to taking the long way—the other bridge—and when he got home, he explained why he was late—his encounter with Shep.

Everyone glanced at each other and then gave Joseph a strange look. Shep, they informed him, had died the previous winter . . .

The next morning they learned that the river had flooded and torn out the middle section of the first bridge. If he had tried to cross (it had been dark), the returning veteran may well have plummeted into the swift current.

Nearly as preternatural are the mundane feats of horses—or so it is alleged. Can anything top the case of Wilhelm Von Osten? (Was it a case of trickery?)

A mathematics teacher, phrenologist, amateur horse trainer—also something of a mystic—Van Osten had a horse named "Hans" who was taught to add, subtract, divide, multiply, work with fractions, tell time, keep track of the calendar, differentiate musical tones, and read, spell, and understand German. Or so it was said.

Addressing his horse, Von Osten posed questions like:

"If the eighth day of the month comes on a Tuesday, what is the date of the following Friday?"

Hans would answer by tapping his hoof.

After Professor E. Clarapede at the University of Geneva tested the stallion for several weeks, he reported that "Hans could do more than mere sums: he knew how to read; he could distinguish between harmonious and dissonant chords of music." (A connoisseur to boot!) His estimated level of intelligence: that of a fourteen-year-old . . .

Was the horse simply taking cues from its trainer and those who tested him?

In another case a horse who had been trained a code suddenly stopped responding and, asked why, tapped out, *"Tired."*

Then he added (via that tap code), *"Pain in leg."*

A similarly adept horse named Muhamed took it to another level: Asked by two Berlin scientists why he didn't simply talk (*a la* "Mr. Ed"), instead of answering with his hooves, the horse made a few pitiful noises (in an effort to verbalize) and after a few frustrating minutes, tapped out letters that formed the words, *"/ h-a-v-e-n-o-t a g-o-o-d v-o-i-c-e."*

And then, stranger, was the African Grey who had been left at home longer than ever before. When his owners returned, and took him out of his cage, he said—and plaintively, to their shock, as they brought in their suitcases—*"Where you been?"*

21

Heart To Heart

Claire Sylvia wasn't the type to snack on chicken nuggets, nor quaff it down with a Bud. At forty-eight, a former dancer and choreographer, she was very particular about her physical condition. In mannerism, she certainly wasn't brusque. In fact she was described as "soft-spoken."

Then Claire began to act in an aggressive way. Impetuous. Compulsive. All of a sudden, it seemed, she was drawn to "cooler" colors—not the bright oranges and reds she'd always favored.

Those nuggets: she could barely keep herself from dashing to Kentucky Fried Chicken.

Also, she suddenly liked *beer.*

If that seemed incomprehensible, to those who knew Claire, so did when and how all these changes occurred: after she'd had a lung-heart transplant at Yale-New Haven Hospital in 1988, the first such operation in New England.

Her donor had been a fellow named Tim Lamirande, who died at eighteen in a motorcycle tragedy. Investigators searching through his clothing after the crash found something both peculiar and relevant: a pack of uneaten Kentucky Fried Chicken nuggets, in a pocket of the young man's jacket.

Tim was a drinker.

His libation of choice: beer.

His own mannerisms: Well, let's say Tim could be a little . . . brusque.

His favorite colors?

The cooler ones.

"Create in me a clean heart, O God, and renew a right spirit within me" (*Psalms* 51:10). "Above all else, guard your heart, for everything you do flows from it (*Proverbs* 4:23).

Such instances—of people who experience personality changes after an organ transplant, especially the heart—are not rare. In a study published in the journal of *Quality of Life Research*, researchers interviewed 47 heart recipients in Vienna and found that while 79 percent did not feel that their personality shifted post-surgery, fifteen percent described a change due to the life-threatening event, and six percent a drastic one. At last count, another researcher logged seventy.

A forty-seven-year-old foundry worker suddenly loves classical music after his transplant. The donor: a teenager who was walking to violin class when he fell victim to a senseless drive-by shooting (and died hugging his violin case . . .).

The hamburger aficionado who suddenly turned vegetarian . . . after receiving the heart of a woman who owned a health-food restaurant.

The organ recipient who suddenly feared water—his donor a person who drowned.

The young man who giggled girlishly, precisely like his deceased female donor.

Claims Dr. Gary E. Schwartz, one of those who has researched this, a Harvard-educated scholar now at the University of Arizona:

"When the organ is placed in the recipient, the information and energy stored in the organ is passed on to the recipient. The theory applies to any organ that has cells that are interconnected. They could be kidneys, liver, and even muscles. The stories we have uncovered are very compelling and are completely consistent."

William Sheridan's drawing skills? Kindergarten level. If he drew, it was stick figures. But as he recovered from a heart transplant, at Mount Sinai Hospital in Manhattan, suddenly and inexplicably he could produce gorgeous, intricate landscapes. His donor turned out to have been an artist. ("Days after his transplant, he began creating this amazing, elaborate artwork," noted Beth DeFuria, the hospital's art therapist.) Yet another scientist put highly sensitive probes on small groups of cells and claimed, on a stack of medical texts, that they reacted to the emotions of their owner . . . who was in another room. (The more superstitious might suspect spirits.)

Serious scientists brook none of this. Quackery. But it was serious business for an eighteen-year-old girl nick-named "Danny" who was afflicted with endocarditis and required a coronary transplant after heart failure.

Once a loud "hell-raiser," she turned inexplicably retiring and quiet after her operation and suddenly wanting to play a musical instrument. Her donor (completely unknown to Danny) was a boy of the same age, the victim of an accident and son of a psychiatrist who later recalled:

"He had decided to donate his organs when he was twelve years old. We thought it was quite strange, but we thought they were talking about it at school. He always wrote poetry. We had waited more than a year to clean out his room after he died. We found a book of poems he had never shown us. One of them has left us shaken emotionally and spiritually. It spoke of his seeing his own death. He was a musician, too, and we found a song."

Title of the composition his parents unearthed: *"Danny, My Heart Is Yours."*

22

Mummies That Curse

Was she cursed?

After her shocking loss in the 2016 U.S. presidential election, Hillary Clinton presented a long list of reasons for her loss. None of them was a "curse."

And yet . . . some were made to wonder.

That's because in 1997, as First Lady, Clinton stopped at a museum in the Russian city of Novosibirsk, where she was treated—if "treated" is the verb—to a private showing of a recently disinterred mummy, one believed to be that of a woman, perhaps a shaman, who died about 2,500 years before.

The Russians dubbed the mummified female Ochi-Bala—princess of the Altai people—with an ominous warning: it was said that anyone who crossed her path would be sorry.

In fact, during removal of her body, scientists testified there had been, on a stormless day, a sudden clap of thunder. Soon after, an earthquake rattled the area. And after that, an upsurge in similar tremors was accompanied by forest fires, windstorms, various illnesses, even a rash of suicides.

Then a helicopter carrying her remains crashed.

And once Ochi-Bala was ensconced at Novosibirsk, all hell seemed to break out in the country, as rebel tanks shelled the Russian parliament.

In the U.S., scandal erupted when Hillary's husband, President William Jefferson Clinton, was caught in the Monica Lewinsky affair . . .

Whether there's a scintilla of validity to the "Ochi-Bala curse," there are other reasons to wonder if things and circumstances and people can be hexed. There is the curse of *Superman*: actors who played that part have run into trouble, starting with the suicide of the original superman, George Reeves and then the tragic accident of Christopher Reeve, who played the superman part in a major movie—and soon after was paralyzed upon falling from a horse.

Not long after, Reeve's wife died of lung cancer (though she didn't smoke); Margot Kidder (who played Lois Lane) developed bipolar disorder and in the end killed herself; a member of a video crew was mugged; and a producer of *Superman* cartoons died in poverty (while a colleague fell down a flight of stairs).

Just happenstance?

Some. Others, perhaps not.

In the six years between the first and third *Poltergeist* movies, four cast members died, and the same woe followed those associated with *The Exorcist*—deaths, accidents, illness; two actors whose characters die in the movie themselves passed away shortly after the movie was done; as shooting began, in 1972, the set used as the home of Regan MacNiel burned down when a bird flew into a circuit box; eerily, the only part to remain untouched by flames was the room used for filming the actual exorcism scenes. That delayed shooting. When it resumed, the star's plane (this Gregory Peck) was hit by lightning on the way across the Atlantic to film it! Evangelist Billy Graham declared the very celluloid as "cursed." In Rome, lightning struck a church across the street from a theatre where it opened . . .

While director Roman Polanski was shooting Rosemary's Baby, his wife, Sharon Tate, was brutally murdered, along with their unborn baby, by the Charles Manson cult. Manson said his inspiration to kill came from the Beatles song, "Helter Skelter."

The devilish movie, starring Mia Farrow (about a woman who gets wrapped up with a strange cult, and gives birth to the devil's spawn), was filmed at the famous Dakota apartments on Manhattan's Upper West Side.

Years later, Beatle John Lennon was killed at the Dakota, where he and Yoko had taken up residence.

The last person his assassin, Mark David Chapman, saw before shooting the rock 'n' roll legend was . . . Mia Farrow . . . who happened to pass by with her dog on the way to Central Park . . .

There are other musicians. There have been other politicians (see, the Kennedys). There are *things*, such as the Hope Diamond—taken from a temple idol in India and bad luck for all those who owned it.

The afflictions suffered are legion.

There is the "Curse of the Oetzi Iceman," a prehistoric man discovered in the Alps in 1991: seven of those who found him have succumbed to accidents, one from an avalanche, a second on the way to a lecture about it, a third by falling off a cliff (near where the iceman was discovered); all within a year.

An hour after funeral services for the fellow who fell off the cliff, the head of the rescue team died of a heart attack.

In Brazil, the national museum tragically burned down in 2018, destroying an estimated twenty million items—including a plethora of mummies, among which was "Luzia"—11,000 years old . . .

Ill fortune likewise fell upon those involved with the tomb of the Egyptian king, Tutankhamun (or "Tut").

In 1922, shortly after opening of the tomb, Howard Carter, a British archeologist who led the team, was informed by messenger that a cobra had slithered into the cage of his pet canary.

That's one story, anyway.

Cobras were symbols of Egyptian pharaohs.

On April 5, 1923, George Edward Stanhope Molyneux Herbert, financial backer of the expedition, was bit by a mosquito and suffered serious infection after he slit the bite while shaving—an infection that caused fatal blood poisoning. Across Cairo, it was reported, the lights went out at the exact time of Herbert's death.

Electrical outages, they point out, were common.

But noted the London *Guardian*: "The media in the 1920s found plenty of evidence that something was punishing the excavators of the most perfect ancient Egyptian burial chamber ever found. His pet bird was eaten by a snake, his dog died back in England almost the exact moment he kicked the bucket in Egypt, and a radiologist who supposedly x-rayed the mummy died of a mysterious illness. A rich American died of pneumonia after visiting the tomb, and a member of Carter's excavation team was said to have died of arsenic poisoning."

When Tut was unwrapped two years after *that*, the mummy was found to have a wound on the left cheek—in perfect correspondence to the location of Herbet's mosquito bite!

Meanwhile, a mummified hand given by Carter as a memento and used as a paperweight (by Sir Bruce Ingram) was adorned, it seems, with a scarab bracelet, the hiero*glyphs of which, we come to learn, said: "Cursed be he who moves my body. To him shall come fire, water and pestilence."*

Shortly after receiving the gift (according to Mideastern historian H. V. F. Winstone), Ingram's house burned down . . . followed by a flood when it was rebuilt.

Myth? No doubt, some is.

But all?

Carter, who lived to a reasonable age, was skeptical of any curse but took note of spotting rare Anubis jackals in 1926, the first he'd ever encountered on the Sahara in three decades of work there—jackals like those depicted in ancient etchings as guardians of the dead.

Within a dozen years, eight of those present at the tomb's opening were dead.

I kept my distance while visiting both Tut's Tomb, in Cairo, and the Hope Diamond, at the Smithsonian . . . though uttering the Name of Jesus would have sufficed. Distancing oneself is a bit more challenging when a "curse" comes from the angry, hateful, or jealous thoughts of another person, particularly someone close to us.

When it comes to mummies, Tut may not have been the worst of it. Once more we find ourselves four hundred miles off frigid Newfoundland. On a luxury ship, author-spiritualist William T. Stead regaled seven fellow passengers on April 12, 1912, and stretching into the wee hours of April 13, with the account of an inscription on the lid of a mummy warning that anyone who spoke the words audibly would meet a violent death.

Stead, in this version of the story, may have recited it— boasting that he was not prone to such nonsense.

At any rate, seven of the eight men, including Stead, died when the ship sank, leaving just one, Fred Seward, to recount it.

Superstition?

The ship, of course, was the *Titanic*.

23

A Miracle in 'Hell'

Some said it was at the intersection leading to the gates of hell. After all, it isn't so far from a mine that's been burning out of control for half a century, rendering a city above a ghost town. It's claimed that a priest put a "curse" on it after attack by a secret society known as the "Molly McGuires," vowing that his church in this eastern Pennsylvania coal city would be the only building left standing. Even horror movies have been based on it. A hellish scenario it was, and remains—fires erupting here and there on the now-abandoned streets, spewing toxic gas. One writer called it "the demon fire."

That's Centralia. But the year after the coal fires started, it was a neighboring city called Sheppton that experienced a disaster at least as horrifying: collapse of an anthracite column that trapped three miners on Tuesday, August 13, 1963: Hank Throne, twenty-eight years of age at the time; David Fellin, part owner of the small company that owned the mine; and another employee, fifty-four-year-old Frank Bova. They were entombed more than three hundred feet below when a runaway cart smashed support columns, Fellin and Throne able to protect themselves in one cubbyhole while Frank was isolated in another.

For those fourteen days, almost sleepless, as they held and rocked each other to remain warm, Fellin and Throne inhaled thick coal-laden daggers of air in the dark and, almost starving, gnawed bark off the timber supports, washing it down with sulfuric water as they crawled about a space no more than fourteen-by-nine-feet, feeling their way through rock piles and excrement—unable in spots to stand fully erect nor to determine if it was day or night, no idea whatsoever, more to the point, if anyone outside would ever be able to reach them—if they even knew where they were. Fellin led prayers. And prayers. Crawl, tap, listen, pray. (*"Lord, help get us out . . ."*). The place seemed consecrated by the devil himself, causing them to wonder if—in exchange for the riches brought by coal—they were a blood sacrifice.

Many above already took them for dead. "Fear Three Area Men Killed in Sheppton Mine," was one immediate headline, and soon that fear was accepted as fate: Funeral rites were planned by St. Joseph Church at what had been the mouth of the shaft before it collapsed . . .

Still, rescuers fought to find them—drilling two six-inch-wide bores—and after six arduous days, detecting sounds. Gigantic machinery was rushed from as far as the oil fields of Texas as workers, first dozens, then hundreds, labored around the clock, gathering the encouragement of Governor William Scranton and U.S. President John F. Kennedy. Massive generators powered a drill that weighed a staggering sixty-five tons, cheers erupting when things went well, then falling when matters took a wrong turn.

The urgent mission: burrowing widely and deeply enough to extract the miners without causing rock slides or gushes of blackened groundwater, sure to drown anyone still alive. And the sounds indicated there *was* life.

All the two miners could do, in the meantime, was listen to the sounds, try to fend off the constant fifty-degree cold, and pray. Throne was enthralled as Fellin, who seemed abnormally calm, spoke of God, salvation, and Jesus. This went on for nearly fourteen days. Food, water, and a microphone were lowered.

Once the burrow was completed, a hoist was lowered and the two men, bouncing against the sides of a large bore, each was painstakingly lifted, staggering when they got to the surface to eruptions of cheers. Bova's ending was not so lucky: he was never seen again.

That was one part of the story—the part focused upon by newsmen. There was, however, a deeper aspect. For when they were debriefed, Fellin and Throne related that the mine compartment in which they were trapped had been like another dimension.

There had been constant visions, the two miners said. There had been angels. There was a spiraling staircase that went up from their position, in endless skyward fashion. There were various illuminations. Oddest were the human-like figures dressed in strange shiny space suits with softly glowing lanterns attached to their helmets, as if looking for them.

Hallucinations?

Booze?

At one point, someone had slipped Fellin's libation of choice—Johnnie Walker Scotch Whiskey—in with the supplies . . .

But that had come at the very end, and the visions were there, they testified, from the beginning. Moreover, both Throne and Fellin witnessed precisely identical phenomena. "The lights and figures always were in front of us," explained Throne to a reporter.

"But the more we crawled toward them, the farther away they got . . ."

On the fourth day—an especially dismal one, with both men left back in total dark, and Throne, in a deep depression, yet clinging to hope—the tomb suddenly had been lit by what seemed like a door outlined in bright blue luminescence, clearer than sunlight. Two ordinary-looking men—decidedly not rescue miners—opened the door to the gorgeous marble steps. Around the vision had been an aurora that shimmered in an effulgence not of this earth, with a massive ethereal construct they described as miles and miles of celestial majesty—a "Golden City."

There was the lambent light. There was exquisite music—penetrating as a trumpet, but sweetly pitched, as soft and gliding as a violin. Fellin spotted deceased relatives. Children and angels were there, interacting. Everything was made of gold, alabaster. The ceiling captured aureate glory (*"When the roll is called up yonder . . ."*).

Stranger still, both miners—one Catholic, one Protestant—insisted that for most of the ordeal they were in the presence of a gently smiling man in a black cassock. He was encompassed by the blue hue and radiating encouragement. From photographs shown them later, they identified the apparition as the youthful visage of Pope John XXIII—who had died weeks before the mine collapse.

Day and night, for more than a week, whenever they opened their eyes, but never uttering a word—at least that we know, they said—was the pontiff, arms folded as if in respect.

It was perhaps worthy of irony that the pope, known for journeys by foot around Rome, had borne the nickname "Johnnie Walker."

Afterwards Throne, not a churchgoer at the time of the accident, founded the Living Savior Church in Hazelton. Fellin maintained his own faith. And, it seems, never revealed all he encountered.

"We saw many other things like that, that you couldn't explain," Fellin told the Philadelphia *Inquirer*, "but I'm not going to tell you about them because I feel too deeply about all this."

And so it was that those secrets would remain as such for nearly three decades . . . going with Fellin to the grave.

24

The Pilots Saw What?

In December of 2017, reports flashed across normally sober publications such as *The New York Times* and *The Washington Post* about a secret government program that monitored UFOs. Needless to say, it raised brows and widened eyes.

It was called the Advanced Aerospace Threat Identification Program, and its budget was almost impossible to find. In the end, it was learned that inspiration for the project had come from a hotel billionaire who holds a fascination for the bizarre and who once bought a ranch on which everything from bigfoot to werewolves were said to have roamed, under strange lights in the sky. As *The Times* put it, "For years, the program investigated reports of unidentified flying objects, according to Defense Department officials, interviews with program participants and records obtained by *The New York Times*. It was run by a military intelligence official, Luis Elizondo, on the fifth floor of the Pentagon's 'C-Ring,' deep within the building's maze. The Defense Department has never before acknowledged the existence of the program, which it says it shut down in 2012. But its backers say that, while the Pentagon ended funding for the effort at that time, the program remains in existence."

Was it science, or did it relate to the warning in *Matthew* 24: 24: "For there shall arise false Christs, and false prophets, and shall shew great signs and wonders; insomuch that, if it were possible, they shall deceive the very elect"? One alleged government study group dubbed the "Collins Elite" supposedly concluded as did others that UFOs were just that—a spiritual issue—and in the words of one writer, "were somehow connected with the realm of the dead and the afterlife." Others fretted they were an end-times deception paving the way for an anti-christ.

Come to learn, from these reports, that, among other evidence, officials ensconced there in the Pentagon had not only reviewed written reports of unidentified flying objects, but had videos showing encounters between American military aircraft and unknown crafts—including a blanched oval one roughly the size of a commercial plane. It had been chased—and recorded (on a cockpit camera), said the report—by two Navy F/A-18F fighter jets from the *Nimitz* a hundred miles off the coast of San Diego, California, in 2004, after two weeks of reports from other pilots. When military types observe such things, not to mention record them—and release the tapes—one tends to pay heed, for admirals and generals and tried-and-true top-gunners are not prone to . . . tomfoolery.

Was it China or Russia, operating spy missions with technology of which our intelligence agencies were incognizant?

Could one or both have developed vehicles the likes of which are at best on the U.S. drawing board—and more likely confined to science fiction?

Improbable, this notion it was Chinese or Russian. The object, which glowed in no known way, "displayed beyond-next-generation capabilities," in the words of a spook who worked in the Pentagon unit. The salient fact: two pilots had seen the same thing at the same time and on the 34-second video-tape for all to hear were their voices speaking excitedly to each other. The ruckus, in that cockpit chatter, was over the speed and maneuverability of *whatever* they were both seeing.

Let's give them their names: Commander David Fravor and Lieutenant Jim Slaight, on a routine training mission in F/A-18F Super Hornets in preparation for deployment to the Persian Gulf. It seems one object, shaped like a forty-foot Tic-Tac, darted erratically, even doing tumbling maneuvers: appearing suddenly at less than a hundred-thousand feet as if to materialize and then hurtling toward ocean waters, before stopping twenty-thousand feet above frothing waves where at least one hovered before disappearing from radar.

How could even the most advanced human ingenuity accomplish that?

Worm holes? Warp drives? It got fanciful.

The radio operator commanded them to investigate.

And as they neared the objects, it seems, Fravor peered down to the sea and the ocean looked like it was boiling beneath a hovering craft—with waves breaking over another strange object that was just below the surface. Whatever this was, down there, underwater, was causing the water to churn!

It was the most unsettling claim since 1952, when what a CIA historian would later describe as a "massive build-up of sightings over the United States" was documented on radar at National Airport—so unnerving that President Harry S. Truman personally asked for an explanation. Spattered throughout the report were certain other eerie findings, including the conclusion that the object "was no known aircraft or air vehicle currently in the inventory of the United States or any foreign nation," one that "possibly demonstrated the ability to 'cloak' or become invisible to the human eye or human observation" and "possibly demonstrated a highly advanced capability to operate undersea completely undetectable by our most advanced sensors."

As they tried to get closer, the object rose to greet them, then sped away. There was now only the clear sky and the normal motion of ocean.

Commander Fravor told *The Times* he had been "pretty weirded out." No plumes of exhaust. No rotors. No wings. At one point it zipped forty miles in less than a minute, "accelerating like nothing I've ever seen."

Another tape released by the investigative unit included a Super Hornet's encounter with an unusual object along the East Coast in 2015. "Oh my gosh, dude," said that pilot of an oval-shaped aircraft that moved with befuddling, astounding speed.

"Wow! What is that, man?" said another. "Look at that flying!"

Asked what he believed he and Slaight had seen, Fravor told a reporter: "Something not from this earth. I have no idea what I saw."

But, he added wryly . . . "I want to fly one."

25

Those Who Can Recall Everything

Memory is a funny thing, a tough thing to lose.

And that's what a man whose adopted name is now Benjamin Kyle did: lost every recollection, his name, where he lived, how he got there.

You see, in 2004, "Kyle" woke up behind a dumpster at Burger King in Richmond, Georgia, devoid of a suitcase, identification, and any knowledge of his past. He was naked and covered with ants. There were three blunt injuries on his head. No idea how that happened. But the effects were obvious. Doctors put a name on it: "retrograde amnesia"— Kyle was unable to remember who he was! And not even the FBI could help. Despite years of effort, no one made a bit of headway, and so Benjamin Kyle became, as one report noted, "the only U.S. citizen in history listed as missing despite his whereabouts being known. When he looked in a mirror, he was twenty years older than he thought he was." Social Security number? No. A record of employment? Forget it—literally. Was there a wife out there, children? He wasn't wearing a wedding ring, and certainly had no photos to show that. Only God knew who he was!

But a clue existed in that Benjamin Kyle, or whatever his name was, could recite presidents up to the twentieth-first century, when, for "Ben," history abruptly ended. Therefore: he'd lost his memory around 2000. He could recall a little about 9/11, and a few things related to Colorado and Indianapolis, as well as tidbits about the restaurant business. But it was all disjointed—far too vague. Skills? If he had any, he couldn't resurrect them. Where to work? A problem, that can be, for someone with not the scantiest résumé. Finally Ben got work as a dishwasher when, seeing him on the news, a local businessman offered "Ben" not only a means for pocket money, as well as an air-conditioned shed (he'd been living in the woods). His identity remained a startling mystery until 2015, when genetic sleuthing of ancestral bloodlines unearthed the name . . . William Burgess Powell.

The other extreme: people who remember *everything.*

That too can be a "curse." Some things: best forgotten!

Yet ask a fellow named Nima Veiseh what he was doing on any particular day during the past fifteen years and he'll run it all down for you, often minute by minute, certainly able to recall, at minimum, what the weather was like and what he did that day. An artist, Nima at last count had visited art galleries in forty countries and could remember every painting on each wall in every section of each museum. It's a condition called "Highly Superior Autobiographical Memory," and there are an estimated fifty people around the world with it. In the case of Veiseh, it began when he met his first girlfriend—an event that obviously triggered something in him. That first girlfriend: unforgettable . . . and everything that followed as well.

There are folks who are nearly extraterrestrial when it comes to their memories.

Robert Owen Evans, a minister from Sydney, Australia, has memorized the foreground and positions of 1,500 galaxies and can detect minute changes with a glance through his telescope. To put this in perspective: It took until the 1990s for computerized telescopes to do the same. Google CEO Sundar Pichai can remember every phone number he has ever seen or heard. "Years ago when Sundar was in school, he came to our house in Mayiladuthurai once," recalled an old acquaintance. "During a conversation, a family friend gave me his phone number. I asked my wife to write it down but she forgot. After some months, I asked Sundar about the number, and he reeled it out instantly."

Others—in just an hour—can memorize the exact order of 1,500 random digits or in half a minute a deck of shuffled playing cards—or (in the case of one Stephen Wiltshire) every building in an urban skyline after flying past it once . . .

For contrary to common thought, the brain stores everything, or nearly everything, that deigns to enter; what "fades" is our ability to retrieve it. Science has shown that, when used in a certain way, the brain can over time even change physiologically—the right posterior hippocampus (a portion of the brain involved in spatial navigation) growing by as much as seven percent in London taxi drivers (as they memorize thousands of streets) . . .

Intelligence is such that: we're not smart enough to *know*, actually, what it is. No matter how much you test or analyze, you can't figure it. The brain can do so many strange things. We are "wonderfully"—and mysteriously— made (*Psalms* 139:14).

Take those who lapse into a coma and then wake up speaking a new language! In most cases this is explained by language courses the person once took, even as long back as grammar school—still there, hiding in the subconscious. The first known case was reported in 1941, when a Norwegian woman suffered shrapnel injuries to the brain during a German bombing run—and started speaking with a German accent.

But wait: this was Norway: where did the German *accent* come from?

There is also the "savant syndrome," when a person has impaired mental faculties (intellectual disability or autism) but can perform wondrous mental gymnastics far beyond what we usually consider an intellectual possibility.

Example: a person (and there is such a case) who can tell you what day of the week a particular date fell on in any specific year going back before the first calendar! (*Quick now:* October 20, 1589. The record: forty thousand years.)

Normally incommunicado, there are savants who are happy to recite every thing they've ever had—time and date—for breakfast. There was Kim Peck, the real "rain man" who at last count had read twelve thousand books and could tell you everything about every one of them!

More incredibly, Kim, who hailed from Utah, and was the subject of a movie, could read and memorize two pages of a book *at the same time* in as few as four seconds. Not bad for a kid who doctors predicted would never be able to read or talk and had an IQ score of 87.

Leslie Lemke's IQ was 58, but after hearing it once, he could flawlessly play any song (including Tchaikovsky's "Piano Concerto Number One").

Also, he could sing: *How Great Thou Art* and *Amazing Grace.*

What about Simplician of Rome, an eidetic friend of St. Augustine's (and certainly no simpleton) who could recite Virgil *backwards*? Others commit to memory 1,700-page dictionaries. Some recall lives, or so we are led to believe, they never lived. A British girl who "recalled" being a wartime soldier with a blue-eyed daughter and could offer details, impossible for her to have known . . .

Is there a cosmic memory? Shared consciousness? Spirits that whisper?

Or is this simple supernatural oddness—the mind traveling back in time?

A funny thing, the brain. There are blind people who claim to have been trained to *feel* colors and others who duck if you throw a ping-pong ball their way. Occult stuff?

Still others can drive blindfolded at nerve-wracking speed—under strict experimental protocols (and not to be attempted by us mortals).

A little . . . peeking?

Stage chicanery?

Or is it as a famous brain surgeon named Wilfred Penfield once said:

"All of the brain is in the mind . . . but not all of the mind is in the brain"?

26

Back to the Past

How about stepping *back* in time? Is it possible to traverse the boundaries of what's defined by calendar and clock—can some transcend that proverbial hourglass?

The answer may be "yes," according to various and sundry testimonies—folks who have visited history.

In 1951, two British sisters-in-law vacationing in Dieppe, France, were awakened by the sounds of warring aircraft, gunships, and rifle shot—what they described as a battle, one they listened to, in all its array, for three full hours there near the English Channel. One can imagine thunderous mortars followed by the agonized howls of wounded, the shouts of hand-to-hand combat (if hand-to-hand combat there was) . . . the frenzied taking of prisoners . . .

There in the dark of night—when, otherwise, in a hotel, there is at most the rumble of a stray car outside—erupted the sounds of a full-fledged military skirmish.

The puzzle: it was 1951. There was no war! It was a battle, but one trapped, apparently, between the wrinkles of time. For when the detailed notes these two bumfuddled, rational women were later analyzed by military historians, those notations perfectly, inexplicably matched something to which the general public was not privy: the minute-to-minute chronological military logs of the "Dieppe Raid," a misbegotten foray nine years before.

That World War Two battle, which foreran Normandy, had pitted German attackers against British, Canadian, and

American troops—misbegotten in that the Allies suffered 3,623 killed, injured, or captured, while Germany counted few losses.

And the diary kept by the two women relived it all. There were bursts of attack, the sound of *Spitfires* and *Hawk Hurricanes* in dogfights with the wily *Luftwaffe*, which in the end claimed the day; there were stretches of calm; then, the sound of landings and whistling howitzers in this hellish encounter.

"5:07: Waves of noise—mainly dive-bombers—but some faint cries in the background," the women took note.

The official military log for the exact same minute said: "Landing craft beached at Puy under heavy fire; then destroyers bombarded Dieppe with shells while aircraft attacked seafront buildings."

And precisely at 5:40? "Silence," recorded the two befuddled tourists.

The military record for 5:40: "Naval bombardment stopped . . ."

Between six and seven a.m.: "all noise died away," then, some "cries, gradually becoming fainter," followed by "uninterrupted silence"—fully documented when the government released logs showing Allied reinforcement had failed and that by 8:30 a.m. the attack had been "repulsed with appalling Canadian casualties . . . Survivors surrendered . . ."

Faint, distant cries; fading indeed. These woman seem to have relived a crucial episode during World War Two.

Residents of Niagara-on-the-Lake, Ontario, swear that soldiers in old war-torn regalia—exhausted, hobbling, perhaps injured—have been witnessed on what is now a park but what in 1812 was . . . a battlefield.

At a fort across the lake, the faint voices of those awaiting execution centuries ago have been heard in a dungeon. One witness was the editor of the Niagara Gazette, who had gone there one Halloween night to spoof the rumor of ghosts and instead of an article, left there terrorized.

In 1901, two esteemed Englishwomen, Charlotte Moberly and Eleanor Jourdain, were visiting the Palace of Versailles in France when they got lost on a maze of roads lining the gardens and wandered toward a little chateau that had belonged to Marie Antoinette.

On the way, odd sights exploded before them: Charlotte saw a woman who looked like she was from the past era, shaking a white cloth out the window of a small stone cottage, while Eleanor suddenly noticed what seemed like a deserted farmhouse with an old plow or wheelbarrow near it. The puzzle in this case: such structures hadn't been there since the late 1700s.

Next, exploding out of *somewhere else*, were "very dignified officials, dressed in long grayish-green coats with small three-cornered hats." It was no re-enactment. There *were* no re-enactments. Was it a *tableau vivant*—the living picture of a scene captured from the past, frozen in time, like waxworks come to life. Both women were extremely credible, respected academicians—Moberly, president of St. Hugh's College at Oxford and Jourdain her assistant. Among others they observed was a man wearing a cloak, his complexion dark (this later identified as a companion of Antoinette's), with the feeling of evil, and another woman who seemed attired in period costume and had come to sketch in the gardens.

After studying a specific portrait of the queen, Moberly would later claim the artistic woman she saw had been Antoinette herself.

A con? A joint delusion? (A place that needed exorcism?)

I remember the account of two couples, traveling through the same nation of France, on the way to a vacation in Spain, who suddenly found themselves on what seemed

like an abnormally quiescent back road near the suspiciously quiet town of Montélimar. There, despite the
uncanny aura, they stopped at a small hotel where they
stayed over night, taken by the quaint, old-fashioned
manner of the couple who owned it and the antiquated style
of the place itself. It was out of a past era. The staff wore
clothes from yesteryear. When they paid the bill they were
delighted at how fantastically inexpensive it was. Leaving
town, they asked a policeman for directions but he seemed
to have no notion of the motorways.

Returning from Spain, the two couples, named Simpson
and Gisby, wanted to overnight there again (the quaintness;
the price!) and found the road with no problem, but not the
hotel.

It no longer existed—and hadn't, they found out, for
decades. (When they developed their film and looked in
earnest for their photos of the hotel, they found
them . . . missing.)

In Scotland, two men climbing the highlands near Loch
Mullardoch in May of 1987 noticed a two-story cottage on the
shore. It was made of granite, in good condition, they noted—
and very confusing, for it was not anywhere on their map.
Members of an official rescue team were Donald Watt and
David Bruce, not the type who tended toward speculation.
"We decided to head for it," said Bruce. "It caught us
completely by surprise. We went on down toward the cottage,
discussing it. We kept it in our sights for some time and then
lost view of it. We assumed that we would see it again when
we got over the crest of a hillock but when we joined the path
along the shore, there was no cottage to be seen."

Later they learned that there once *had* been a cottage at
the loch, but a dam built decades before had put all the
buildings, including the cottage, deep under water.

In 1995, a couple traveling to the Barossa Valley in
Australia passed through a small town they had seen many

times before. Now, however, something was different—even wrong. Recalled the husband: "I was entering a straight level stretch of road from some hills and I could see the small town ahead called Allendale North, which is just outside of Kapunda. Looking ahead, I saw a large group of people milling about the hotel. This interested me as there had only ever been a couple of cars outside the hotel at anytime when I had traveled through.

"As I got closer, I could see the group in closer detail. These people were at a fair or reunion of some kind. Every person was dressed in early–1800s style. Very Victorian-era. I needed to slow down, and I recall that on my left was a horse and buggy.

"As I traveled through the group, there was a boy about seven years old holding onto a woman's hand, who I presumed to be his mother. The boy watched intently as I approached and drove past. He was close to the road, dressed in a navy-blue sailor outfit with white frills [and possessed of] the most penetrating blue eyes. No one else seemed to notice my travel through the group, but his eyes did not leave me.

"My wife stirred from a nap and asked where we were. I told her and suggested we stop, at which point I looked in the rear-view mirror."

There was nothing there! No crowd. No reunion. Just: "an empty street."

The town had disappeared.

If this was not a hallucination, the question:

Was that youngster clinging to his mother witness to an event in the future—while the stranger in a contraption called the car was viewing the past?

27

A Trail of Cloven Hoofs

Around the world and throughout history have been accounts of strange footprints—or more to the issue, *hoof* prints. In some cases, cloven ones.

The question here is not whether a mammal with cloven feet can imprint itself in snow or mud—it certainly can—but how one could leave marks indicating it was bipedal: that at the time of the prints, it was walking on two legs, not four.

And not just on the ground . . . but across rooftops.

There are a number of animals with cloven hoofs: deer, antelope, gazelles, goats, sheep, and cattle. None of these walk upright, or right through fences and walls. And yet, that's precisely what has been reported: an unseen two-legged animal that has left puzzling tracks—tracks that, even from the annals of history, taunt us.

The most famous occurred across Devonshire, England, on February 8, 1855. In this case the hoofed animal—if an animal it was—left a trail reported variously as between forty and a hundred miles long, in fresh snow. More inexplicably, the tracks, about three inches across, and generally parted by eight inches, were noted in a continuous pattern in yards, the estuary of a river, and even up one side of a fourteen-foot barricade and down the other.

A badger; a donkey?

An imported *kangaroo*?

The trail became known as the "devil's footprints," and as one commentator said, "What made it all even stranger was the bizarre route that these prints took, going right up over walls, along narrow fencing, over house roofs, through barns, haystacks, gardens and courtyards, across frozen lakes, fields, and spookily often seeming to come right to people's front doors, as if whatever had made them had been intently investigating these homes. Oddly, in some cases it seemed as if the prints had entered and exited pipes that were only around four inches in diameter, passed through locked gates, or seemed to wander straight up trees, as well as in totally enclosed or locked off areas and other improbable places. The weird story took off and was widely publicized in newspapers of the time. The people of the area were spooked to say the least, and began to strongly believe that these were not the tracks of any normal animal, but rather those of the Devil himself. Many were afraid to leave their homes at night, terrified that the Devil was still out there roaming about and that he could sniff out their sins. More rational explanations have encompassed everything from hoaxes or the distorted tracks of mice, birds, rabbits, badgers, ponies, horses . . . to things like raindrops falling and creating the depressions—and even the far-out idea that a weather balloon had drifted down to drag along the ground. None of these fully explain the mystery, and the 'Devil's Footprints' of Devon have largely remained an enduring mystery."

There are still accounts. In 2009, an Englishwoman named Jill Wade reported the same prints in the fresh snow of her garden and in the same area of Devon. The size: a precise match, a century and a half later.

And again, the shape of a cloven hoof, with no other marks in the snow.

Similar footprints have been associated with the legend of the "Jersey Devil" in the Pine Barrens north of Philadelphia.

But none are more dramatic than the prints near Route 1334, three miles west of Bath, North Carolina.

There, in the first part of the nineteenth century, was a gambling, hard-drinking, profane fellow named Jesse Elliott who made it a habit to race horses on Sunday, despite the urgent admonitions of a religious wife.

Bold?

Elliott would take on anyone who challenged him—sure his horse was the fastest in the area. When he stood next to that stallion, he stood as a man who owned the world.

And so it came to be that in the quiet hours one Sunday morning during 1802 (some records say August, others autumn), Jesse, getting ready for the day (and certainly not for church) watched the approach of a dark stranger on a midnight-black horse who proclaimed that his stallion could beat Jesse's, offering to bet a hundred dollars on it.

"I'll meet you at the track in an hour," replied Elliott, perhaps with false confidence; for he found the stranger's horse a bit fearsome. Still, he no doubt conjured a confident if not arrogant timbre.

Returning to his house, Elliott donned riding boots and – the day's octane—chugged two glasses of straight whiskey as his wife again warned about the Sabbath and listened as he cursed in response. "I hope you'll be sent to hell this very day!" his exasperated wife shouted back, according to lore, unable to contain dismay over her unheeded admonitions.

Was it all a piece of fiction designed for pulpits?

There are even disagreements over the year. Some say 1813. At any rate:

Elliott left in a huff—perhaps with another curse—and set out in his standard thrasonical manner for a rudimentary woodland track, where, true to his words, the challenger was waiting for him—calm but earnest, as they came to terms. It was said, by the few who accompanied Elliott, that something about the stranger's froideur bothered them, but no witnesses offered detailed testimony.

We know only that the race was on, and down the lane both horses bounded. Relaxed and lagging a length behind, the stranger's horse suddenly burst forward toward the finish, pulling alongside at a curve. Elliott had one more curse left in him. "Take me in a winner," he supposedly barked at his own stallion or take me to hell!"

At that moment, it's said, the horse twisted its head and suddenly shied, digging its hooves into the ground and rearing up such that Jesse Elliott was sent sprawling head-first into a large pine, his death instantaneous, strands of his hair imbedded in bark. The stranger dismounted, looked over the corpse, and was never seen again.

To this day, it is said, the prints are still visible, rain or shine, four to five inches deep, with sloping sides of six to ten inches—in loamy soil near Goose Creek State Park on what is now private land.

And though unsheltered, it's said that not only, after two centuries, do the marks evade erosion, but no pine needles, grass, dirt, or leaves ever accumulate in the holes. Are these just vents for a subterranean pocket of water, as some scientists speculate, or the result of salt veins?

The current owner offers no response to my calls. The library knows only the main bulk of the tale. Many take it as fact, not parable. Chickens, it is said, would eat corn scattered around the holes but not kernels placed in the holes themselves.

They are always clean and empty, those prints, and if there is a bit of debris, it's usually gone . . . within hours; or at least by the following morning.

Nothing covers the tracks for long. In the mid–1900s, a newsreel cameraman named Earl Harrell tested the legend and placed corn in the holes, noting birds ate the area around the indentations clean but nothing from the holes. Intrigued, he tried a second experiment, filling each depression with detritus, dirt, and stone, then constructing a network of black thread over the holes. When he came by the next morning, the net was undisturbed, but the holes, as always, were empty, perhaps half a dozen of them.

Had the swarthy stranger arrived, in the 1800s, to take Elliott to a netherworld? A local minister at St. Thomas Church thought so, declaring, with no mean measure of self-righteousness, that the hoof prints were left, indeed—in fact —by "a man on his way to hell."

28

Claws and Fangs

The headlines were hair-raising: "Girl Faints As Spirits Bite," "Manila Mayor Confirms 'Spooky' Attacks On Girl," and "The 'Thing' Bites Girl Again."

The details were even more so . . .

Clarita Villanueva was a 17-year-old Filipino girl whose life could be summed up in one word: tragedy. Her dad died when she was too young to remember, and her mother turned to spiritism—telling fortunes, holding séances—to make money, laughing at the gullible behind their backs. She thought it was just a game. Her daughter was to learn the hard way it was not.

Soon, by the tender age of twelve, Clarita's mother was also dead, and with no one to care for her, the girl fell into a circle of harlots who turned her onto the streets. Eventually, Clarita worked her way up to the huge city of Manila. By the time she was seventeen, she was well versed in the ways of the streets, frequenting bars as a "taxi driver" and seducing men of all stripes.

Like so many ill-fated who fall into this lifestyle, Clarita found herself arrested late one night—having propositioned an undercover cop—and tossed into the city's three-hundred-year-old Bilibid Prison, really a city gaol. There was a bit of history to the place: now basically a jail, it had been used during the war as a place of torture. Did that factor into what was about to transpire? Or was it all about her mother's spiritism and her own wayward life?

Whatever the answer, one can determine the episode began about two days after incarceration, in May of 1953. Suddenly—screamed the young woman—something was biting her. Actually, two things were attacking. And she had the welts, bruises, and bite marks—in spots that rendered self-infliction impossible—to prove it. Her wounds—in some cases, deep ugly bruises and bite marks, outlined in saliva—simultaneously materialized on her legs, arms, and back, including the *back* of her neck. Writhing on a cot, the girl fainted and was taken to the prison hospital, where nurses and doctors encountered something they had never seen before. Other medical professionals swarmed in— American doctors, university professors, and psychologists—to stare in wonder at the wounds, some of which appeared before their eyes.

If that wasn't alarming enough, there was her description of the two spirits: one, with bulgy eyes, buck teeth, and two fangs, wearing a cape and with curly hair all over his large body, perhaps ten-feet tall, and a smaller one, almost a dwarf, with an angelic face and large incongruous mustache. The tall entity was black and hirsute, with fangs that came down on each side of his mouth, as well as buck teeth not just in front but all the way around. Doctors said the bite marks matched just such a description. The one in the cape, she said, could levitate and come right through her cell bars. It climbed up her body to bite her upper torso. Doctors confirmed that the bite marks had been incised by buck teeth and fangs.

Some of the observers, however, didn't believe their lying eyes. The "bite" marks, hypothesized skeptical psychologists, were the result of a condition called "hysterical fugue": the amazing "psycho-emotional" ability of the human subconscious to cause red marks on flesh. It was a convenient theory, but hardly a proven one, and what was occurring, it became obvious, went well beyond a rash. And it went on for three weeks. Blood flowed beneath her skin. The press was soon calling her the "Dracula girl."

Terror spread afresh when a doctor accused her of putting on an act and, in a trancelike state, Clarita's eyes turned snakelike. *"You will die,"* she uttered. The physician, thought to have been healthy, expired with no known cause the next day. This was no tall tale. These were all documented—and widely reported—facts. The chief jailer also had a confrontation with Clarita, who looked at him with cold, inhuman eyes—fulminating with hatred—and leveled the same curse. Four days later, he too was dead . . .

"I walked into Bilibid Prison just as the funeral cortege moved out," wrote one witness, the local evangelical preacher from the U.S., Lester Sumrall, whose faith obviously overcame any fear. "The prison guards had paid their last respects to their chief. Dr. Mariano Lara, the chief medical officer, and his staff were deeply concerned. They had a prisoner who was not crazy, but who was being wildly attacked by unseen entities and being bitten deeply on all parts of her body by creatures no one else could see. I have never seen such a fearful and perplexed group of people as those I met in that prison that day."

Such attacks are hardly unknown to demonology. Bites and scratches inflicted were in similar fashion in the 1920s upon a Romanian woman named Eleanor Zügun, and in 1974 was the case of bleeding claw marks endured by Anthony Rossi of East Hartford, Connecticut. In 2009 came the account of a teen who fled to a church because "he was being haunted by a little green 'man' that was hissing and growling, and chasing him about the house . . ." Church folk went to his house and conducted their own version of a deliverance.

But Clarita was in a category unto itself—if for no reason other than the witnesses. As chronicled by United Press International, "Manila's tough Mayor Arsenio

(Arsenic) Lacson said Tuesday he would ask the archbishop to exorcise the 'invisible tormentors' of a teen-aged girl in the city jail. Lacson said he had heard reports that 'evil spirits' had been pestering Clarita Villanueva for nine days and ordered her brought to the city morgue so he could see for himself. The hard-boiled mayor took along Medical Examiner Mariano Lara and other observers, including a group of newsmen. Lacson said that within fifteen minutes while he was sitting beside her the girl had two attacks and was 'bitten' on the index finger and neck. [He] said he saw marks of human teeth where Clarita had been 'bitten,' and they 'were not made by her. Clarita's hand was bitten while I was holding it,' Lacson said. 'The finger was bitten under my palm.'" He added that a doctor present was "scared stiff."

When the girl tried to draw a picture of her assailants, according to the mayor, the pencil "flew off her hand." Clarita savagely began eating the paper and biting the writing utensil.

It didn't sound like mere psychology.

The archbishop, it seems, declined the request for an exorcism—understandably concerned for the safety of his priests—and so it was left to Reverend Sumrall, the evangelical, who went into a prolonged period of prayer, Bible-reading, and fasting, before seeking permission (he said God was directing him) to help the teen.

This he did despite warnings. And though Clarita recoiled at the sight of him, screaming hateful threatening words, the preacher proceeded to cast out what was in and around her.

Now a headline read: "Devil Loses Round One."

As it turned out, the alien entities, the devils—whatever they were—lost the entire game. Clarita saw them flee out a window. And soon she was just a normal young woman, one who eventually would marry and start a family. So grateful was the mayor, he gave Lester permission to hold a six-week revival in a park downtown. About 150,000 attended. The mayor also granted him a permit to build a new church. People on the street bowed to the heroic minister. For so frightening had it been that guards, policemen, inmates, and reporters had been brought to tears. As the mayor had noted, "What it was is beyond me.

"This is something that goes way back to the dark, dim past . . ."

29

Stranger than Roswell

Many believe—wrongly—that an incident near Roswell, New Mexico, in 1947 was the first-known case whereby actual physical evidence was left behind by a UFO, or what the Air Force itself at first called a "flying saucer" (later modifying the description to "weather balloon").

Whether or not Roswell bears credence, it is not the first such alleged instance—no, not when stood next to what UFO buffs call "MO-41."

The 41 is for the year, 1941. Some believe the date was April 12. The "MO" is for Missouri, where the crash is said to have occurred.

There is as much reason to believe this case as there is Roswell.

Unless a preacher named Reverend William Guy Huffman, Sr. in the quiet town of Cape Girardeau was a liar, that Saturday night—Holy Saturday, the night before Easter—he witnessed not only an extraterrestrial craft that had fallen from the sky in a fireball, but also three occupants.

Believable?

Everyone described Huffman, 52, from a struggling Baptist church called Red Star Tabernacle, as impeccably honest—a straightforward man whose devotion was to church and his family. He was not an insistent type. Fire and brimstone were not part of his repertoire. Perhaps, one could say, in his quiet humble way: exemplary. No one, said friends, was further from a proclivity for hallucination (or prevarication).

But that's the only explanation for what Reverend Huffman, balding and on the portly side, said he and others lay witness to that spring night when informed by someone attached to the Cape Girardeau police department that his services—last rites—were needed at the site of what sounded like a plane accident.

There was no time for hesitation. The crash site was outside of town by a bit more than a dozen miles, some-where east of a small town called Chaffee, perhaps near Route 62, toward Scott City, perhaps closer to Benton. To this day, no one is sure—or will say—precisely where. All we know is that it most probably was on the patch quilt of farmland amid undulating rock hills not far from the Missis-sippi.

Was it, as estimated, between eight and 8:30 p.m.?

What can be ascertained is that someone saw the orange inferno and called police on one of the few phones in the area. Firemen scrambled. Locals rushed to the scene. What we know is mainly what Reverend Huffman described to his wife and two sons. "I'll tell you this once," he had intoned, "and then I'm never going to speak of it again."

Moreover, he said, before offering details, "you can never repeat it either."

It was a pledge he and his family tried to keep—spooked, perhaps, by warnings from military officials at the scene—whether Army or Air Corps from the Missouri Insti-tute of Aeronautics, 309th Detachment, of this too no one is certain. They were in plain clothes—white shirts, fedoras—as well as uniforms. And once they arrived, and compre-hended what was there, they had demanded secrecy.

But nothing could erase what Reverend Huffman's own eyes had processed, and that, he told his small family, was not a small prop plane engulfed by flames but a rivetless, oddly rounded, and gray-silver craft, surrounded by scattered shiny fragments. In the scorched grass, which was several inches high, said Huffman, he spotted the three victims. Wrinkled and not quite human, of stature comparable to children, but with large bulbous heads, rubbery limbs (at the end of which were a thumb and three long fingers), and gray skin or body suits, two were clearly dead. It was said a bystander who belonged to Huffman's denomination or possibly a newspaperman who knew the minister arrived, snuck out a camera, and snapped at least one photo (with a Miniature Speed Graphic or new Kodak Brownie), positioning one of the entities between two men who held it up as Huffman finished his prayers, before the site was secured by government personnel.

Officials "surrounded the site at first, and moved quickly," the preacher told wife Floy and their boys. Firefighters put out the blaze. There may have been trainees from the airport in Sikeston. Only one of the entities, about four feet in height, but now stretched on a yard or unplowed field, seemed to be alive: barely. "Granddad said that when he got to him, his breathing was shallow," related Charlette Huffman Mann, the only family member who later talked, adding that Huffman referred to them as "creatures" or "little people," according to a native of the area, Paul Blake Smith, who did yeoman's work researching and writing about it.

Charlette, who gathered the details from Grandmother Floy (just before the latter's death), said there had been no visible injuries and the bodies were soon whisked away. The creatures were identical, as if clones—their eyes large and almond-shaped, jet black, almost reaching like goggles around the side of the head, with hauntingly empty stares.

Were they fallen angels, demons from hell? Had the devil crafted one of his more elaborate deceptions? This Huffman no doubt pondered. When it looked at such cases, it has been alleged that a secretive government group concluded black helicopters, "men-in-black," and abductions aboard flying saucers were hallucinations, "sophisticated imagery generated by demons and fallen angels and projected into the minds" of supposed witnesses, noted writer Nick Redfern.

As for the craft, it supposedly had no visible engine or wings. The preacher said that through a gaping hole in the fuselage he could make out an interior compartment with small metallic seats, an instrument panel, and strange hieroglyphic-like script on a metal band around a curved, seamless interior. Though largely mum, Charlette further asserted that the copy of a three-by-four-inch black and white photograph snapped at the scene, and now dog-eared, with scalloped edges, would be passed around at several special family gatherings—only to vanish in 1953, when a visitor to the Huffmans', believed to be connected with military intelligence, borrowed and never returned it. The face? Two small holes for a nose, above a mere slit for a mouth. No ears. "You couldn't see those eyes and not be affected," said Charlette in the early 1990s—when she broke the family *omerta*.

Others in town remembered hearing about the event from those related to additional witnesses, none of whom would speak for the public record. Charlette's grandmother didn't give her testimony until she lay dying, and the same was true of others. According to Smith, in the 1940s another man of the cloth, Church of Christ pastor Turner H. Holt from Ohio, claimed to have been taken by his trusted friend and cousin Cordell Hull—U.S. secretary of state—to a subbasement of the Capitol in Washington, where in a secured storage room he was shown a metallic-like wreck that fit descriptions of what allegedly transpired in 1941. He, too, kept it secret, except for closest relatives.

This is what, in any case, was averred to have happened six years before Roswell, where debris and bodies from a crashed UFO were said to have been confiscated by officials from the Roswell Army Air Field after it was discovered by an awe-struck local rancher. That same year—1947—an entirely credible pilot named Kenneth Arnold was flying over Mount Rainier (in the state of Washington, which, intriguingly, is also known for big foot) when he spotted objects flitting with preternatural speed—like "a saucer if you skip it across water," he said (thus: flying saucers). Interesting it was that the territory below was known for bigfoot sightings, and likewise that Arnold's experiences reportedly went beyond the event in 1947: that there were later other sightings, including "floating orbs" in his own home. Strange to say the least . . . He came to believe, some claim, that it was a spiritual experience. And that UFOs were like living organisms that could change their density. One he saw was no solid spaceship but "semi-transparent."

It was the beginning, if we can believe these testimonies, of a major extraterrestrial visitation (some said "invasion") that would peak in 1952, with documented radar sightings of "aerodynes" over Virginia and near National Airport in D.C.—so many that President Truman, a Missourian, ordered a special investigation.

A CIA historian would later describe the period of 1941 to 1952 as a "massive build-up of sightings over the United States."

A leaked memo from Dr. Edward Teller to President Ronald Reagan—who went on to famously ponder an alien invasion—had reportedly included the phrase, "1939, two years before a captured UFO." Another purported memo, this from a former C.I.A. agent named Tom Cantwheel, referred to "an aerodyne recovered in 1941 that crashed in southwestern Missouri" (actually, south*eastern*). By 1942, General George C. Marshall was urging FDR to create a special group to study claimed unidentified objects in U.S skies.

How could it be that these craft, seen by capable, experienced pilots, so suddenly vanished, contradicting our notions of time and space? How was it that strange orbs of luminosity, which some referred to as "spirit lights," have long been reported south of Cape Girardeau—orbs that zigzagged and then rejoined like a single star? (I witnessed this phenomenon at a religious site in Bosnia-Hercegovina.)

Were these things extraterrestrial, or extra-dimensional?

And why did it start during the 1940s?

Why this part of Missouri? Was the Chaffee area as Indians claimed—a center or "vortex" of power?

As for Roswell, some wondered if that had occurred because it was the beginning of the "Cold War" (an interesting observation in that such sightings' would later occur over atomic test sites, nuclear reactors, and military bases, including missile silos).

One thing most agreed on: the government went out of its way to conceal sightings, let alone crashes, which could produce technology the military could secretly attempt to replicate. Was it also afraid of public panic—what had ensued a few short years before, during the "War of the Worlds" broadcast in 1938?

Or had Reverend Huffman, and others, lapsed into an inexplicable mental state?

Not according to firefighter Walter Reynolds, who many years later, in a rushed interview at the end of a battle with cancer, supposedly stated, in the words of Smith, who quoted a Reynolds' nephew, that "*it was just as Charlette Mann said*"—dramatic contact between earthlings and beings from . . . let's just say, somewhere else.

30

The Most Amazing Miracle?

What is the most amazing miracle in religious circles?

No answer to that. Catholics might say the sun miracle of Fatima—tens of thousands witnessed it. Pentecostals might point to healings that defy all medical science—bones that materialize in a body that was missing them. There are Lazarus reports. Still others, secularists these, might declaim all of the above.

One contender: what happened—and not just once—to the mystical woman from Venezuela, Maria Esperanza. On sixteen occasions during her life (she died in 2004), a rose—*an actual flower*—was said to have erupted from her chest. From her body! One would dismiss this out of hand were it not for the witnesses: doctors, a television-news crew, a radio host from Philadelphia, among dozens of others.

The occurrences, which can only be described as inconceivable, began on January 18, 1986. Those who witnessed it—including Caracas newswoman Carolina Fuenmayor of Venevision—said it looked as if Maria was having severe heart palpitations. The woman would sit or lie down, clutch her chest, and a rose would break through her skin, push its way out, and open as if in slow-motion photography—with little sparkles of water, I was told by a son-in-law, Carlos Barrero, who was there during an occurrence on August 15, 1995. Maria claimed to have visions of Jesus.

Another witness, former CBS radioman John Marion, recalled, "My travel agent and I were down there on business, a hot summer night, and it was close to one o'clock in the morning. We were seated in a compound [near a shrine], wondering why Maria [currently up for sainthood] had kept us waiting—four to five hours. While we were waiting we heard a cry from Maria's son-in-law: *'John, John, hurry! Come over here!'* What they had done was set a chair in the compound area for Maria and helped by some family members, they placed her in the chair. They told me to keep looking. I couldn't imagine what would happen. She was experiencing some kind of pain. She was very uncomfortable in the chair.

"Maria sort of parted the blouse she was wearing and a red spot began to appear. I stared. It kept getting bigger and bigger and Maria was really in pain. Then this red spot began to take a shape and I recognized the shape as that of a rose—a deep red rose, first budlike as she continued to force it out right through her skin, excruciating pain—until finally it was through and fully in bloom and there was this big red beautiful rose!

"I couldn't believe it," John told me. "I turned to my travel agent in amazement. He said, `I know, I know. I see it!' After the rose cleared Maria's body, you could see about two inches of stem, and Maria broke it off, then she handed a petal first to a priest, three nuns, and then she called me over and gave me a piece. The next day I was told she passed the rest of the stem, with thorns on it. It was like she was giving birth—the same expression and same kind of pain and couldn't wait to get it out, then she held it lovingly in her hands. If you went into a florist shop for a single long-stemmed red rose in full bloom—that was what it looked like. It was absolutely beautiful, such a phenomenon that I couldn't believe my eyes."

Was there a conspiracy of fabrication here? That's what it would have to have been. And there was no sign of that whatsoever. But where is the final proof—for example, that video of it?

According to Maria's daughter, Coromoto, they are waiting for the permission of church authorities, who will release it, they say, when they deem it prudent.

31

A Bible 'Marvel'

In 2017 a member of a small evangelical prayer group noticed something very different. It was Friday, January 27, and when he picked up his Bible to continue his reading, he noticed spots of liquid from Psalm 39 to 63.

Did their great grandchild spill something on it, he wondered?

His name was Jerry Pierce and the spots were wet. But not water. He and those Jerry showed it to agreed that it had the distinct consistency of oil.

Over the next month, the stain grew—to the point where it saturated his Bible from Psalm 39 all the way through to the Book of Revelation!

It next appeared in Genesis 1 and continued, page by page, until it was back to Psalms 39, now saturating the entire book.

It was at that juncture that Jerry, a bald fellow with suspenders and a backcountry goatee, was forced to place it in a plastic container, where the oil not only continued to exude—but filled up the container!

By April, he was on his fourth container—and filling little vials, which he dispensed free of charge to people who requested it for healing, with the mysterious fluid. It overflowed the large container on two occasions. Eventually more than 90,000 vials would be distributed. Gallons of it!

A gimmick? It didn't seem that way. I went to Lake City, Florida, to view it (they travel around to churches with the

Bible) and there under the pulpit during a rousing service: the King James inside a large container steeped in at least five inches of yellowish fluid they said was analyzed and most resembled mineral oil. Said a woman named Jan Bare: "I received a bottle of flowing oil a few weeks ago. I felt like I should give it to my pastor. Last Sunday he had us anoint a number of people with it. It was a third to a half gone when we were through, but by the time we were ready to go home, the bottle was completely full!"

Similar "miracles" have been alleged in Orthodox, Jewish, and Catholic circles. In Las Cruces, New Mexico, a diocesan investigation was launched into a statue of the Virgin Mary as depicted at Guadalupe, Mexico, after it "wept" oil, and many are those who have entire collections of statues that oil, as if the phenomenon is contagious. People bring statues and *they* begin to exude or lachrymate in a way that sometimes defies ready explanation. In a suburb of Toronto I held a small hollow plastic statue as it shed oil—and as I looked inside.

In Georgia, the oiling Bible was accompanied by a similar viscous substance flowing from walls in a prayer room where it has been kept. "The chemist said that it had some of the characteristics of mineral oil but was not manu-factured," said a fellow named Johnny Taylor who is involved with it. "The best they could tell us . . . they don't know where it came from." Some think it's a sign of "end times." They claim it has various fragrances.

Does it damage the paper? No. Even the highlights have not blurred. The binding is intact. Does it heal? That's what some claim. Was it a manifestation showing, as Scripture says, that anything is possible (*Matthew* 19:26)?

32

Move Over, Rip

What's the longest anyone has slept?

Move over, Mr. Van Winkle. Here we get into comas.

On Aug. 6, 1941, six-year-old Elaine Esposito went to the hospital for a routine appendectomy—that *should* have been routine. She was put under a general anesthetic . . . and never came out. Dubbed the "sleeping beauty," Elaine stayed in a coma for thirty-seven years and 111 days before succumbing in 1978—the longest coma ever, according to Guinness World Records.

It can get perplexing.

The Gao family of Huizhou, China, was struggling. They didn't have money, lived in a community facility, and picked up what little coinage they could collecting and selling trash for cash. Wretched poverty—but at least they had each other.

Until . . .

One hot summer's day in Huizhou, Mrs. Gao and her daughter Ya Wen were out at the market, pawning some of their "wares," or trying to. It wasn't easy, conducting a sale and watching the inquisitive, independent, and as it turned out, precocious Ya Wen at the same time.

Just three years old, the intrepid Ya Wen, never known to be especially wary of roaming from mom, walked away while Mrs. Gao was talking to another vendor. As she had been taught, the girl looked both ways before crossing the nearby street. But suddenly a speeding van careened out of nowhere—and struck her.

Fighting panic, Mrs. Gao and her husband bolted into action, getting the girl to the hospital as fast as they could, with help from passersby, although the damage had been done. Ya Wen was so severely injured she lapsed into a coma. All her parents could do was, wait . . .

For five days, the Gaos held vigil at their daughter's bedside, hoping for the impossible and praying with no small measure of desperation. The van had hit the girl with full might and doctors were realistic, conveying to the parents that even if Ya Wen did ever wake, in all probability, she would not be the same. As it turned out, how right they were!

The Gaos worried about brain, nerve, and muscle damage. But whatever it might be, they wanted their little girl back. Finally, on the fifth day, Ya Wen awoke. Thankfully, but for some lacerations and bruises, the girl was amazingly healthy, and quick to recover.

But where was the *little* girl? Their tot comported herself more like an adult man—one they'd find in the bathroom puffing her dad's cigarettes. It turned out that Ya Wen was smoking up to a pack a day, going to the store to buy her own. She also began drinking alcohol. Had a spirit entered? ("Three beers," Mrs. Gao told reporters, was "nothing to her.") Eventually her taste in clothes changed and she only liked male ones . . .

In 1984, Terry Wallis's pickup jettisoned off a small bridge and into a creek in Stone County, Arkansas. The crash left him quadriplegic and with brain damage—again in a coma. But—astoundingly—still alive (he had been in the car for a full day before rescue).

After a few months, Wallis's coma stabilized into a "minimally conscious state." There was little reason to believe he would ever regain full cognition. And the odds looked grimmer by the week.

Months turned into years.

Wallis's wife, Sandi, and newborn daughter, Amber, were left to question if they would ever see Wallis "alive" again.

Their questions were answered on June 11, 2003, when, incredibly, Wallis awoke from what turned out to be a 19-year coma—making him the survivor of the longest comatose state. (Actually, that was a year shy of Van Winkle.)

His first word upon awakening was "Mum." His second: "Pepsi."

Asked by his mother who the president was, he replied: "Ronald Reagan."

Like Rip, who, when he awoke, didn't recognize the world, the brain damage left Wallis with very poor short-term memory—stuck in 1984.

But lucky. He had crashed off that bridge on a Friday the 13th, and nearly twenty years later started talking, in a true reversal of fortune, on . . . Friday the 13th.

33

The 'Dancing Plague'

One day a cheerleader in Upstate New York awoke from a nap and right away knew something was amiss. Her chin was jutting forward—beyond her ability to control it—and her face was a tangle of spasms.

Her name: Katie Krautwurst. She was still twitching weeks later—though no longer alone. Another cheerleader, Thera Sanchez, took a similar nap and woke up *stuttering*. Her arms whipped about. Her head kept jerking—contractions, spasms.

Then a third—in that case, wild tics and strange sounds. Humming. Bizarre movements. Soon the number was eighteen in a small school. There were kids with bruises from hitting themselves.

Stranger yet: no cause was ever found. While the contagion eased and finally faded, medical experts at first wondered if it was "Tourette syndrome." Once considered a rare and bizarre syndrome, it is often associated with the exclamation of obscene words or socially inappropriate and derogatory remarks. But jerking and uncontrolled body movements—out of nowhere? We see this also in the Bible. "While he was coming, the demon threw him to the ground and convulsed him, but Jesus rebuked the unclean spirit and healed the boy, and gave him back to his father," says *Luke* (9:42).

A three-month-long investigation by the school district and state health department uncovered no communicable ailment. Grasping for an explanation, psychiatrists settled for "mass psychogenic illness," a polite way of saying mass hysteria.

Still others wondered if it was due to toxic chemicals. Those inclined to the esoteric had this to ponder: LeRoy is smack amid a stretch of New York Thruway nicknamed the "Psychic Highway." From Hydesville to just east of Buffalo are towns that have spawned everything from the spiritualism movement to American Masonry.

History is replete with strange mental epidemics. In July of 1518, "the Dancing Plague" was a case of a mania that occurred in Strasbourg, France. Numerous people took to dancing for days without rest, and over the period of about one month, most of the people died from heart attack, stroke, or exhaustion. In the 1960s, dozens of students on the western shore of Lake Victoria in Africa were struck with fits of uncontrollable laughter that lasted for weeks. In Amsterdam in 1566, thirty children were afflicted in such a way that without warning they would be seized by a violent frenzy, fall to the earth, and lapse into convulsions. Once they ended, the kids had no memory of what occurred. Some of them regurgitated strange objects, like pins and shards of glass. In more recent days, schools in Kenya's Central province have been closed and students sent home following perceived invasions by "ghosts." In one case, ten times the number of Amsterdam—three hundred students—were affected. Kenya's education minister dismissed it as the imagination. Others blamed drugs and music. "The affected children, mostly consisting of girls and just a few boys, are seen running and screaming from invisible apparitions that often instruct them to gaze into a nearby pond," said a report. "In this pond they are shown a list of students targeted by the demons, to whom they run and inform of their discovery. The children claim that they hear the principal's voice in their heads telling them to drink from the school's tap. They see visions, speak in strange languages, and if held down, they writhe and scream in agony. There have been many other outbreaks on the Dark Continent—where tribal occultic religions, with their witch doctors, are so focused. In 2015 Bumula Girls School in Kenya hurriedly and indefinitely closed when a flurry of youngsters became hysterical, wailing all over the school compound that spirits were invading. Fifteen years before, two boarding schools west of Nairobi were afflicted in a similar way, with a hail of stones raining down upon the roof at night. Witch doctors have taken some of the blame. There were claims of sexual assault. Said an article in "Bumula Girls closed after demons in the compound":

"Since time immemorial there have been claims of satanism in schools and the presence of demons. This has hence led to fear in both students, teachers and parents of the concerned schools and also other schools. This has been experienced in various counties in the country and various remedies have been applied to the situations. The recent case comes from Bumula Girls High school in Bungoma county. Students want a priest sent to their school to exorcise demons they claim are haunting the school. Speaking to Citizen Television after staging a demonstration on Monday, the girls say they are terrified by the alleged demons after seeing strange things happen every night. During the day, the girls say that they see lots of cash littered all over the school compound without a clear source. This, they say, has caused them distress and anxiety and have called for a priest to exorcise the evil spirits behind the strange phenomena in the school so that learning can continue. The school was completely deserted following the demonstration after the girls were sent home indefinitely as a solution is sought to solve the issue."

Noted a government study by the U.S. Institutes of Health, "In 2009, a wave of mass hysteria overcame a

Pretoria high school in South Africa as dozens of children collapsed, screaming in unexplained convulsions and fits. The hysteria started when a Grade 9 girl collapsed at her desk at Daspoort Secondary School in Claremont. Within moments of the unexplained attack about 25 pupils in various classes and grades were affected and started screaming hysterically, fainting and convulsed as they succumbed to the strange occurrence. The attacks came two weeks after a pupil at the school committed suicide. It was said that the hysteria also affected schools in Sunnyside and Laudium the previous week. The community attributed the incident to an evil spirit around the school and said Satanism items had been discovered around the school recently and they were believed to be some of the causes. Nothing medically wrong could be found with any of the pupils and all the narcotics tests were negative. The situation returned to normal after the school was closed for a while and the students were assured that the source of the outbreak has been dealt with. A few days before the outbreak of the epidemic it was noted that during the morning prayers a few female students had fallen down 'unconscious.' They were taken to the staff room and a few minutes later regained consciousness. The pupils went on to attend classes as usual. On the morning of 21 May 1999 during the morning prayers, female students started screaming and falling in rapid succession. A total of 50 students out of a population of 765 were involved. There was complete pandemonium at the school. Ambulances and private cars were used to ferry those affected to the local hospital and clinics."

Can we so easily brush it away as "kid's stuff"?

In the literature of parapsychology, it is well known that adolescents, particularly girls going through puberty (when so much nervous energy is released), are most prone to the "poltergeist" (noisy or violent "ghost") syndrome.

How much of this is actual hysteria? No doubt, some (the power of suggestion is very strong with the young). How much has another root? "Everyday I see people who are experiencing some type of possession, some manifestation of the spiritual battle," a psychiatric nurse-practitioner from Georgia, Kimberly H. Littrell, president of the Promedical Psychiatry Group and Research Center in Loganville, told me. "There are things that are clearly out of the diagnostic categories. Most people in the field want to give it a nice psychiatric code and move on. But the enemy is not just imbalances in [the neurotransmitters] dopamine and serotonin."

Tourette syndrome?

Mass hysteria?

Or just plain . . . strange?

In one case, said Kimberly, more than a dozen people who were waking up at precisely the same time—3:31 a.m.—came to see her.

That was nearly as difficult to explain as the psychiatric patient who coughed up a *nail* . . .

34

Modern-Day Lazaruses

Can people really return from the dead?

We all have heard about "near-death experiences": folks who report a glimpse of the hereafter during a medical crisis. There are millions of such cases—literally. By 1984, pollster George Gallup estimated more than twelve million people in America alone had some form of unusual experience tied to a clinical emergency. The number has only swung decidedly upward since that time.

But what about someone who *announces* a "death" in advance—and then goes about dying in front of witnesses?

This actually occurred in the dirt-poor village of Kibeho in Rwanda—again, Africa. Again, a school; this time, the dirt-poor western part of the country.

There, a 16-year-old Catholic schoolgirl named Alphonsine Mumureke stood before the principal one day in 1982 and told her that soon she would be traveling to a "special place" (according to a mystical message she had "received"). "My body will look dead, and you'll think that I'm dead," the girl forewarned, "but please don't bury me!"

The director, understandably startled, asked where it was Alphonsine thought she was going!

"Heaven," the girl announced, with not a hint of jocularity. "My body will be here, but I'll be away until Sunday." The Virgin Mary would be stopping by the dormitory that Saturday, she said, to take her on an excursion. A note to the same effect was sent to the bishop, who had set up a panel to study alleged supernatural occurrences at the school.

It would be an "overnight trip," Alphonsine was "told"—with a "return" on the girl's seventeenth birthday. Quite a gift! And on the surface, an exercise in obvious absurdity—or pious drivel. Except: it happened.

On that Saturday, March 20, when a nun went to check on the girl—who had failed to show for dinner—she found Alphonsine lying on her bed in what appeared to be a deep slumber, still fully attired, her skin pallid—waxen—her hands neatly folded over her chest—as if in a casket! So deep was the schoolgirl's "sleep" that shaking her caused not a twitch or budge, even when the nun pushed as hard as she could and then tried shouting, full-throttled, into Alphonsine's oblivious ears . . . Listening carefully near the girl's mouth, in a vain effort to detect respiration, the nun jumped back after several minutes, crossed herself, and dashed off to the school director to announce the obvious: Alphonsine had expired.

Next on the bizarre scene was the school nurse, along with other staff. Abbot Augustin Misago, who would later become bishop, was summoned. Peering with disbelief at Alphonsine's rigid "corpse," the words she had written, in her note, came flooding back: *"My body will look dead . . . but please don't bury me!"* A nurse listened through a stethoscope while an official from Red Cross probed the girl's neck for indication of a pulse. In short order, every school official was in the dorm room, eyes wide, mouths agape. Silence said everything. Again they listened with a stethoscope. A faint pulse—but impossibly slow—was finally notated, as was very low blood pressure, the girl's chest rising and falling almost imperceptibly but enough, apparently, to send critical oxygen to her tissues.

Still, those standing around her felt they were staring at a corpse. Four men tried to roll Alphonsine on her side—but were unable to. She was preternaturally heavy. And no matter how hard they tried, they couldn't separate her clasped hands. Two more men drew close, so that now half a dozen men strained with all the force they could summon to lift the thin girl from the bed, before giving up in frustration. Alphonsine may have been a sliver of a girl, but she was heavier than a slab of granite!

Desperate, medical personnel pinched her, pulled her hair hard, and stuck needles under her fingernails. Incredibly, no response. Nothing. The conclusion: a coma, but a short one. Eighteen hours after lapsing into this condition, Alphonsine awoke, her eyes shining, livelier than ever, her face vivified and radiant with happiness. Hardly the pallor of death!

She was smiling, and why not . . . it was her birthday!

As she would later tell officials as well as enthralled classmates: The first place she was taken was "filled with shadows and groans of sadness and pain." She called it "the Place of Despair, where the road leading away from God's light ends.

"Our travels were many," she continued, to witnesses who were forced to suspend their disbelief—these events eventually accepted as authentic by the Vatican.

"We moved across the stars until we arrived in a place of golden light filled with happiness and laughter and songs sung by so many joyous voices that I thought the souls of all the people who once had lived were floating around singing praises to God."

Next up was Anathalie Mukamazimpaka, another student who was claiming mystical experiences, one whom I met when I visited. Her "trip" took seven hours—and left her in a state of silence and immobility for two full days. When finally Anathalie spoke, it was to describe a surreal, luminous destination with verdant hillocks, soaring mountains, and lush valleys composed of colors unlike any on earth, so lucid as to seem like fire-color. How to describe a place, she said, where you could breathe water and drink light?

In one part of this place, which was illuminated by a brilliant white light, said Anathalie, were seven handsome ethereal men in pure-white cloaks standing in a circle and "creating the most beautiful music without any instruments—each note a different sensation of contentment and joy" (in the words of writer Immaculée Ilibagiza). This, Anathalie was informed, was *"Isangano,"* which means "the Place of Communion."

And the men?

They, she was told, were angels.

And their job?

Watching over earth, it was explained—and aiding humanity when humanity needed it.

In all, Anathalie claimed to have visited three realms, spotting people dressed in white in a second heavenly place. There were countless happy, robed folks there. Radiant. Below that was a level that was dull, like dusk, not nearly as vibrant. Dull robes. Lonely. And a last place below *that* which she described as horrible, a "land of twilight where the only illumination was an unpleasant shade of red that reminded me of congealed blood."

The heat, Anathalie said, was dry and suffocating—so intense that she feared it would blister her skin.

Last but not least was Vestine Salima, who "succumbed" at three p.m. on Good Friday—once more leaving physicians and other medical observers dumbfounded and aghast. "The young woman simply stopped breathing," wrote Ilibagiza. "They couldn't hear her heartbeat or detect her pulse; and it was noted that her blood pressure had dropped to zero. The doctors sat staring at her for more than an hour, trying to decide if they should pronounce her dead and announce publicly that Vestine had passed away in her sleep."

Dead? Vestine took a breath every hour or two. *How could she be dead?*

They waited nearly two full days.

Then: "Good morning, everyone," said Vestine, rubbing her eyes, stretching her limbs, and releasing a gaping yawn when her coma was over—as alert as had been Alphonsine upon her revival.

It was daybreak, April 11, 1982 . . . Easter Sunday.

She had been "dead" for most of three days.

35

Devil's Hole

Hidden in U.S. history may be a curse as consequential as that involving the archduke of Austria. Instead of a car, the hex, if hex there is, may be attached to a place—more precisely, a cave.

This is Niagara Falls, at the bottom of the gorge, a mere couple miles downriver from the famous cataracts and known as "Devil's Hole" because it's at the site, this twenty-foot cave, of an old massacre. As kids we used to visit it with our grandfather. Actually, there's an entire glen carved out of the gorge and it was where Senecas had slain Brits and thrown them, after taking their scalps, into the caldron of rapids.

The cave was rumored to have had dark charisma even before then, the Indians believing a giant snake resided there next to the river. Noises likened to thunder and shrieks and groans were said to issue from the ravine, and when one young brave insisted on visiting the cave (brave indeed!), legend has it he was never seen again. When another descended the gorge and entered, he returned a raving maniac, states Seneca lore—his once glossy black hair horror-movie white.

Of all that was Francis de la Salle apprised, and yet the French explorer still insisted on visiting the mysterious hole. During his expedition it's said he heard voices warning him away. More to the point: soon after, he was murdered by members of his expedition.

That was in 1687 and is not the only historical flourish. No. Not by any measure. It was seventy years later that more than eighty British troops and family members met their end, thrown into the gorge, near a tributary that became known as "Bloody Run."

"Violent deaths at this most baleful location have been attributed to suicide, murder, and the occasional slip-and-fall 'accident,'" said a local newspaper one Halloween. "Visitors tell of hearing strange, mournful voices and sighting mysterious lights in the vicinity, called by one visiting writer a place 'cursed by an aura of sheer bad luck.'"

In fact, hardly a summer goes by without news of someone lost near Devil's Hole or falling into the roiling, boiling waters. Just upriver is a whirlpool to nowhere . . .

One woman who fell in but was rescued said she was shoved off a rock by hands unseen.

She isn't alone in feeling those hands . . .

Once upon a time a trolley ran along the base of the gorge and past the shallow cave, carrying tourists from Niagara to Buffalo—which takes us to the momentousness of this "curse."

In one case, a trolley car flew off the tracks, causing fatalities. That was long ago.

In 1965 a strange glitch in the massive hydroelectric circuitry caused a great blackout which darkened not only Niagara but everything from there to Boston, New York City, and Washington. A small variation of power originating from the Robert Moses Generating Plant (a stone's throw from Devil's Hole) caused the relay to trip, disabling a main power line heading into Southern Ontario and tripping lines into a massive overload.

During the blackout came reports of strange luminosities in the sky . . .

In 1978, it was found that dioxin—the most toxic synthetic compound known to man—was leaking from a dumpsite and through the creek—upstream from the water supply for a city called Toronto.

A college basketball star known to jog near it (and sip the water) died from a rare malignancy . . .

Others encountered bodily mishaps.

In some cases, bodies were never recovered.

Meanwhile, in 1901, President William McKinley passed by Devil's Hole on a trolley at the base of the gorge before heading to the escarpment for Buffalo for an appearance at the World's Fair. A historic day for sure—was September 14, 1901.

For just a few hours later, President McKinley, like the archduke, was . . . assassinated.

36

Those Mutilated Cows

Almost certainly you have heard of what has been called "cattle mutilations." A great mystery: cows and horses found dead, missing organs, lips, and eyes—and often all their blood. Who? What? Why? Satanists? But there are no track marks around them.

Called, in 1967, to one scene, pathologist John Altshuler told a journalist, "I have done hundreds of autopsies. You can't cut into a body without getting some blood. But there was no blood on the skin or the ground. No blood anywhere [around a mutilated horse]. The outer edges of the skin were cut firm, almost as if they had been cauterized by a modern-day laser. But there was no cauterizing laser technology like that in 1967."

Adding to the mystery, the horse's tracks ended a hundred feet from where it was found, as if the carcass had been picked up and then deposited a short distance away, in a formation that looked like a circle or where some sort of a tripod had settled down. Quite a riddle.

Did a group of scientists solve it?

In the 1990s, a small cadre in Nevada called the National Institute for Discovery Science issued a paper speculating that there perhaps was a covert government monitoring program seeking to track the spread of bio-warfare agents which had escaped, infecting first deer and then farm stock. The researchers' fear: that genetic meddling had set loose certain arcane proteins, causing a brain-wasting pathogen.

They never delivered a smoking gun, but they did find it more than peculiar, when they surveyed maps of cattle mutilation, that they seemed prevalent near military installations. "In the 1970s, in addition to the scores of cases in Colorado, hundreds, perhaps thousands, of animal mutilation reports were investigated by local law enforcement with cases occurring in fifteen states, from South Dakota and Montana to New Mexico and Texas," said the institute. "Chronic waste disease was first seen in 1967 in captive deer at Colorado State University research station in Fort Collins, Colorado. Shortly after the animal mutilation epidemic in Colorado died down, beginning in 1981, cases of chronic-wasting disease were found in free-ranging elk and deer."

So extensive was the phenomenon that then Colorado Governor Richard D. Lamm denounced it "one of the greatest outrages in the history of the western cattle industry," adding it was "no longer possible to blame predators."

The Nevada group's conclusion was chilling: the mutilations, they deduced, were linked to an infectious protein known as "prions" and coincided with both biological warfare experimentation. While in Europe it had burst into headlines as "mad-cow disease" (causing panic and the culling of animals by the thousands during the early 2000s), the intrepid researchers wondered if the disease had taken a silent, "subclinical" form across North America: In other words, it hadn't broken into the open as yet—was not at the level of an epidemic—but someone was trying to keep tabs on it.

The implications—and questions—were vast . . .

Was the plague they hypothesized silently but insidiously contaminating beef—threatening the American food supply? How many deer hunters might harbor it?

"One of the highest profile early series of mutilations occurred near Socorro, New Mexico," said the study. "Socorro is located at the northern end of White Sands Missile Range. In late 2002-early 2003, out of twenty-five mule deer tested from White Sands, four tested positive [for chronic-wasting]"—which in deer, they pointed out, had now spread as far east as Michigan.

In Canada, said the report, "there is considerable geographical overlap between the locations of the chronic-wasting disease epicenter in Saskatchewan and the locations where animal mutilations were reported since 1994. We hypothesize that the animal mutilations reported in northwestern Saskatchewan in the past several years may have been a covert prion sampling operation by perpetrators who knew that the infectious agent was spreading from farmed elk and deer to wild deer and thence to cattle." The institute's deputy administrator, Dr. Colm Kelleher, pointedly noted that an online report from his group received "thousands" of hits over a short period from computers originating at the U.S. Department of Defense.

The military? A private company? Terrorists?

It certainly seemed sinister.

But if it was the government, why were there strange lights—"UFOs"—associated with some cases? Why did certain of the instances happen near mysterious crop circles? And why was it such a worldwide phenomenon—witnessed from Australia to Russia?

37

The Wheels of Ezekiel

Are ancient biblical mysteries still unfolding around us?

If so, an example may be objects in our own time that have resembled the fiery "wheel" described in *Ezekiel*.

Let's quickly revisit his strange visions.

"The appearance of the wheels and their workmanship was like sparkling beryl, and all four of them had the same form, their appearance and workmanship being as if one wheel were within another," he said (1:16-21). *"Whenever they moved, they moved in any of their four directions without turning as they moved.*

"As for their rims they were lofty and awesome, and the rims of all four of them were full of eyes round about.

"Whenever the living beings moved, the wheels moved with them. And whenever the living beings rose from the earth, the wheels rose also. Wherever the spirit was about to go, they would go in that direction. And the wheels rose close beside them; for the spirit of the living beings was in the wheels. Whenever those went, these went; and whenever those stood still, these stood still. And whenever those rose from the earth, the wheels rose close beside them; for the spirit of the living beings was in the wheels."

That was six centuries before Christ.

Fast forward to . . . May, 1880, when, according to a passenger, Lee Fore Brace, heading up the Persian Gulf aboard the British India Company's *Patna*—"there suddenly appeared on each side of the ship an enormous luminous wheel, whirling around, the spokes of which seemed to brush the ship along. The spokes would be two or three hundred yards long . . ."

There was a luminosity ("fire") that he compared to a phosphorescent "gleam." It was also witnessed by the captain and third officer.

On December 20, 1893, half a world away, many in the states of Virginia, North Carolina, and South Carolina reported a luminous body that passed overhead moving west. At one point it stood still for twenty minutes—an enormous wheel of brilliant white that suddenly disappeared. (Caution: one sighting in 1848 included a strong sulfurous odor . . .) In 1891, a report was sent to admiralty by another captain who served as a hydrographer in the British Navy. Like the first instance, this too—curiously— occurred in the Persian Gulf.

One of the nations that border the gulf is Iraq.

Ezekiel lived in a town called Tel Abib.

That's in what is now Iraq.

The date: May 15, 1879. The ship: *Vulture*. This time, the object appeared just below the waves. "On looking toward the east, the appearance was that of a revolving wheel with a center on that bearing, and whose spokes were illuminated, and looking toward the west, a similar wheel appeared to be revolving, but in the opposite direction," wrote commander J. E. Pringle.

In 2018, UFO enthusiasts (and in some case fantasists) proclaimed the sighting of a fiery, rotating, circular aerial object over a London rooftop, with a smaller rotating "fire" inside it, captured on a cell camera. This seemed to fit what Ezekiel described (1:4) as "a whirlwind [that] came out of the north, a great cloud, and a fire enfolding itself, and a brightness was about it, and out of the midst thereof as the color of amber, out of the midst of the fire." What Ezekiel described seemed more like a spiritual manifestation; he even said as much when he wrote that "the spirit of the living creature was in the wheels" (1:20). During the last century—on June 10, 1909, at that curious hour of three a.m., according to the *Nautical Meteorological Annual* reported—the captain of a steamship called *Bintang*, sailing placidly through the Strait of Malacca (between the Malay Peninsula and Sumatra), suddenly and of course quite unexpectedly saw a gigantic revolving wheel with "long arms" issuing from the center around which the whole thing seemed to rotate. It was flat on the water. In this case: an unidentified *floating* object (if it was anything). He watched it for a full fifteen minutes, moving and vanishing when it was just ahead of the *Bintang* . . .

Hallucination or optical illusions at sea (known, for sure, to occur; see, mermaids)?

In 1910, another was seen in the air, rotating with flashes . . . In 2004 two Navy pilots off the coast of California spotted a flying object hovering over a disturbance that looked like frothy waves and foam, as if the water were boiling. Hallucination does not seem to fit in those cases.

Christopher Columbus and his crew saw a strange fire on their first voyage to what became known as the Americas . . . Scholars still argue over what *that* could have been.

38

Not of This World

In the time of Noah, we're told, there was much merriment and uproarious celebration. Tremendous entertainment. There was partying. There was violence and carousing. Lasciviousness. But there was also an evil greater and darker than any other. *"The Nephilim appeared on earth in those days, as well as later, after the sons of God had intercourse with the daughters of human beings, who bore them sons,"* states the Bible of Noah's era (*Genesis* 6: 12-4)—alien entities bred with humans.

Nothing is stranger than this particular account—and the fact that some believe it is repeating . . .

Those who propound this often start in 1957, when a 23-year-old law student named Antonio Villas Boas in Brazil claimed a strange object in the sky had abducted him while he was driving a tractor at his father's ranch. The case was so bizarre it wasn't even taken seriously by "UFO" researchers—his assertion that he was taken aboard a "craft" and made to mate with a female-human-looking and yet non-human entity after his body was coated with a thick clear odorless liquid. On September 19, 1971, a couple named Barney and Betty Hill made a similar claim, that they were abducted while driving on a rural road near Indian Head, New Hampshire, and held aboard until early the next day. Although understandably embarrassed to discuss it, Betty and Barney claimed that what they first thought was a plane descended rapidly, hovered directly over their Chevrolet Bel-

Air, which was forced to stop on Route 3, and Barney, who got out to approach it, glimpsed nine to eleven "beings" in the window, entities that were "somehow not human." They tried to drive away at high speed, but the object, shaped like a pancake, remained overhead as buzzing sounds pinged and vibrated off the automobile. Plunged into an alternate state of consciousness, the next thing the couple knew it was hours later—dawn when they straggled back home, later to recount what seemed like memories of beings aboard the "craft" removing their clothes, examining them, taking tissue samples, and in Barney's case, extracting sperm. Betty insisted that a painful needle was thrust into her navel. The case made headlines because Barney was a member of a civil rights commission and postal worker—seemed credible— and Betty a social worker whose notes about the episode are kept at her *alma mater*, the University of New Hampshire. So famous was their case that the site of "abduction" is now indicated by an official historical marker.

They were hardly alone. That same decade, on January 25, 1967, was the case of a devout Christian named Betty Andreasson who was in her kitchen in South Ashburnham, Massachusetts, when the lights blinked off and her father claimed to see diminutive beings "hopping" toward the house. The next thing Betty knew, she attested, everyone seemed to be in a trance while she was led outside (again, to a "craft") by entities similar to those depicted in other accounts: three or four feet in height, grayish, with pear-shaped heads and wide, catlike wraparound eyes, plus tiny ears and nearly no nose or mouth, communicating telepathically and subjecting her to a physical examination with unfamiliar equipment.

It was the beginning of many other reported cases—so widespread they were even studied at Harvard, where a famous psychiatrist, Dr. John Mack, looked into the matter and though expecting it to be a study of strong psychosis, ended up . . . believing many claims. A retired professor, Dr. David M. Jacobs, of Temple University, believes beings from another planet (or *somewhere*) have been extracting reproductive tissue, including ova and sperm, and merging it with DNA from aliens to create "hybrids" that will be integrated, or *are* being integrated, according to recollections under hypnosis, with the human genome.

Is it *all* delusion—concoctions made in an altered state of consciousness, which is inherently suspect? Few cases have caused the stir of one studied far more recently by Luigi Vendittelli, a businessman and researcher in Montreal, where a tall blonde French-speaking woman—six-foot-three—believes she is a "hybrid": that she was genetically engineered by extraterrestrials that implanted or modified her in her mother's womb. The story—detailed during a video-taped interview with Vendittelli that went "viral" is that Lisa's "old-school French-Canadian" mother had an experience when she was pregnant that involved strange supposed life forms that took her aboard a "ship" and into a sort of laboratory/examining room and meddled with her reproductive system.

Vendittelli cites as evidence the fact that Lisa is a twin but doctors never detected her during her mother's pregnancy, despite regular sonograms.

The "abduction" supposedly happened when the mom, pregnant, and taking a break from housework, went to lie down in her bedroom and suddenly found herself unable to move.

"She saw two 'grays' to the right side of the bed and a craft come through the wall," Vendittelli told me. "This was in a really rural area called Rouyn-Noranda, way out in the sticks. Suddenly she felt the presence of two beings, and turned her eyes to see the two tiny little beings from a "vehicle" that had come through the wall. The aliens were skinny and had big heads, black eyes—terrified her. "For many many years [the mother] was very angry with them—

in no way did she find it very cool," says the businessman. "Today she feels they're still in contact with her. She has had many UFO experiences." As they examined her, she heard one saying, 'She's not ready yet' and the other reply, 'Yes she is.'" A month later, claims Vendittelli, "she gives birth and they had always confirmed that there was only one baby. Her mother delivered a baby boy and the doctor walked out of the room because everything was done, but shortly after the nurses were screaming that there was another baby and the doctor said that was impossible—there had been no evidence of a second baby"—but there was Lisa. Many years after, in the woman's teenage years, her mother claimed she was visited by a being, "this time," says Vendittelli, "a human-looking being, very tall with jumpsuit-like pants and like a doctor's coat and the medical symbol of a snake."

That's not all that made Lisa think she was born a hybrid. Now 43, with a daughter of her own, she always had a funny feeling about herself—set apart, she told Vendittelli, who says she has insisted on anonymity (though she appears, seated next to Vendittelli in the video—displaying unusual eyes).

"She sticks out in a crowd, like it's out of this world. Very tall and very good looking. Her mother doesn't say she is a hybrid. She simply says she can't explain what happened. She doesn't like to say she is a hybrid because they don't know. Lisa has felt very, very alone from day one. She never felt like she belonged to us, that she was connecting with regular people. She's still looking for the missing piece. She still hasn't figured it out and still questions it. She has had out-of-body experiences. That started when she was younger but she never made the connection. She did have an experience at age five. They were living in a rural area, with a big field next the house, and in the middle of the night her cousin rushed to her and said, 'Come and see—there is a circus!' When Lisa peered out the window to the field, she saw an oval object with a ton of lights on it. The next day nothing was there."

The woman feels she has some sort of mission. She feels there are "many" similar hybrids. She can sense them immediately. When, in the presence of Vendittelli, she met one and was able to converse with her even though they spoke different languages (Lisa, Francophone, the other English).

Mental illness? Simple obsession?

Those are the obvious questions. As Vendittelli acknowledges, "one must be careful because the beings are very deceiving and what people recall can be very fictitious."

Lisa reportedly senses she is here for a special reason, a mission. "She keeps saying all the time, 'Something has to happen. Something has to change in the world.'" Major events are coming. Fundamental transformation. Aboard the "crafts," some abductees have been shown a multitude of images of our planet's future: atomic explosions; meteorites striking the earth; ecological disaster; all the trees destroyed; suffocating humans; the world cracking apart. Black clouds everywhere. Mountains collapsing. In other words: you name it. As one "hybrid" told a researcher named Claudia Negron, "Soon all life will be changed. People will be different." Some sort of major change is coming. It has to. There will be only one form of government, abductees are told. There will be no need for nations.

And who will be in charge? Who are the saviors? In comparing UFOs with supernatural lore, one scholar, Jacques Vallee, noted that such encounters share much with fairies of folklore. And with accounts of witchcraft: dwarfish figures, paralysis, subsequent illness, bedroom intrusions, the soul leaving the body (and encountering entities), electromagnetic interference, gruesome examinations, and henceforth, shamanic equivalences. Curious it was how "contactees" in the 1950s began "channeling" that led to the New Age movement, and curious too how accounts of satanic abuse and UFO abductions emerged at about the same time, with many parallels (scary eyes, babies important, amnesia, forced against will, and an examining table in one case, an altar in the case of Satanism). As an Anglican priest and UFO researcher in Nebraska named Ray Boeche—speaking of two Christians he said were in the Department of Defense—reportedly said, "They came to believe that the nonhuman entities were not extraterrestrial at all; they believed they were some sort of demonic entities. And that regardless of how benevolent or beneficial any of the contact they had with these entities seemed to be, it always ended up being tainted . . . with something that ultimately turned out to be bad. From what they told me, it seemed like someone had invoked something and it opened a doorway to let these things in." There were those who claimed that famed rocket scientist Jack Parsons, widely known to have been involved in satanic rituals (at a place near the Jet Propulsion Laboratory called Devil's Gate Dam), had done precisely this—held rituals invoking such entities—in 1947 (the year Kenneth Arnold had that sighting, and also the year of Roswell). But could spirits cause physical effects like *pregnancy?* Both Saint Thomas Aquinas, Saint Albertus Magnus, and Martin Luther believed the answer was . . . yes. "The demons are called animals of the atmosphere because their nature is akin to that of aerial bodies," Aquinas had said. Saint Augustine said that evil spirits could have sexual interaction with humans.

Take it all—the modern hybrid claims—with a grain of salt, or not at all. Or take this: Another abduction researcher, Joe Jordan, who has interviewed hundreds of such people, and works for a military contractor, told me there is no sound physical evidence for abductions, and that in virtually every case he has investigated, when the Name of Jesus is invoked, the "aliens" flee.

39

The Case of the Restless Tombs

Everyone gets a little spooked at the notion of graveyards. Conjure up the image of old, tilted stones, bedecked with spider webs, and you are raising the specter of ghouls, kobolds, the living dead—or at least luminous and uncanny orbs: if nowhere other than in the imagination.

Or does it only make sense, for those who believe that souls can linger (in need of prayer), that they would do so near their graves?

Not many, however skeptical, would spend the night at one!

Sunbathe?

In their youth, John Lennon and Paul McCartney took shortcuts through St. Peter's Graveyard in Woolton near Liverpool, basking in the sun there, taking naps (and in the case of Lennon, rendezvousing with female fancies).

Do such things rub off?

"I felt like a hollow temple filled with many spirits," John Lennon said many years later, in discussing his songwriting, "each inhabiting me for a little time and then leaving, to be replaced by another." The name on one of the grave markers at St. Peter's: Eleanor Rigby.

But this is taking us off course. We are here to speak of graves. Aside from the spookiness, there is mystery. When the body of a 17th-century Anglican bishop, Peder Winstrup, was exhumed at London's Lund Cathedral in

2015, the corpse of a fetus . . . an unborn child . . . was found at his feet.

Who? Why?

Was it the *bishop's* child?

The Merchants, a family in Marion, Ohio, marked the grave of a family patriarch Charles, who had made a fortune in the locomotive industry, with a stone plinth and a huge granite ball on top of it. Proudly, they had it stained and polished to a fine shine, but for a rough spot where, out of obvious necessity, the ball, which weighed more than two tons, touched the plinth. All well and good, except that within a few years, it was discovered that the ball was spinning. This was clear because the rough spot underneath was now . . . visible. *Who or what could manipulate a stone spheroid weighing five thousand pounds?* Unhappy with that turn of events, the family had a crane hoist the monument and returned it to its original orientation. That was in 1898. The top of the ball was even secured with a dollop of tar. But to no avail. The ball continued to spin—and does to this day, with no one quite sure why (though science will doubtless offer mundane explanations, or try to). Is it from an imperceptible vibration, or something a bit spookier? "No matter the cause," says an observer, "the Merchant ball rolls on."

Other mysteries go beyond. Case in point: the moving coffins of Barbados. These were in a family vault at Christ Parish Church, the tomb purchased in 1808 by the family of a rather reviled local businessman named Thomas Chase. First to die was his beloved daughter, Mary Ann. Into the vault she went. Next was daughter Dorcas, who may have killed herself—perhaps because she had been abused.

And after her? Just a month subsequently, Thomas likewise committed suicide. No happiness in this clan!

It was upon the burial of Thomas that the disturbance was noted: opening the crypt to inter him, workmen discovered the coffins of both daughters had been tossed around and violently, now upended and propped against a wall. Dorcas's was upside-down (as if in protest of dad's arrival) . . .

Had water somehow entered, floated the lead coffins, and then drained out of the mausoleum—which was located on Pleistocene coral-reef limestone, a highly porous rock that could allow water to percolate through it?

That sounded logical, but there had been no flash flood and graves nearby were fully intact. Nor is Barbados known for earthquakes.

At any rate, the coffins were placed back in order and a massive marble stone was rolled in front of the entrance to inhibit pranksters.

When Lord Vincent Combermere, the governor of Barbados, went to see for himself—tired of the wild stories that abounded and might spook tourists—he too observed coffins wildly out of place and ordered sand spread on the floor to detect any entry.

Once more the crypt was closed and a heavy marble slab was placed at the door and mortared in place. Then Lord Combermere pressed his signet ring in the wet cement—as a seal to detect tampering.

But when he returned, on April 20, 1820—eight months later—and the vault was reopened, the macabre sight of displaced coffins again greeted onlookers. This time Thomas's was against the entrance and one coffin thrown so forcefully that a corner of it had fractured. Yet, there were no footprints in the sand and the official seal was still in place.

Strapped for an explanation, the governor had the coffins removed and buried elsewhere. He should have put a cross there.

Or anointed oil.

What about a Bible open to *Ephesians* 6?

And so it is: the original vault remains vacant, the only way, apparently, of halting future disturbances. The final question: does anyone still hear what passersby had: shrieks from the crypt, and screams?

40

Living Fossils

What about animals that seemed dead—or should be?

Through the centuries have come reports of small creatures, entombed in rocks, coal, or wood, that suddenly revive, despite suspended animation for decades.

In the 1400s, it was reported that a small living snake was found encased in a chunk of marble stone, though there was no visible crack or hole that could have allowed the serpent to enter or air to sustain the animal. Or so it was reported.

Often, it's frogs or toads. Sometimes lizards.

Is it simply hibernation?

Once more, the wonders of God's Creation.

In 1733—May 8, to be exact—two quarry laborers named Olof Sigräfwer and Anders Halfwarder dashed to their inspector, telling him that Anders had seen a frog sitting in the middle—inside—a large boulder he'd just cut in half.

The inspector—a fellow named Johan Gråberg—did the logical thing: followed the two frenzied men into the quarry, where his eyes set upon a frog, grayish in color, with a mouth sealed by a yellowish membrane. To see if it was alive, he touched it. Not excessively patient, Gråberg grew miffed when the animal failed to adequately react, grabbed a shovel, and beat it to death! Regret soon consumed him, and in writing he swore sorrow for "being the Slayer of that extraordinary Animal, which might have lived for many hundreds of years within its stony Prison." As a sort of penance, he assumed the mission of taking the squashed frog to scholars, one of whom—a physician and amateur naturalist named Dr. Johan Phil—studied it and concluded that frog spawn somehow had found its way into the rock, developing, over the years, into a full-grown amphibian. This he presented with requisite evidence to the Swedish Academy of Sciences, which promptly rejected his paper at its next meeting, filing it, with a huff, in the academy's archives. (The frog itself was whisked off to the natural history collection of a brilliant count, Carl Gustaf Tessin, at Akerö Castle.)

In 1761, Ambroise Pare, physician to Henry III of France, wrote of his own experience. "Being at my seat near the village of Meudon," he said, in the *Annual Register*, "and overlooking a quarryman whom I had sent to break some very large and hard stones, in the middle of one we found a huge toad, full of life and without any visible aperture by which he could get in there. The laborer told me it was not the first time he had met with a toad and like creatures within huge blocks of stone . . ."

Was it that the skin of certain animals absorbed all the necessary oxygen from molecules of air that found their way through exquisitely small pores in the rock? And might it be that certain boulders or chunks of coal have been formulated more recently than suspected?

Benjamin Franklin wrote of four live toads entombed in limestone.

A few decades later a British geologist and theologian named William Buckland, skeptical of such accounts, sealed more than twenty toads in blocks of sandstone and limestone, burying them in his backyard. In 1826, after a year, he chipped away the rock and found that all the toads in the sandstone were goners. The opposite, however, was true of the limestone: frogs survived in that, and two even seemed to have gained weight! When Buckland buried the toads for another year, and sealed the stone, there were no survivors.

End of story?

As one chronicler of the arcane has pointed out, the shape of the entombment often exactly fits the animal's size—seemingly impossible when it's a rock that takes (or is believed to take) eons to form. Simply put, a toad can't hibernate that long. What about coal? Neither is that created overnight! Yet, there have been such living fossils in coal— more than two hundred, at last reckoning.

In 1865 the Hartlepool *Free Press* brought forth the news of a block of magnesium limestone with a toad in a cavity that "was no larger than its body and presented the appearance of being a cast of it."

In 1928, a toad was found in the stone of a twenty-year-old hotel in Emerson, Manitoba. It was shrunken and covered with dust—this poor reptile—but, reported the Ottawa Citizen, "when touched it moved with a healthy hop." Not easily explained.

On April 22, 1881, a fellow named Joseph Molino was using a sledge hammer twenty yards down in a Nevada mine when to his surprise a rock fell with a cavity the size of his fist. Inside were white worms that put him in mind of maggots, "dead" at first but reviving with exposure to air. After a full hour they were crawling around the ground— witnessed not only by Molino but other miners!

What about beetle remains discovered on August 13, 1892, in iron ore: This at the Longfellow Mine, Chilton, Arizona. When the ore was smashed open, Z. T. White saw a dull red something in the close-fitting hole—a hole that, again, precisely fit the tiny carcass.

Amazed, White reportedly placed the insect on a cloth and on the way home the matter took a stranger turn when he saw a smaller, *living* beetle emerge from the dead one like a butterfly from a cocoon—crawling out of the entombment!

How can stone that may take hundreds, thousands, or millions of years to form harbor animals that may have normal longevity of several years?

Flags of caution wave when one reads that English archeologist Charles Dawson—he of the infamous "Piltdown Man" hoax—years earlier had presented the Brighton "toad in a hole" (entombed in a flint nodule, and likely another forgery).

In 1975: construction workers in Fort Worth, Texas, were breaking up concrete that had been set just a year before when they happened upon a living green turtle that obviously—by the shape of the hole—had been trapped as they poured the concrete. Jackhammers can wake anything up!

41

Strangeness in the Night

It's said one of Elvis's experiences with strange lights took place en route from Memphis to Las Vegas when, as he crossed New Mexico, in the late 1960s, Presley claimed he and two companions, Jerry Schilling and Larry Geller, watched a saucer cross the night sky in a huge arc, growing larger and more brilliant until it cut a sudden ninety-degree turn and slung itself into the unobservable distance.

We don't have a fix on what city they were near. We do know that afterwards, Presley took to reading the Book of Ezekiel. We also know the highway he was on: Route 66.

Therein lies the mystery—or better said, mysteries (plural). For as it crosses New Mexico, Route 66 passes through a nondescript town called Gallup, where a branch of the highway veers north and, because it's the sixth "leg," was officially designated "Route 666"—a road bedeviled not only by its ominous numbers but the lore (some would say, the curse) that went along with it. No joy ride, this: travelers suffered more than the expected number of accidents or break-downs—especially unexplained electrical disruptions and encounters of the phantasmagoric kind. Some called it "Satan's Speedway" and with grim recollection (and straight faces) reported everything from apparitional hitch-hikers and a phantom truck to a pack of vicious dogs that somehow could keep up with any vehicle and glowered with luminous eyes.

Did the juxtaposition inflame imaginations? According to researcher Dr. Avery Teicher of Phoenix, several of the

167

accounts were well documented. One involved unworldly canines that chased a group of motorcyclists, two of whom were badly mauled, medical records show. Others insisted they saw a woman in white hitchhiking along the side of the route or even standing in the center of the pavement before vanishing. And then there is the black sedan—some say a 1930s-era Pierce-Arrow roadster that roared alongside in a most threatening manner. As the sun sets, flickering head-lights were and perhaps still are spotted, moving inexorably closer. Some say the sedan has bumped into them or, honking angrily, has forced them off the road. When folks try to see who's driving, what they observe are only dark-ened windows—or suddenly, no car at all . . . This aston-ished me because in July 1993, while visiting Lewiston, New York, my wife and I spotted a shiny black Lincoln all but blocking our access to the parking lot of a restaurant. From a block away—somehow—we could see the driver: stocky, with a round austere face, not friendly at all, the inte-rior of the car swathed in an unusual reddish glow. When, peeved, I squeezed past and pulled up behind it, the license—as if to mock us—was "666." The car then pulled out of the entrance onto the street and out of sight . . .

Another who has written of the route in New Mexico, author Linda Dunning, said on one drive near Gallup (a one-stoplight-type town composed mainly, on the route, by gas stations, diners, and motels), her husband encountered a phantasmal semi that "looked like it was on fire heading straight for him, right down the middle of the highway. It was going so fast that sparks were flying up off the wheels and flames from the smokestack. He pulled over and got out of his car and walked way off the road into the desert till the truck passed him going what he estimated was a hundred and thirty miles an hour."

"Walked"? (Rather hurriedly, one imagines.)

Some of the accidents—if not all—can be rationalized. Route 666 had four hundred curves in one stretch of just sixty miles—ascending and descending steep, dangerous highlands. In 2002 a female driver suffered a heart attack and drove head-on into a speeding truck, injuring a baby and costing four others their lives. Once known as the Old Mexico Trail, Route 66 coursed not only across the sweeping deserts of New Mexico but also the bony western spur of Colorado and into Utah, slicing through a huge Indian Reservation and a towering natural monument called Shiprock . . . which Navajos believed was magical and gave roost to flesh-eating bird-monsters . . .

More modern accounts tell the tale of folks who, encountering car trouble, have walked along the ominous trail, only to disappear with no trace—in some cases, leaving their vehicles behind, in other cases, their cars disappearing with them.

In still other cases, people have vanished for hours or days. When they resurface, they experience what is known as "missing time": unable to recall where they went and how long they were gone. In Utah, north of where 666 ended, and along Route 66, similar phenomena (bigfoot, UFOs, and crop circles) are reported at Skinwalker Ranch— land that was under study by the same billionaire who funded the Nevada institute studying mutilations; for there were mutilations here also. I found the same upon journeying on a similar aggregation of bizarre occurrences called Clinton Road in West Milford, New Jersey: accounts of a preternatural pickup, roadside apparitions, ineffable creatures, and the omnipresent aerial lights and crop circles. Old ritual grounds, they said. There had been covens. And Masonic meetings. The Mafia (this is Sopranos territory) supposedly dumped bodies there.

In New Mexico, fears were assuaged when the U.S Department of Transportation renumbered the road in 2003.

That was done after the three states petitioned the department with a resolution that included such clauses as:

WHEREAS, people living near the road already live under the cloud of opprobrium created by having a road that many believe is cursed running near their homes and through their homeland; and

WHEREAS, the number "666" carries the stigma of being the mark of the beast, the mark of the devil, which was described in the Book of Revelation in the Bible; and

WHEREAS, there are people who refuse to travel the road, not because of the issue of safety, but because of the fear that the devil controls events along United States route 666; and

WHEREAS, the economy in the area is greatly depressed when compared with many parts of the United States, and the infamy brought by the inopportune naming of the road will only make development in the area more difficult . . .

[And in the New Mexico application, let it be known that]: "There has been such an outcry from people living on or near US 66 in New Mexico and from the traveling public who avoid traveling on US 666, that House Joint Memorial 60 and Senate Joint Memorial 49 were passed by the 2003 Legislature of the State of New Mexico, to request assignment of a new designation for US 666 as quickly as possible."

Has it worked?

Noted Dunning: "In Arizona the road is now Highway 191. In Utah it is known as New 491/Old 666. This new moniker has not stopped the strange incidents from happening on the road, nor has it stopped people from telling stories about it.

"Drive Route 666 at night, and you drive at your own risk."

42

Sinister Wings

How can we reconcile the almost constant reports of strange creatures around us? Might it be a "sign of the times"—an indication of a great upturn in the presence, in countless ways, in countless places, of evil? An official Catholic exorcist I know named Father Chad Ripperger says "one of the things that we exorcists have noticed is the resilience of demons now is unprecedented. Historically, when you talk to priests who had been exorcists back in the Fifties and Sixties, they said before the mid-sixties, when you got faculties for a case of possession, it was *over*. Within a day to two days, ninety-nine percent of the time the demons were out, maybe on the outside a week. The average case of possession now takes somewhere between ten months and two years to break. The demons are extraordinarily resilient to your prayers in ways that exorcists say they never saw in the past." My own take on it: everyone is called to deliverance, and with enough fasting and Bible-quoting and prayer, in the Name of Jesus, any demon can be rather promptly cast out.

Bigfoot is one thing—in our time, nearly *passé*. The same is true of Loch Ness: as we've seen, lake "monsters" are claimed everywhere, along with assorted other beasts. In the U.S. alone, three hundred of them! On land, there's also the "Flathead Monster" in Montana. There's "Michigan Dog Man." In Ukraine there was the "Blackbird of Chernobyl" (spotted a year before the nuclear disaster). Back at

Mount St. Helens was "batsquatch" (accompanying those ape-men), and "thunderbird," in North Dakota. A large black figure with red eyes was spotted at Fukushima just before the tsunami, once more a harbinger. ("It sat there for about five seconds, then it unfurled a large set of what I could only describe as large, black wings," claimed Marcus Pules, a visiting American who reported it.)

But none have been more surreal than the famous "mothman" of West Virginia . . .

Perhaps you've heard of it—or seen the movie. But there are stranger aspects to it. In a nutshell, during November 1966, two couples driving in a souped-up 1957 Chevrolet took a right off Route 62 and drove about half a mile to another rural route north of Point Pleasant before taking a left onto a gravel road and entering an abandoned government munitions facility called the "old TNT." That sobriquet was from World War II, when the more than 8,000 acres were devoted to an ammunition manufacturing facility. For reasons of safety, the explosives were stored in camouflaged bunkers—or "igloos"—scattered across the terrain (and later used, when it closed, for satanic rituals).

The mission, for the foursome, was to have a little fun, chasing away "parkers" (in an area now used for car racing and as lovers' lane).

But there was an eerie feeling in the air when they climbed out and looked around. It was about 11:30 p.m.— the night clear and cold, the drama unfolding as they topped a hill. It was then their headlights exploded upon a slender figure along the road that on closer inspection seemed like a man, colored a dirty gray, who stood six-feet tall, perhaps seven, and had wings they recalled as ashen white, the tips of which were seen over his muscular shoulders.

Blasted by the headlights, the creature had stared hard at them—the Scarberrys, Roger and Linda; the Mallettes, Steve and Mary—looking wobbly, perhaps even scared, and making its way quickly for an old power plant. At one point it seemed to be trying to free one of the wings from a guide wire, Linda later testified. It had a face, but they barely recalled further details, consumed, as they were, with its large eyes, which glowed in the headlights. "We were all screaming, 'Go! Go! Go!' but, we couldn't perform the actual action of leaving the scene," said Linda, whose husband was driving. "It was like we were hypnotized. It finally got its wing loose from the wire and ran into the power plant." And they finally freed themselves of their hypnotic hesitation—backing up, tires spinning. As they did, they could hear screeching and a strange humming. Rumor was there had been satanic rituals there.

Racing back down the small gravel road and turning back onto what was called Fairground Road, the two couples realized the creature was pursuing them—managing to easily keep up with the car even when it reached a hundred miles an hour. At one point it seemed over the back of the car, its wingtips scraping it. It broke off pursuit, reappeared; was suddenly standing by the road. At another juncture, it was along the road sitting in a crouched position. It seemed *everywhere*. And the way it flew: when they'd left the TNT, it shot straight up and vanished—at least for a few minutes. Nearby, they spotted a strangely dead animal—a dog—near the road, and then the creature again.

Making a mad dash for town, they stopped at a diner and had someone call the police, last spotting the entity sitting on top of a flood wall in a crouched manner, its wings now folded. "It was like the creature was trying to communicate with us," Linda later said. "We were very confused and scared. We didn't know what to do, where it came from, or what it was going to do."

An officer went back with them, and they filed a formal report, which was picked up by the *Point Pleasant Register*:

"Couples See Man-Sized Bird . . . Creature . . . Something."
The wings, which may have spanned ten feet, led the newspaper to coin the moniker "mothman."

The more newsmen looked into it, the stranger it got. They were to learn, for instance, that several days earlier, on November 12, in Clendin, five gravediggers had seen a man-beast winging over treetops and described the same nacreous red eyes. Clendin was forty-nine miles away.

A *graveyard*.

In the following months, others would report a similarly winged entity, their terror reaching beyond what one would expect with the sighting of a new zoological specimen—though that's what a local wildlife biologist, Dr. Robert L. Smith, of West Virginia University, tried to tell reporters, postulating, with a serious face, that "mothman" was . . . a large sandhill crane.

Perhaps, said Dr. Smith, one had strayed from a migratory route and was mistaken by four local residents unfamiliar with such an animal, which is native to Nebraska.

The questions were as obvious as they were unanswerable. Did sandhill cranes follow people? Did they have huge eyes? And what about the humanoid characteristics?

Moreover, it seemed to *haunt* folks. There were sounds. There were eerie beeping, screeching phone calls. Linda would soon see it at her home, and the same night as the TNT sighting, Merle Partridge, a contractor who lived ninety miles away, watched as his television blinked dark and a strange pattern emerged, accompanied by a high-pitched noise that buzzed around his home. When Partridge went to investigate, he had spotted two large red orbs that reminded him of "bicycle reflectors."

More unnerving still, Partridge's dog tore after the "animal . . ." and was never seen again.

Was it the dog the Scarberrys and Mallettes had seen?

And was there a relation to other animals—including cows—that had or would be mutilated in the region?

In flooded similar reports—five hundred at one newspaper. Was mothman part a *hex*?

When, in the late 1700s, a Shawnee leader named Chief Cornstalk was executed by white settlers, it was said he levied a curse on the area that would become known as Point Pleasant—and a subsequent sighting of mothman was near . . . the Chief Cornstalk Reservation.

A hagridden vicinity, this: plagued by coal-mine accidents, a major train derailment, and plane crashes. When the Scarberrys reached out for local ministers, no one responded.

On December 15, 1967—just over a year after the encounter at the Old TNT—a bridge linking Point Pleasant to Gallipolis, Ohio, collapsed into the Ohio River—killing 46. A harbinger, as the many reports of monsters in our own time—now so multiplied—may be harbingers of larger events? Some claim mothman was seen at the bridge just before the calamity.

That marked the last major encounters in Point Pleasant . . .

But will it ever really end? To this day, mysterious humming is heard; strange lights are seen in the sky (near the Old TNT); in some homes, electricity is disrupted, a common signal of demonic interference. UFOs and "men in black" are reported.

In Guadalajara, Mexico, a winged entity with glowing eyes (and an icy stare) was seen at a sinister cemetery called Panteon de Belen (before disappearing into roiled clouds). That was tame compared to the winged woman of Da Nang, witnessed by U.S. Marines during the Vietnam War, and casting a greenish glow, before disappearing.

Centuries ago, a creature standing seven feet tall with signature glowing red eyes was seen in London at Highgate Cemetery.

And similar reports have been generated at another World War Two munitions facility, the Lake Ontario Ordnance Works, near Lewiston, New York, which like Point Pleasant had strange aerial lights, creature sightings, and the requisite Indian burial mound—a graveyard.

I personally had a friend who was racing around the area in a new car late one night and died in a crash on his way back (this in 1988; his last name: Mallette).

Strangest of all: the nickname for the secret woodland in Upstate New York is identical. Locals long have known it as the "Old TNT."

43

A Most Incredible Cure

In the annals of miraculous healings, perhaps none stands out like what happened to a poor blind girl from Palermo, Italy, named Anna Maria Gemma DiGiorgio.

"I had no pupils in my eyes," recounted Gemma in 1971. "I had no sight at all. When I was three months old, my mother took me to a very famous eye doctor in Palermo. He told her that, without pupils, I would never be able to see."

No *pupils*?

Dire indeed.

A life of darkness . . .

Some claimed she may have had pupils, but that her birth defect was so severe they were not recognized as such. In looking at photos, I couldn't tell either way.

Whatever—in 1946, when the girl was seven, a nun took it upon herself to write the famous stigmatic priest Padre Pio on Anna's behalf and received a note saying she should be brought to Padre Pio in San Giovanni Rotundo. I've been there. This is rather barren territory. A damp cold in the autumn and winter—austere like the monk was austere. Many thousands sought his counsel or healing effects.

That's exactly what Gemma's grandmother did: brought the girl to see the famous Capuchin, who heard the child's first confession and gave her communion—then made the sign of the Cross on her eyes.

After the visit, Gemma was able to see. It's a fact that's beyond question, confirmed by amazed doctors. Did she really lack pupils? Or was her entire eye one large pupil (making it seem that way)? We know only that there was a severe defect and that although the physical defect remained unchanged, afterward Gemma was able to see normally.

More astounding still may be the thoroughly-documented cure of a construction worker named Giovanni Savino, severely injured on February 15, 1949, in a dynamite mishap while preparing to blast a boulder for a friary annex. It was Giovanni's routine to head for church each morning before setting off for work, and afterward, like many others, he would wait outside of the sacristy for the holy man's blessing.

This day, when Giovanni asked for his anointing, Pio gave the workman a warm hug and said only, "Courage! I am praying to the Lord that you will not die."

What?

Die?

One can imagine Giovanni's upset. Pio was known as a prophet, one who usually was, if we can excuse the expression, dead-on.

Giovanni was petrified. "Padre Pio, what is going to happen to me?" he asked, in dread and earnest.

Pio answered with . . . silence.

The following three mornings, when Giovanni went for his customary blessing, Pio said the same, upsetting thing. And Giovanni reacted with the same fright and stupefaction. When the same ominous words were uttered on the fourth day, the worker had had enough and wondered aloud if they should call off work for the time being. The crew, however, intent on its work, went ahead leveling the earth for the addition.

That afternoon, Giovanni and his partner placed a charge of dynamite under a boulder, lit the fuse, and then waited as it failed to detonate. *What was wrong?* After a short while, they went to find out, checking the charge— which blew up in Giovanni's face.

The workman was in a bad way. A shower of rocks had felled him—embedded in his flesh. His face was scorched— much of his facial skin torn off. Most relevantly: where once there had been a right eye, there was now a pulpy mess. Dr. Guglielmo Sanguinetti, a physician, and Padre Raffaele, another Capuchin, as well as a Father Dominic Meyer, rushed to the injured man's side. All three noted that among Savino's numerous injuries, his right eye was entirely gone. On this they concurred: the socket was empty. Other doctors confirmed the eye had been annihilated and Giovanni's other badly damaged. Like Gemma, it looked like Savino was also going to be totally blind . . .

Informed of the terrible event—that the devout Christian laborer, so diligent, and prayerful, had been robbed of his sight—Pio digested the news of blindness and replied succinctly and cryptically, *"That is not for certain yet."*

It was three days before the workman came to, his head and face swathed in bandages. Who knows what went through his mind as he lay, pondering a dark future! Nurses tended to him. One dismal day segued into the next. A tragic episode. On the evening of his tenth day in the hospital, the blinded laborer was praying the rosary when he smelled what he later called "the aroma of paradise," a gorgeous, heavenly smell, as if someone with perfume or cologne was standing next to his bed. He felt, with a sixth sense, that it was Pio standing next to him. "Give me back my sight, Padre Pio, or let me die!" pleaded Savino. "I cannot live like this!"

A week later, on February 25, 1949, at about one a.m., Savino felt a slap on the right side of his face—the side where the eye had been. "I asked, 'Who touched me?'" testified the injured workman. "There was nobody. But again I smelled the aroma. It was beautiful."

When later his ophthalmologist—an atheist—came to examine the remaining eye—shock. "To their amazement," writes a biographer, "the doctors found that his shattered face was fully healed and covered with new skin." But what most amazed and elated Savino was the fact that he . . . had regained his vision. "I can see you!" he shouted to the specialist.

And indeed, as is medically documented, to his "utter astonishment," the doctor saw that Savino had his right eye back.

He wasn't seeing out of the badly damaged one—rather the one that had been turned to a bloody gel yet somehow was reconstituted. It left the doctors no doubt they had witnessed a miracle, according to a Protestant writer, Bernard Ruffin, who reviewed all the records.

Once released from the hospital, Giovanni naturally beat a path to the friary to thank Padre Pio. The mysterious monk, who fasted constantly, and often suffered for the infirm, said just, "If only you knew what this cost me!"

It's tremendous to hear about those healed of diabetes or arthritis or even cancer leaving a person.

For a missing part of the body to be restored is another matter entirely . . .

44

Fiery Phantoms

While researchers have come up with some interesting and perhaps imaginative physical—natural—explanations for the cases of spontaneous human combustion, more difficult to dismiss, by far, are instances in which it's not just a single fire but sometimes dozens, or even hundreds, of them. In one case of human combustion, normal explanations flew out the window when unconnected fires erupted elsewhere in the home—including a closet.

And there were no gas leaks, or anything.

"Outstanding puzzlements," a chronicler of oddities, Charles Fort, labeled them—citing the account whereby a person had picked up a pillow only to watch as it suddenly turned incandescent with heat; in another case, damp clothes tossed in a bin were found issuing licks of fire in the morning.

But let's talk volume here. Once more the pages of time turn back, here to April 19, 1941, when the Travelers Insurance Company reported fantastic fires at the home of a farmer named William Hacker near Odon, Indiana. The initial blaze had gathered the response of firemen that morning—on the second floor of the west side of the house—but no sooner had they returned to the station than they had to head right back to extinguish flames consuming a layer of *paper*—just the paper—that separated a mattress and the box springs in a bedroom on the first floor.

Other fires followed in quick order.

"Some were so strange as to tax the belief of the most credulous persons who visited the place," the company's report said. "A calendar on a wall went up in a quick puff of smoke. Another fire started in a pair of overalls hanging on a door. A bedroom was reduced to ashes while neighbors, standing in the room, stared in amazement. A book taken from a drawer of a desk was found to be burning inside."

Before midnight that day, thirty fires had caused isolated damage: hard to explain, especially in that none occurred in the kitchen . . . and the home was not wired for electricity.

From 1979 to 1981, a family in Ashton, Iowa, reported buttons continually fused to a plastic box that contained them.

And on September 9, 1945, one Mrs. Annie Bryan of Midland, Arkansas, discovered flames licking up from the drawer of a table. Within a week, thirty other unexplained fires were recorded in her abode—damaging curtains, clothes, wall paper, and furnishings, according to another prodigious collector of the arcane, Vincent Gaddis.

Thirteen years later, in Paris, Kentucky, the Charles Johnson family incurred thirteen minor blazes in the course of three short days.

More curiously . . . the fires seemed intent on destroying bedclothes.

One family was plagued so badly during Lent that an exorcist was summoned – for a pair of shoes had ignited just as the man of the house was putting them on!

Few pyrotechnic oddities surpassed a case in 1973 whereby smoke coming from a mortuary was urgently traced by firefighters to the inside of a coffin bearing remains of the recently deceased Betty Satlow . . . of Hoquiam, Washington.

But it was around the world, in Sicily, that the most baffling, and sinister, and frightening, case would unfold . . . two days before Christmas, 2003.

That was when, during dinner, a resident named Antonino Pezzino in a small fishing hamlet called Canneto di Caronia on the island's northern coast discovered a fuse box in his house engulfed by flames.

This one could fathom: glitches do occur in things electrical. It seemed like a normal, if unwelcome, eventuality. Or was it?

Several days after, the television, a kitchen fan, and other appliances caught fire.

Defective wiring?

That seemed plausible enough, though the extent was curious. For in the weeks that followed, little infernos likewise afflicted Pezzino's parents, aunts, and cousins, who lived in five attached homes.

The wiring was changed. The stoves were checked.

The fires continued.

This is where it gets very strange.

Reported *The New York Times*, "Fuse boxes then blew in houses all along the Via Mare. Air-conditioners erupted even when unplugged. Fires started spontaneously. Kitchen appliances went up in smoke. A roomful of wedding gifts was crisped. Computers jammed. Cell phones rang when no one was calling, and electronic door locks in empty cars went demonically up and down. Before long, the mainly Roman Catholic populace professed to see the hand of the devil at work, turning their postcard-perfect paradise into a place possessed of evil, embers, and ash."

Was it the electric grid?

That was a question for ENEL, the national electric and gas provider—which cut off power to the homes. Yet, even with the central source of electricity off—guaranteeing that stray energy was not the issue—the entire village now seemed subject to an unseen immolator.

Odd it was how throughout the community (as another publication, *Atavist* Magazine, put it), "metal, plastic, and insulation all burned . . . outlets burned red hot through the holes—cords lit up like sparklers, an electrical motor melted. Appliances rebelled against their owners."

From January to March, there were more than ninety fires!

Mattresses caught fire as villagers slept on them.

What do you say into a cell phone that rings when it's *off*?

During the second week of February, one neighbor sought refuge at the police station when his shoes went up in flames.

Move in investigators—first from the public prosecutor's office, soon from the National Institute of Geophysics and Volcanology—for this is a region famous for eruptions of lava that can cause a charge of electricity. During volcanic episodes, lightning is often seen amid the smoke.

And all this was true, except for one wrench in the theory: there was no recent evidence for unusual volcanic activity of any kind in the region.

But could it not be that hot lava moving without detection underneath was unleashing enough ions to upset wiring?

"The internal forces of the earth cannot cause reactions of this magnitude, and especially in a tiny area," said the president of the institute after investigating a possible seismic source. At the Italian Center for Electro-technical Experimentation in Milan—Gianfranco Allegra concurred: "No one knows what the cause of these fires is. They are inexplicable."

Those who sought a superstitious explanation could be excused for noting that historically, the area was named, on maps, as "Devil's Valley"—due to vampire lore.

Lo! Residents had to be evacuated. Their sooty furniture sat along streets. Was it *gas* from magma?

The antenna on a car heated to the point of cracking the windshield.

Compasses spun.

There didn't really seem to be a geothermal justification.

How about military experiments?

NATO and the U.S. Navy were known to conduct exercises in the Tyrrhenian Sea, upon which Canneto di Caronia sits. The problem: electromagnetic emissions would not be able to cause the type of fires logged in this wearied community. If it was a laser, the question was why it didn't burn the *exterior* of homes as well.

Those who thought of secret weapons—and they are out there, perhaps directed by satellite—were caught off-guard, however, when tubes and pipes in town began developing holes, flooding homes now with *water*.

A new research group, formed by the national government hurried to Canneto di Caronia and just as quickly excluded a natural cause. Strangest of all: when the investigators surveyed the region by helicopter, something hit several of the rotors, causing clear dints in the blades . . . as if thrown upward . . . from the village.

They also reported what were perceived as strange objects in the sky—ones that would disappear, in the words of the team coordinator, "with great speed."

Drones?

Not likely.

Finally, after sporadic eruptions for several years, the fires halted as inexplicably as they had begun—for a period.

Extraterrestrials?

A leaked government report concluded that "aliens testing secret weapons" were responsible.

That's how baffling it was: many began pointing fingers upward!

That new report—which cost the Civil Protection Department two million dollars—also cited a possible UFO landing close to Caronia where "imprints which have not been explained were found in a field."

What about a simple arsonist?

Possibly. One young man, aching to capitalize on the fanfare, set a number of them (to keep the fanfare going).

Experts knew that while some of the fires rekindled in 2014 were set, a single person or even *team* of arsonists could not have caused all the effects that were witnessed in *2003*—fires coming as fast as anyone could put them out, in various parts of town, eighteen in forty-eight hours. This led a city council member to declare that it was the work of an "entity" that transferred "from one house to another."

Whatever it, he, or she was, it was relentless: one television set caught fire five times.

An unplugged hairdryer caught fire.

Balls of light had been reported during broad daylight . . .

The mayor of Santo Stefano, who witnessed many of the fires, could be excused for saying he was "filled with doubts" . . . over the arson explanation.

45

Stranger Than Harry Potter

The crisis, for an executive from Birmingham, England, began while he and his family were in the U.S. on a holiday in quaint, cozy New England, watching a Harry Potter movie. In a hotel, erasing cares, he was all too soon distracted by an intense, persistent itching. *Where did this come from?* It felt, reported a newspaper, like there were "fleas all over." Bedbugs? That wasn't it.

It was something much worse . . .

As the itching continued, the Brit began to notice little pimples dotting his skin—pimples with strange tiny spikes . piercing out. Seems "Paul," as he was identified by the newspaper, had "Morgellons disease"—an anomalous condition whereby threads or fibers, often of various colors—especially blue and red—poke from lesions or papules and form what look and feel like tiny cotton balls or—in certain cases—a black, tarry exudation. More star- tling, it's estimated ten thousand people have been thusly infected and afflicted—some so beside themselves with the constant itching and inability of medical science to reckon with it that they've committed suicide. For years, doctors scoffed at the notion that fibers or hollow tubules—and colorful to boot!—could be produced from human skin, and armed with that surety, hesitated not at all in diagnosing those with it as "delusional." For *it* is odd.

Maddening.

Fungus? Or perhaps simply fibers of cotton—mistaken as insects, by neurotics? A spiritual infestation?

One notes that exorcists say some cases of possession include materialization of strange fibers.

Many compare them to minuscule worms—ones that, to make it creepier, seem alive . . . the threads wiggling back into the skin. A famous singer, Joni Mitchell, described her own Morgellons as "this weird incurable disease *that seems to come from outer space.*" And in fact theories on its etiology run the gamut from bacteria brought back to earth by space missions to something implanted by aliens—or perhaps, back down on earth, to newly invented nano-particles that have run amuck.

It just isn't normal, its name bequeathed by Mary Leitao, a mom in Pennsylvania whose son had it. When Mary examined him (with his toy microscope, no less), what she had seen was nothing to play with: inexplicable red, black, blue, and white filaments around his mouth.

To her further shock, she watched them coming out of his skin . . .

Researching it in libraries and online, Leitao discovered that there'd been a similarly pestiferous condition back in the 1400s at Languendoc, France, the children itching so badly they convulsed!

There it was described as "coarse hairs." Here, call it simple mystery . . . for Morgellons fibers match not a single one of eight hundred known fibers or organic compounds in the data banks of forensic pathologists. It's neither animal, vegetable, nor mineral. "You feel the sensation of something trying to come out of your skin," said one doctor, Dr. Greg Smith, who had it himself—waxy scars all over his body—and found himself obsessively trying to pluck the "threads" out, as he fought off an intense burning sensation over his entire body.

To make matters more confusing, not only did it act like no biological organism, but one victim claimed to have watched a filament burrow its way into a pair of glasses . . .

Visio imaginitiva?

It went beyond hallucination.

Nanotechnology?

That didn't exist in the fifteenth century!

Yet while we may now know *where* it originated.

When I contacted the director of the Charles E. Holman Morgellons Disease Foundation, she explained that the latest in DNA analysis had proven it to be an infection by *Borrelia* spirochetes—a spiraling, tick-borne bacteria that activates the skin into producing the transmundane results. That bacterium traces back to Lyme disease, a widespread affliction so named because its first cluster was in Lyme, Connecticut, where it was first noted in association with deer insects . . .

They had gotten it by way of ticks!

If that seemed to finally solve it, it also made it more of a mystery, with clandestine subplots.

For the eponymous town in Connecticut is near the body of water known as Long Island Sound that separates Connecticut from the eastern suburbs of New York, and ten miles across that is an island where enigmas rise like cinematic fog.

Once a military installation, it's known as Plum Island and was used, beginning in 1954, for top-secret research on biological weapons—specifically, bacteria and viruses that *afflicted livestock.*

Was it dangerous?

No one worked inside without protective gear nor left without showering. And yet, ducks and cows began suspiciously wasting away on farms in the area.

The dark history began after World War Two, when an ex-Nazi named Erich Traub, whose expertise included warfare pathogens, was recruited by the United States in what was known as Operation Paperclip. Traub had once worked in a germ-warfare lab on an island in the Baltic Sea and helped establish Plum once the war was over. Among the disease carriers (or "vectors") Traub studied for use in disseminating bio-warfare agents were . . . *ticks.*

Did Lyme find its way out of the flasks? Might an animal or human infected with it have brought it away from the strict confines of Plum?

Might it have become airborne?

Or hitched a ride on deer that can easily swim to and from the island? Insects?

More than a million birds flap around, over, or overnight on the island as they migrate each year, many of them en route to estuaries in Connecticut . . . and specifically that quaint and once sleepy but now infamous town of Lyme.

Rumors swirl that West Nile virus—which has killed millions of crows on the East Coast, and threatened humans as well—was likewise on Plum (and at other military facilities). Intriguing it is that Morgellons shares characteristics with the effects of an organism that was isolated from veterans afflicted with Gulf War syndrome (and also bore similarities with juvenile rheumatoid arthritis and fibromyalgia). Suspicions gained currency when a government lab at Texas A & M was closed due to bacteria that had escaped. In Reston, Virginia, ebola once got out of a lab. We have discussed the "prions" suspected of causing "mad cow."

Back on Long Island, it got stranger.

On July 12, 2008, a woman named Jenna Hewitt and three companions stumbled upon a dead, waterlogged creature that had washed ashore at Ditch Plains Beach and resembled no known animal. They stood aghast at its appearance. Almost furless, with pronounced teeth and a purpled, leathery, bloated body, it looked like a skinless hound of the Baskervilles.

Biologists opined that it was a turtle without its shell (this later discounted), a decomposed pig (perhaps), or a partially decayed raccoon (missing its upper jaw). Take your pick.

Raccoons have prominent teeth and upper jaw, though shorter legs (in proportion to their bodies) than the "Montauk monster." Neither did it seem like a lamb: fierce-looking eyes, described as almond-shaped, and the sharp, pronounced front teeth made sure of that!

If it was a canine, it had been a dog one with a beak, for a large bone protruded from the middle of the face!

Other creature reports are also in the record of that area.

The simple process of decay? Or: mammals that, like bacteria and viruses, had been modified at Plum Island?

Perhaps it *was* a raccoon.

Perhaps not.

We may never know. For the "monster" was spirited away, with no one sure of its resting place.

46

Alien Sounds

And then there are the sounds. They are being heard—
unexplained—around the world. They seem to be coming
from somewhere very deep below. Or are they from above?

At five a.m. on November 9, 2013, Ernie Werezak of
Saskatoon in the Canadian province of Saskatchewan was
jarred out of sleep by the sudden onslaught of strange
omnipresent reverberations. It was the wail from an
unknown animal combined with a discordant trumpet and
instrumented by the grinding of heavy equipment or . . .
perhaps a braking locomotive. Unlike any Ernie, a technology expert, had heretofore experienced.

There was also a hum: bass vibrations. Varying sounds
intermingled in the auricular assault, as if vying with each
other.

His cat strutted into the bedroom, peered toward the
window, and looked unnerved.

Despite that trepidation, Werezak went to investigate in
the morning dark . . . and along with neighbors, could
deduce no explanation. "I grabbed my camera quick and
recorded it—not deafening but extremely loud," Ernie told
me. "I was raised on a farm with heavy equipment, and I
knew it wasn't anything like that. The vibrations went right
through me. I could feel it in my chest. I think it lasted a few
minutes, so loud that it was like a rock concert. When I real-

ized it was vibrating on my body and I couldn't pinpoint where it was—it scared me."

Such is also the case in countless other locales: long, hollow, echoing "trumpets" and grinding crashing sounds, a robotic groan, and "howls"—those wails—that seem to ascend from way below or descend from the clouds in nations as diverse as the United States, Britain, Germany, Denmark, Sweden, Costa Rica, Czechoslovakia, Hungary, Australia, Ukraine, Romania, and Byelorus.

In a Canadian forest far from any urbanity, residents wondered if what they heard was from aliens. More brontides. That was Conklin, Alberta.

Days later, a video with an uncannily similar sound surfaced six hundred miles away, in lake-laden Manitoba.

In 2017, such sounds—sometimes like a snow plow blade dropping and grinding against asphalt, but *louder*—were reported in at least sixty locations. A precursor to the end of an age—related to *Isaiah*, which said that the defilements of men caused the earth to groan and travail? "You shalt be visited by the Lord of hosts with thunder, and with earthquake, and great noise, with storm and tempest," says *Isaiah* (29:6).

A noise, says *Jeremiah* (25:31) "shall come even to the ends of the earth."

Difficult it was to explain when during November 2014, eerie sounds, including loud bangs that caused dogs to go into a tizzy, were generated not only in Western New York—Buffalo and Niagara Falls—but the breadth of the state, and in fact across three thousand miles of Atlantic to England and Scotland, all at the same time. Noted News Corp Australia: "Mystery booming sounds have left people baffled all over the planet. The terrifying noises have been recorded everywhere from the Middle East to the East Midlands this year and Australia—with the majority heard on America's eastern coast. The latest boom came to light this week scaring residents in the U.S. state of Alabama."

Sometimes, it's like the first chords of a "death-metal" song (as a hip witness phrased it), or the opening percussions of a horror movie. 911 is called. Police roar to the neighborhood. They listen. They scratch their heads. The more fearful of citizenry fear an apocalypse. *Where is it from?*

At Mount St. Helens, reports of strange rumblings could be simple seismic activity. This *is*, after all, a volcano! The same may be true—seismicity—in Moodus, Connecticut, where thunderous subterranean echoes are the norm (and the name for the very place, *Machimoodus*, derives from Indian for "the place of bad noises").

Mystery lingers. And the explanations of the rationalists satisfy few of those who have listened to recordings from dozens—hundreds—of locales, as if in nefarious orchestration. Was it, they wondered, secret government weapon testing; or more in the way of the mystical: a signal of the apocalypse (sounding, as it can, like the ancient shofar Israelis used to warn of invasion); or—as the conspiratorial prefer—some sort of hidden subterranean construction project; perhaps even extraterrestrial? Was the U.S. or Russia experimenting with low-frequency waves that somehow caused this? "In a moment, in the twinkling of an eye, at the last trumpet: for the trumpet shall sound, and the dead shall be raised incorruptible, and we shall be changed (1 *Corinthians* 15:52). "I saw the seven angels which stood before God, and to them were given seven trumpets. And the seven angels which had the seven trumpets prepared themselves to SOUND."

That's in the Book of Revelation (8).

The more mundane said it was a reverberation from the grinding of gigantic tectonic plates. For there are also resounding *booms*. These, it has been feared, could foretell of future massive earthquakes (perhaps in areas not currently known for faults). In recent years, odd deep quakes have been registered miles and miles below—as far as four miles below the seafloor. *Is the core shifting?* There are some who speculate that there are dramatic "compositional changes" occurring at its mantle boundary. *Is the axis moving just a bit?* In England, a droning was reported in dozens of towns . . .

"Folks in the back mountain heard a loud rumble, some even saying it shook their home,'" said a report on local television station WNEP in Scranton. "It takes a lot to wake up 12-year-old Kendra Steltz of Lake Township. 'I was sleeping and all I heard was a big bang,' she said. A big bang heard by more than just her.'" Even pigs and cows took cover.

Loud as an explosion . . . for miles.

Could it be spiritual?

History taunts us. Take Moodus. Witches were said to inhabit the region. One preacher described that spot as "where the Indians drove a prodigious trade at worshipping the devil." That was in 1729. In the 1840s, a comet was witnessed with blazing crosslike luminosities and strange, accompanying sounds.

A hundred miles away, in Littletown, Connecticut, a humming was heard in 1980 but with no explanation. That town is known for shamans and a pond which harbored "Ap'cinic"—a tentacled, horn-headed water monster. Millerites had settled in and around Littleton, preaching the end of the world.

Strange and stranger: none more so than what happened on October 26, 1958, when Alvin Cohen and Phillip Small were taking a ride along the Loch Raven Reservoir near Towson, Maryland, when they spotted what a newspaper described as "a great, iridescent, egg-shaped object" over a bridge. "The young men inched closer and the car stopped— no headlights, no engine, no ignition, as if the entire electrical system had given out," said the Baltimore *Sun*. Had they been able, said Cohen, they would have fled, for as he told an Air Force investigator, in a report that has been declassified, and still stamps the case as unsolved, "we were terrified at what we saw"—the object hovering and then a flash of light and noise—a loud boom—and heat that they claimed caused red marks some compared to radiation burns.

In recent times? For seven days in 1980, a humming was heard from the ground—most audible near a church. In the historic annals of Littleton it is recorded that folks went into trance and rocks were flung by invisible hands down chimneys . . . There was what historian Daniel Boudillian describes as "an extraordinary, explosive, all-pervading boom" on January 23, 1990, causing homes to sway. In 2012, booms that have gone unexplained were reported simultaneously in five Georgia counties.

In some cases, the sounds are suspiciously near oil fracking operations. "A spate of mysterious booms that has been shaking central Oklahoma returned for a second day Friday, again rattling houses and frightening livestock," reported the Associated Press in January 2015. "It sounded like thunder, you could feel the ground shake, but it was nothing like an earthquake," offered one more witness. Numerous others had been reported in the same area at about the same time.

Many seem unrelated to seismicity—to be coming, in fact, from the sky.

Some resemble the musical lights of that craft in *Close Encounters*.

Others are taken as hints of prophecy.

During Hurricane Sandy, an eerie keening was heard from the Freedom Tower—thought to have been wind through steel girders during construction but then heard, too, after *completion* of the New York skyscraper.

Coming, as they often do, in winter, they may in some cases be frostquakes ("cryoseism"—a sudden cracking of frozen soil). In Upstate New York, residents reported loud booms to officials who could trace no seismic cause, nor anything related to other potential sources, such as sewers or gas pipelines or jets overhead—actually, louder than a sonic boom, said a resident named Randy Smith, who heard it thrice and said that "as soon as it goes off, the dog starts growling . . ."

Quarry blasts? Secret military testing? The B-1 "Lancer"? These no doubt cause many of the booms—do recent tests. Propane guns used on farms to scare away . . . animals?

Or if you prefer: bubbles of methane reverberating as they burst from the ocean floor?

Perhaps vibrations from the aurora borealis, strumming chords in the magnetosphere?

Or is a "veil" thinning?

Said an article in a British tabloid, "It's the dead of night and you are driving through rural Scotland when suddenly this strange object appears out of nowhere making a noise like 'a thousand Hoovers.' Pretty scary, right? Well, John Macdonald says that is exactly what happened to him and he's convinced it is a UFO . . ."

The mystery endured from mountainous areas to the shores of oceans to the mists that enshroud woodlands to the deserts of Arizona (also for Indian burial mounds), echoing like a legend, but *not* a legend . . . rumbles from the rocks and buttes of mystical New Age Sedona.

Said Werezak back there in Manitoba: "I've seen the northern lights all my life and they don't make sounds like this, and the strangest thing is that my video of it, which I later put on YouTube, shot up to 80,000 hits . . . before it was taken down for no reason."

47

When Dreams Turn Into Nightmares

Clifford Maxwell of Brooklyn is living proof, to hear the media tell it, that you should pay attention to the voices in your head. They could make you forty million dollars richer!

That's if it's the *right* kind of voice.

Is there such a thing?

Holy men receive what they believe are voices of heavenly figures, mainly angels, or Jesus, and in some cases, perhaps they do. So do those who are demented—schizophrenics. And spiritualists, who "communicate" in draped and darkened rooms. In one survey researchers at the University of Chicago found that nearly seventy percent of adults claim to have foreseen eventualities through a "sixth sense"—what those in tweed jackets call "precognition."

Maxwell was none of the above, just a retired father of five who happened to be riding a bus past a regular lottery outlet in 2004 when an "inner voice" nudged him—more like *pushed* him—into getting off and purchasing a ticket, even though he already had three squirreled away in his wallet.

Sure as fate, several days later, the sixty-one-year-old former transit worker watched in shock as his numbers, seven of them, scrawled across his television.

The impulse to hop off the bus ended up being worth $40 million to him. "I am truly blessed," he remarked, with admirable understatement, and perhaps no little self-satisfaction. For he did what most of us too often don't: followed a hunch, even if it was inconvenient and . . . illogical.

Logic is a funny thing; sometimes it helps; sometimes it blinds us to other forms of reality. He recalled how he had been half asleep when the lottery drawing started, but found his eyes flashing open when he heard the announcer, Yolanda Vega, call out the incredible winning numbers. It was almost too difficult to believe. When he was sure it was true, "the first thing I did," Maxwell told the New York *Post*, "was pray to God." The next was to wake up Arlene, his wife. One can only imagine the look on her face when Clifford dashed into the bedroom. But he soon calmed down. A patient man, he decided to wait until Christmas breakfast with his children to break the unimaginable news. *Flabbergasted*? Their little retirement fund was about to get a heap bigger. After taxes, the lump sum was still over $20 million—enough to buy two hundred Mercedes SL roadsters, or 666 of his own buses, if he so desired anything of that particular number! (Instead, he planned to give a chunk of it to charities and his local church.)

Then there was the geological statistician from Toronto named Mohan Srivastava, who after winning a small sum via a tic-tac-toe scratch ticket ingeniously discovered, with mere use of his calculator, that the numbers on "scratchers" were not really random.

"I swear I'm not the kind of guy who hears voices," he said. "But that night, as I passed the station, I heard a little voice coming from the back of my head. I'll never forget what it said: *'If you do it that way, if you use that algorithm, there will be a flaw. The game will be flawed. You will be able to crack the ticket. You will be able to plunder the lottery.'*" The algorithm he had deciphered—the one in question—was used to formulate the lottery.

At first Mohan tried to brush it off. It *couldn't* be true. The Ontario lottery officials surely knew what they were doing! But looking at more tickets and stabbing at the calculator, Srivastava learned that visible numbers revealed crucial information about digits hidden under the latex coating!

Nothing needed to be scratched to win, discovered Srivastava—if you knew the secret code. One had only to survey face numbers at the gas station.

The next day, Srivastava stopped at the station, and sure enough saw that every ticket he purchased had the telltale pattern. He picked up other tickets from other outlets and was able to choose winning tickets an astounding ninety percent of the time. The problem: most winnings were a pittance; he'd have to spend all his time buying tickets to make a living . . .

Instead he informed officials of his discovery.

They altered the algorithm.

More profitable were the voices that reputedly made Arthur Stilwell from Indiana a very rich man. He was a lowly freight wagon driver and had been hearing voices—locutions—since he was a kid. When they told him to move to Kansas City—and build a railroad—he listened!

Finding work as a clerk, Arthur gained enough trust over his first few years for bankers to finance the "idea" he had: a railroad linking the Gulf of Mexico to farms in Kansas. Little by little did he build upon the inspiration. And the result was the Kansas City Belt Line Railroad—a massive transportation network that led to establishment of forty towns and the City of Port Arthur, Texas (named for him).

Whenever Arthur was troubled or needed to make a major decision, he retired to a quiet place, usually his office, drew the shades and . . . listened. At one point the voices even had him divert his railroad away from Galveston, Texas—a good piece of advice, for Galveston was soon decimated by a hurricane. But all earthly luck comes to an end.

Store not treasures of this world! In 1928, age 69, Arthur died of apoplexy. Distraught, wife Genevieve stepped out onto the ledge of a skyscraper window two weeks later (they had moved to New York) and joined Arthur in eternity . . .

Sometimes, bad luck haunts the moneyed . . . particularly those lottery winners. Mammon, mammon.

Conmen ring the doorbell. Thieves watch the house. Relatives unknown—third, fourth cousins—come calling. Wives turn on husbands (and vice versa). There have even been murders . . . as in the case of Urooj Khan from Chicago, who never did cash a lottery check for $425,000; he was pronounced dead of cyanide poisoning the next day.

There was Andrew Whittaker of West Virginia. He won $315 million in 2002 during a Powerball drawing, this on top of the $17 million he was already worth as owner of a construction firm. Inner demons got the best of him, however, and plagued by personal as well as legal difficulties, Whittaker began overdrinking and frequenting sordid nightclubs—where robbers broke in his car and stole $545,000.

That was followed by another theft, and then plain bad family luck: His granddaughter's boyfriend was found dead from a drug overdose (in Whittaker's home) and three months after *that*, the granddaughter followed her boyfriend to the grave (likewise overdosing). Whittaker's daughter— mother of the ill-fated granddaughter—died five years later. "I wish I'd torn that ticket up," sobbed Whittaker, who, we might add, was sued by an Atlantic City casino for bouncing more than a million in checks . . . to cover gambling losses.

Everybody dreams of winning the lottery, unaware that some of those dreams can be nightmares and that money (mammon) is not the only thing, whilst gambling, that we risk.

48

Otherworldly 'Apes'

Is there an abominable snowman—in Florida?

It may come as a surprise that the state with the third most sightings is precisely the Sunshine State (after California and Washington). That's my home state, and of course there isn't snow there—instead, legends have it, skunk ape. I became interested in skunk ape (or more politely, "swamp ape") in 2012, while kayaking the lower Myakka River in the west-central part of the state with my youngest daughter, who was startled when she spotted what she insisted was a tall furry human-like creature that stood up on two legs before disappearing behind the sable palms, oaks, and palmettos. We certainly hadn't been talking of these things. We were out there looking for gators. These she wasn't frightened by; the creature along the shore was another issue! I told her it must have been a bear, but she never accepted that explanation, and when we saw how obsessed she was, we did a quick internet search that now left *me* startled: such a creature not only was known to Florida, but had been photographed—at Myakka!

A hoax? An orangutan on the loose? Or transmundane? And, if just a case of biological relics—cryptids—why are these "creatures" so often connected to burial grounds, "UFOs," and the occult?

There are primate laboratories in the state, including a secretive government one in the Everglades. Was it something that escaped from research labs? Or perhaps

202

descended from apes used in old television shows shot in Florida (including "Tarzan"—never mind movies such as *Creature from the Black Lagoon*)? I have seen mountain gorillas and other primates in the wilds of Africa, but skunk ape, so fleeting and ephemeral, seemed like no known primate—if an animal it is. The "skunk" in its appellation is due to a sulfurous redolence, and there have been more than two hundred sightings, from the sandy shores of the Atlantic intracoastal—where witnesses claimed to see it opening oyster shells in Flagler County—to Ocala National Forest and vicinity, where hunters claim even to have stumbled on abandoned nests.

If it really exists, and if it was of a mundane nature, how could forest rangers never have spotted anything like it (at least not the ones with whom I spoke) and where is the physical evidence: tufts of fur snagged by the thorny brush, or some form of bone fragment?

The paucity of proof doesn't stop reports, especially in the Everglades. At Joanie's Blue Crab Café, the clerk at the register told me she once heard ungodly nocturnal howls that caused enough fright to flee her home. A waitress recounted her own terror on a dirt road nearby when at dusk something minatory jumped on the tailgate of her parked pick-up . . . or was it lifting it up and down? A nearby resident spotted what he described to me as a large humanoid dashing across Tamiami Trail (the road in front of Joanie's). They are smaller than the classic bigfoot but large enough. Was one reason few saw them because they are often in trees? And is their widely reported, rancid smell because they reside in holes dug into creek beds by gators during winter months? (Alligators, to be polite, are odiferous.) Far to the north, a 67-year-old preacher named S. L. Whatley from Fort McCoy Baptist Church had claimed to have seen one in 1977 while vacationing in the Ocala woodlands. Scrubby bush and dense palmetto underbrush can hide anything under the canopy of stock-still, sun-reaching pines . . .

But when one thinks of bigfoot, what comes to mind are places like the Himalayas and Oregon, as well as California and the state of Washington, which is famous for its UFOs. Airport newsstands sell souvenir shot glasses and refrigerator magnets in Portland and Seattle with images of the imposing brute on them. Hotel gift shops hawk yeti T-shirts. The sightings are endless.

It was in Washington, on a southeastern shoulder of Mount St. Helens, near Spirit Lake, in 1924, after weeks of hearing strange noises at night, and spotting large tracks near a creek, that four gold prospectors trying their luck at a claim called Vander White are said not only to have spotted the maddeningly elusive yeti, but to have been attacked by them.

This stark terror went on for hours. Or so we are asked to believe by the last living witness, Fred Beck of Kelso. "Each of us settled down in his crude, but welcomed bed, and soon fell asleep," he wrote of an episode involving creatures standing seven or eight feet, with massive shoulders (though svelte waists) and covered with hair from their large heads to big feet, known in Indian lore as "mountain devils," if that is any sort of hint.

"About midnight, we were all awakened. [A fellow miner named] Hank, who was sleeping on the floor, was yelling and kicking.

"But the noise that had awakened us was a tremendous thud against the cabin wall. Some of the chinking had been knocked loose from between the logs and had fallen across Hank's chest. Then we heard a great commotion outside; it sounded like a number of feet trampling and rattling over a pile of our unused shakes.

"We grabbed our guns. Hank squinted through the space left by the chinking. By actual count, we saw only three of the creatures together at one time, but it sounded like there were many more. We had to brace the hewed-log door with a long pole taken from the bunk bed. The creatures were pushing against it and the whole door vibrated from the impact. We responded by firing rounds through the door. They pushed against the walls of the cabin as if trying to push the cabin over, but this was pretty much an impossibility—the cabin was sturdy. They are not entirely of the world. I know that the reaction we experienced as these beings attacked our cabin impressed many with the concept of great ape-like men dwelling in the mountains. And I can say that we genuinely fought and were quite fearful. But I was always conscious that we were dealing with supernatural beings, and I know the other members of the party felt the same. Hank and I did most of the shooting—the rest of the party crowded to the far end of the cabin, guns in their hands. One had a pistol, which still is in my family's possession, the others clutched their rifles. They seemed stunned and incredulous. We could have had clear shots at them through the opening left by the chinking had we chosen to shoot. We did shoot, however, when they climbed up on our roof. We shot round after round through the roof. A most profound and frightening experience occurred when one of the creatures, close to the cabin, reached an arm through the chinking space and seized one of our axes by the handle—a much written-about incident, and a true one. Before the thing could pull the axe out, I swiftly turned the head of the axe upright, so that it caught on the logs; and at the same time Hank shot, barely missing my hand. The creature let go, and I pulled the handle back in and put the axe in a safe place. The attack continued the remainder of the night, with only short intervals between."

I spoke to a ranger in New Mexico who told me he and his partner had large rocks thrown at them while investigating a bigfoot sighting—tossed from someone or something unseen that was about five hundred feet away. He kept the rocks. One weighed twenty-five pounds! He didn't believe these were terrestrial creatures, because when they followed tracks—up to a mile—they went through brush that was left undisturbed, which simply couldn't happen with a large mammal. They also investigated . . . UFOs in the area. Perhaps better described as a "boggart"—specters of fields, mountains, and other terrain.

Back in Florida was the much more obscure account of an executive at a multi-national Orlando company who liked to hike around the old Indian grounds of Ocala National Forest and recalled a terrifying encounter on the verdant edges in 2012 near Lake Mack, where all notions of a relaxing afternoon fled when his car got stuck on a sandy service road. As the Florida man dug with bare hands around his tires, he said a rock suddenly pelted him on his left hip. Quickly peering around, the businessman, who requested anonymity (he oversaw a thousand employees), noticed something causing movement in the scrub. That was followed by what sounded like a large person taking a single step on the desiccated fronds . . .

This was fifteen feet into the brush, and he felt surrounded: movement on both sides of the narrow path.

A bear, coyotes, feral pigs?

Hogs, bears, and coyotes didn't pitch rocks.

Fear mounted. He remembered pepper spray he'd bought in Tennessee, rummaging urgently through a backpack in his trunk. As he slammed it shut, a noise from some kind of unfamiliar creature came in response.

It was like a loud "hiss," he told investigators, along with what he described as sort of a *yowl* reminiscent of the Kelso account (interspersed with an odd gurgling).

Surging with alarm, the executive had thrown himself back into the car. As he slammed a door several times—a vain effort to scare whatever it was away—he spotted a bipedal creature fifteen feet into the woods, upright on two legs and facing east—perhaps eight-feet-tall and of remarkable girth, with black-gray hair that seemed slick and tamped down, as if it had taken a bath (a spring was nearby), and strands of long hair or fur hanging from its hands. It tossed clumps of viscous mud across the trunk and hood of the car until it crossed the road.

Locking the car doors in a fit of panic, the Orlando executive claimed it was close enough to discern a broad mouth, enormous, sunken, but human-like nostrils, and massive lips. Out of sight for a minute, the "animal," when it returned to view, reached into the brush and plucked out a juvenile that wrapped itself around the back and stomach of the larger creature as it crossed back over . . . and disappeared, this time for good, into the scrub.

Soon a pickup truck materialized, hunters who hopped out to help yank the car out of the sand—oblivious to what had transpired. Once he got back to asphalt, the businessman told investigators, he'd had no time for speed limits, putting his pedal to the metal and careening past quiet homes in neighborhoods across the road from the mystery forest . . .

49

Those Who Eat the Most (and the Least)

How much can a person eat?

And how fast?

What's the most a person has ingested at a single sitting?

Let's take gluttony to its extreme: A fellow named Takeru Kobayashi ate thirteen grilled cheese sandwiches . . . in one minute.

A Connecticut man, Name: Jamie McDonald (no relation to Ronald): sixty Krispy Creme doughnuts—five *dozen*—in a bit over nine minutes. Speaking of McDonalds: the record for Chicken McNuggets is forty—in seventeen seconds. Hopefully, that's without the Spicy Buffalo sauce.

Imagine eating an entire pizza pie in thirty seconds (it's been done).

How about crunching through thirty-nine potato chips . . . in one bite? Or one hundred and thirteen pancakes, clocked at eight minutes?

There's a fellow who downed a hundred and twenty-one Twinkies in thirteen minutes.

It doesn't say how many Rolaids he had for dessert.

The largest meal in modern history was eaten by a twenty-three-year-old *woman* and consisted of (roll the credits): a pound of liver; two pounds of kidneys; an eight-ounce steak; a couple eggs; a pound of cheese; *two* pounds of carrots; two glasses of milk; a pound of mushrooms; two large slices of bread; a whole cauliflower; ten peaches; four bananas; two pounds worth of plums (helps with digestion);

four pears; and: two pounds of grapes. Grand total was sixteen pounds.

The problem: she couldn't digest it all and later died "following attempts to have the undigested food surgically removed," according to *The Lancet*, a medical journal.

When it comes to extremes—and dangerous eating—I remember visiting a shop that specialized in hot sauce in Charleston, South Carolina, and noting that the hottest offering was called "Flashbang" and came with a warning (posted above the cash register) that it could cause death.

Recommended amount: no more than a single drop per two to four gallons of chili. (Their latest such product is called The End.)

We'll leave such things to Ripley. I'm interested in strange. And more odd than how much a person can eat are those who . . . don't eat at all.

Or so it is stated.

In this regard was a woman named Alexandrina da Costa in Balasar, Portugal, bedridden for thirty years with spinal paralysis. From March 27, 1942, until her death in 1955, Alexandrina ate not a single meal, at least not that anyone saw—and at one point, hospitalized, Alexandrina was constantly monitored by skeptical medical personnel. "The strict surveillance by relays of doctors and nurses continued," she later recalled. "Never for one moment was I left alone. The door of my room opened only to admit doctors and nurses. The improvement in my condition failed to convince any of them. They said it was impossible to live without nourishment and they tried to intimidate me, using soothing, persuasive tones to induce me to take food. But all their efforts were in vain. On one occasion I heard them affirm that my case could be one of hysteria . . . or a phenomenon still unknown to medical science."

The doctors themselves, Dr. C. A. di Lima, professor of the Faculty of Medicine of Oporto, and Dr. E. A. D. de

Azevedo, a graduate of that same faculty, testified that, "having examined Alexandrina Maria da Costa, aged 39, born and resident at Balasar, of the district of Povoa de Varzim . . . have confirmed her paralysis . . . And we also testify that the bedridden woman, from 10 June to 20 July 1943, remained in the sector for infantile paralysis at the Hospital of Foce del Duro, under the direction of Dr. Araujo and under the day and night surveillance by impartial persons desirous of discovering the truth of her fast. Her abstinence from solids and liquids was absolute during all that time. We testify also that she retained her weight, and her temperature, breathing, blood pressure, pulse, and blood were normal, while her mental faculties were constant and lucid and she had not, during these forty days, any natural necessities."

Except for a host, Alexandrina (who was quite devout) did not eat a single thing . . .

A second certification was presented by a medical professor named Ruj. Joao Marques and a researcher, Professor Recife, president of the Society of Gastroenterology and Nutrition, both in Pernambuco. What they were sure she had done—or more accurately, not done—was, they wrote, "incompatible with life" and could not be explained . . . "by purely natural means."

We know Christ fasted for forty days and forty nights, in preparation for public ministry.

I knew a charismatic who did the same and felt great spiritual power (though, of course, not to be compared to Jesus!).

In 1981, in Ireland, eight men, Brendan Hughes, Tommy McKearney, Raymond McCartney, Tom McFeeley, Sean McKenna, Leo Green, John Nixon and Laurence McKeown, abstained from food for fifty-three days and lived to tell it. That was a prison hunger strike. Not advisable: several others died when they tried to exceed this, lapsing into comas.

Yet, some mystics, it has been claimed, have gone on for years. An 82-year-old man in Indian, Prahlad Jani, observed in a Gurjarat hospital, under strict protocols, claimed to have abstained from food and drink for seventy years (since 1940). Doctors from the Indian military allegedly studied him to learn his secret. He said he drew nourishment from air and meditation.

Prana, prana.

Most such claims can not be verified.

But the document on Alexandrina continued:

"An examination of the blood, made three weeks after her arrival in the hospital, is attached to this certificate and from it one sees how, considering the aforesaid abstinence from solids and liquids, science naturally has no explanation. The laws of physiology and biochemistry cannot account for the survival of this sick woman for forty days of absolute fast in the hospital, more so in that she replied daily to many interrogations and sustained very many conversations, showing an excellent disposition and a perfect lucidity of spirit. As for the phenomena observed every Friday at about three p.m. (i.e. ecstasies), we believe they belong to the mystical order . . . For the sake of the truth, we have prepared this certificate which we sign . . . *(Oporto , 26 July 1943)*."

50

America's Stonehenge

W ho built the "Georgia Guidestones"?

In June 1979, a courtly well-dressed man who called himself "Robert C. Christian" entered the far-flung town of Elberton—ninety miles east of Atlanta—with an eccentric request. Plopping down a cool $10,000 as down payment, he wanted a set of granite monuments erected just outside town in a paddle-wheel formation, like Stonehenge.

His real name was not Christian, and he refused to identify the small group he said he represented, flying in each time from a different airport and never mailing correspondence from the same place. The group's project entailed four "pyramid-blue" granite megaliths that at nineteen feet were actually taller than those at Stonehenge, surmounted by a roof-like capstone and in the aggregate weighing 237,746 pounds, according to the granite company. The stones were set in an exquisite astronomical design with round openings and a slot such that the sun pours through them at the equinox or solstice while the North Star is always visible through one alignment and at noon each day the sun beams through an aperture that illuminates the day of the year on the central column.

It's one matter that these strange stone structures (the largest and most exquisite project in the history of Elberton, which is the world's "granite capital") would be so precisely aligned with astronomical bodies—and solid enough, at Christian's direction, to survive any disaster—but what captivated everyone, from globalist Yoko Ono to alarmed Christian fundamentalists, were the messages. For etched in the capstone on all four sides were the words *"Let These Be Guidestones to Reason."* They are spelled out in hieroglyphics, classical Greek, Babylonian cuneiform, and Sanskrit.

On the megaliths that hold up the capstone—in *eight* languages (English, Spanish, Arabic, Chinese, Hebrew, Russian, Hindi, and Swahili)—are what some call New Age commandments for those who survive a future apocalypse:

MAINTAIN HUMANITY UNDER 500,000,000
IN PERPETUAL BALANCE WITH NATURE
GUIDE REPRODUCTION WISELY –
IMPROVING FITNESS AND DIVERSITY
UNITE HUMANITY WITH A LIVING
NEW LANGUAGE
RULE PASSION – FAITH – TRADITION
AND ALL THINGS
WITH TEMPERED REASON
PROTECT PEOPLE AND NATIONS
WITH FAIR LAWS AND JUST COURTS.
LET ALL NATIONS RULE INTERNALLY
RESOLVING EXTERNAL DISPUTES
IN A WORLD COURT
AVOID PETTY LAWS AND USELESS
OFFICIALS
BALANCE PERSONAL RIGHTS WITH
SOCIAL DUTIES
PRIZE TRUTH – BEAUTY – LOVE –
SEEKING HARMONY WITH THE
INFINITE
BE NOT A CANCER ON THE EARTH –
LEAVE ROOM FOR NATURE –
LEAVE ROOM FOR NATURE

Christian, who is now believed to be deceased, said he was a spokesman "for a small group of perhaps half-a-dozen people who believe in God and country seeking to erect a monument to help in some way to improve this world and this world's people," according to a booklet later released by the Elberton Granite Finishing Company, and chose Elberton for its high-quality rock and mild climate. Others point out that Elberton had been considered to be the center of the world by some Indians and conforms with occult "ley" lines (geographical tracks that link prehistoric monuments and some believe carry spiritual power). "It is very probable that humankind now possesses the knowledge needed to establish an effective world government," the group is quoted as saying in the booklet. "In some way that knowledge must be widely seeded in the consciousness of all mankind. Very soon the hearts of our human family must be touched and warmed so we will welcome a global rule of reason. We are entering a critical era. Population pressures will soon create political and economic crisis throughout the world. These will make more difficult and at the same time more needed the building of a rational world society. The approaching crisis may make mankind willing to accept a system of world law that will stress the responsibility of individual nations in managing internal affairs, and which will assist them in the peaceful management of external frictions.

"We, the sponsors of the Georgia Guidestones, are a small group of Americans who wish to focus attention on problems central to the present quandary of humanity. We have chosen to remain anonymous in order to avoid debate and contention which might confuse our meaning, and which might delay a considered review of our thoughts.

"The celestial alignments of the stones symbolize the need for humanity to be square with external principles which are manifest in our own nature, and the universe around us. We must live in harmony with the infinite.

"We profess no divine inspiration beyond that which can be found in all human minds."

Some have speculated that R. C. Christian plays on "Roman Catholic," but more convincing are those who argue that there is a link between the name and a man with the same initials as "Rose Cross," short for "Rosicrucianism"— the ancient school of thought which some date back to the first century (others somewhat later, to the ancient Druids, who are also linked to Stonehenge). Rosicrucianism laid the foundation for Freemasonry.

What disaster is foreseen?

Could a secret cabal really know anything about it?

A strange aura encompasses the area. When I visited, a very low, dark cloud suddenly scutted over the monument on an otherwise completely cloudless day. I learned that various occultists have conducted rituals here. Unusual people are drawn here. Across the road I found a local man, Jeffrey Allen and his mother, who told me they have seen unexplained lights at night at or above the monument (decidedly not flashlights, which Allen proved when he drove there to investigate), and that during hot summer days neighbors claim to witness hay swirling above in a little vortex on windless days.

Just west of the stones is a large plaque set in the ground above a time capsule.

Perhaps most hauntingly, there is a plaque to the west engraved with the words, *"Time capsule placed six feet below this spot on _____"* (there is a blank space) and *"To be opened on _____ (another blank space).*

Who will fill in those blanks?

51

Was It a Comet?

The mystery endures to this day.

What caused the greatest wildfire in American history?

Was it a presage of the Apocalypse?

This was the Peshtigo conflagration in Wisconsin in 1871. The damage: 1.2 million acres up in fire—flames that created fiery whirlwinds at a hundred miles an hour across the terrain, with the temperatures of a crematorium.

To grasp the extent of it, the great Camp Fire during 2018 in California consumed 100,000 acres—less than a tenth Peshtigo.

Back in 1871, with far less in the way of firefighting and rescue capability, anyone in its path—nor any *thing*—survived. Even the roots of trees burned, as did farm families who had sought refuge in wet blankets on pastures away from the combustion. By the time it was over, a region of America was a sea of ash. There were strange effects. Fire seemed to fall from *above* in some cases. Coins were found fused together in the pockets of victims who were not themselves incinerated, as if by an inexplicable electrical mechanism. A literal ceiling of fire hung over a major river where hundreds sought protection—killing virtually all of them, according to the chronicles of a priest who miraculously survived.

Was it loggers or hunters with their haphazard campfires? Rail workers?

No question, the forests had become a tinderbox. Conditions were abnormally windy and dry. And who could doubt that around those campfires, drinking and other careless carousing had taken place. But odd too: a dozen years before, a devout local woman predicted a cataclysm.

Fourteen thousand were killed. Had it occurred in our current day, the casualties would have been phenomenal. Once more: *how did it start?* How did it keep up such a path of utter incineration? Why did it seem like there was not just a horizontal sweep of inferno, but from above the blackened trees? Strange black clouds, floating like balloons, were recorded. So were flaming, wafting orbs. And those hellish tornadoes!

Now let's take the mystery yet deeper: *On the exact same day* that Peshtigo started—some say the same hour—so did the Great Chicago Fire, the worst *urban* blaze in American history: lasting—as did Peshtigo—from October 8 to 10. Quite a coincidence! Here, too, were peculiarities. The fire moved up and down streets that seemed like blowtorches. Virtually identical accounts described "freakish wind" that "whipped flames in great walls of fire more than a hundred feet high," a meteorological phenomenon known as "convection swirls"—masses of overheated air rushing upward and spinning violently upon contact with cooler influxes. "The wind, blowing like a hurricane, howling like a myriad of evil spirits, drove the flames before it with a force and fierceness which could never be described or imagined," wrote one eyewitness.

It sounded, said one firefighter, like a "million valkyries."

It even melted windows at the weather station.

North and east did it move, destroying 17,000 structures. Legend had it a cow kicked over a lantern in a barn owned by a family named the O'Learys, igniting the horror, but that's now dismissed as ludicrous. Other theories hold that humans caused it. To this day, like Peshtigo more than two hundred miles to the north, no one really knows. But there *is* one tantalizing theory: that both fires, and also wild-fires that erupted in far western Michigan at the same time, though widely separated, were caused by a visitor from space in the way of a bolide, which is to say comet or asteroid. Perhaps better stated: the *gases* from a passing object.

There may even be a name for it—Biela. Discovered in the 1770s, that was a comet first that swept across the earth's path every seven or so years, meaning that earth passed where it had been a few weeks after it swept by. It was the only comet known to intersect the earth's orbit, which made it of particular interest during the 19th century. A few weeks sooner, in its arrival, of course, and the comet itself, on one of its sojourns, would have impacted earth. The possibility comes into sharper focus when we learn that in 1846, stargazers noted there was no longer one comet but now two—that Biela had split apart. There were now a swirling debris field and between the two bolides a soft glow from a gaseous cloud, or "prolongation," that hypothetically lingered between them. A year after the fires, a bright meteor display was witnessed in the same area as Biela. Could it be that earth, and specifically that region of the Midwest, touched the fiery gases on 1871—that the comet's orbit had shifted or left lagging debris and volatile gas, out of its normal chronicity?

Astronomers are wont to scoff at such a notion. But every now and then through history a series of unusual, even inexplicable, events have occurred, events that hint at asteroid or comet impacts. There have been mysterious mass migrations. There are times when abnormal temperatures suddenly have besieged parts of the planet. Populations in places such as Turkey (Anatolia) or the Middle East have shifted suddenly, with dozens of towns . . . vanishing. In

South America, Indians once fled from the coast, as if haunted by disease or tsunamis. Across Europe, astonishing evidence indicates periods of tremendous rainfall and flooding. If you look back to periods such as 2500 B.C. and then 1500 B.C., and 1000 B.C., you'll see the strange decline or even abrupt end of certain regional populations.

We're talking *major* swerves in climate, not just a bit of flux. In that rough time-frame of 1000 B.C., a very strange series of events seems to have occurred on the earth. "From many other sources of information it is obvious that these events were sudden and occurred worldwide," wrote two Swedish researchers, Lars Franzén and Thomas B. Larsson—who found deposits, indicating an unrecognized flooding catastrophe. In one period, a vast section of the Hungarian Plain went under water. "During these generations the changes that came about are little short of fantastic," wrote another scholar, V. R. Desborough. "The craftsmen and artists seem to have vanished almost without trace."

Again, why? How?

By the end of the twelfth century A.D., during another such period, the population in major parts around the Mediterranean appears to have dwindled to one-tenth of what it had been little over a century before.

"This is no normal decline," Desborough had noted. "And the circumstances and events obviously have a considerable bearing on the nature of the subsequent Dark Ages, and must be in part at least a cause of its existence."

But what was it?

During the 1,000 B.C. events, Franzén and Larsson found something that enthralled them. The periodicity seemed to be about 550 years, and during those episodes, said the two Swedish scientists, they found, in the strati-graphical record—soil analyses—"small glassy spherules with varying compositions," including iron, which is common in asteroids. These occurred in conjunction with dramatic climate swerves, including severe ground frost in Tunisia. Their conclusion was unnerving: that the spherules—melted rock—had been formed by "relatively large asteroids or comets that hit somewhere in the eastern Atlantic, possibly at the shelf of the Atlantic west coast of Africa and Europe around 1500 B.C. and 1000 B.C."—affecting the British Isles, southeastern and central Europe, northern Africa, and the Near and Middle East. Other researchers pointed to those times when the Aztecs suddenly fled in a mass movement from the Pacific Coast. "Why did they move from a coastal region to a highland?" asked one whose research team, conjecturing "that similar to what happened to the coastal region of Peru, the Pacific region of Mexico was [also] affected by a huge tsunami. The surviving people were immensely scared and took refuge up to the Mexican plateau marshes of Lake Texcoco . . . "

I once met with an astronomer at the Jet Propulsion Laboratory who was known for her discoveries of asteroids not just from the far reaches beyond Mars and Jupiter, but between earth and the sun. She had seen some objects that had scared her—and caused meetings on whether the public should be alerted. These are the objects most likely, she said, to "whomp us."

Have they already? Without prayer, when will they again?

52

Angry Ghosts

It was strange enough—was it not?—when that massive tsunami swept across southern Asia in 2004. There was the quake—"a megathrust." There was the water—uncannily drawing back and exposing stranded fish. There was the roar—sea displaced by the quake and returning with towering, furious vengeance.

The resultant surge in some instances reached a hundred feet. It frothed five miles inland, turning a coastline into a wasteland of more than 225,000 dead.

The idea of the sea retreating, laying bare the ocean floor, then rushing back, is uncanny. Eerier still is what was reported in its wake.

Across Indonesia, survivors insisted that the shore-line—hundreds of miles of it—was now haunted by the dead. Were they souls in need of prayer, or devils in masquerade?

The word is "ghosts," a term Jesus and His apostles used (*Matthew* 14:26); in the Old Testament, one was witnessed by Saul (1 *Samuel* 28). Whether or not one subscribes to this fare, after the wave, tales of spirit sightings grew to epidemic proportion.

In Phuket, a taxi driver was hailed by four western tourists who asked to go to the airport. The driver chatted as he drove, watching the busy traffic weave in and out in front of him, concentrating on that, but when he pulled up to the terminal, silence; his passengers were gone; no one was with him in the vehicle, not a soul, front or back. Yet, no door could have opened before the stop. That's according to *National Geographic.*

Indonesians believe that spirits unhappy due to a violent death or undignified burial cling to earth, resentful of (and as such, aggressive *toward*) the living. These suffering entities are known there as *gui*, meaning hungry and angry ghost. Hangry. Not a happy hereafter—and the tsunami was registered in fourteen countries!

So feared were lingering spirits it caused tourism to plummet and prompted a plea from the president of Indonesia. "There are no ghosts!" he stated, pleadingly . . .

The accounts—endless. Not just from taxi drivers!

"Other apparitions which have been reported include a foreign woman, whose screams echo through the night from the wreckage of a hotel that was particularly badly hit," reported BBC. "A security guard on the site has already left his job because he could not bear it anymore. In Khao Lak, a local family say their telephone constantly rings through the day and night. When answered, the voices of friends and relatives cry out to be rescued from the flames of the crematorium."

Late the night of January 6, 2005, seven passengers at Patong Sea Shore clambered into a *tuk tuk* minivan owned by a fellow named Lek, commanding him to "go to Kata Beach" (agreed fare: 200 baht).

Fair enough—but Lek started to feel strange; inexplicably, numb all over.

When he looked around, his passengers, as in Phuket, were gone.

Lek decided to look for another line of work . . .

Other drivers swore they picked up a foreigner and his Thai girlfriend heading to the airport, only to then look in the rear-view mirror at an . . . empty seat. One minute there, the next not.

Ghosts? Demons?

After the tsunami in northern Japan, in 2011, were similar reports—perhaps more pernicious ones. Hundreds claimed to have become *possessed*. Noted Richard Lloyd Parry, a writer for the *Times* of London, "They were mainly ghosts of people who had died in the tsunami. For a lot of people, it was simply strange and disturbing or sometimes comforting dreams about their lost loved ones. Other people who hadn't experienced loss saw spooky figures on the beach. There was one man who hated to go out because he saw eyes of people in puddles. But then [a Buddhist priest] Reverend Taio Kaneda also had a couple of even stranger cases of people who actually seemed to be possessed by spirits of people who died in the tsunami."

Parry reports that a man who out of curiosity went to the devastated area "came back that evening, sat down for dinner with his family, had his tea, a can of beer and then began rolling around on the ground making animal noises, running out into the field behind his house rolling in the mud, to the horror of his wife and his mother. He woke up the next day not knowing anything about this. And this continued for three days."

Laugh if you will, but while in Indonesia, take an early cab.

Guards at a beachfront plaza said one employee quit after hearing a foreign woman cry "Help me!" all night long. That was in Patong.

Another wraith was seen walking the shore calling for her child.

Post-traumatic stress disorder?

Try telling that to residents.

Buddhist "exorcists" were called on in Indonesia, too. There were even special offerings of pizza to sate the "hunger" of foreigners who died!

"As clouds of incense drifted down the white sand and over the calm blue waters, the troubled spirits of the dead and missing were urged to return home," BBC reported . . . "for the sake of the peace of mind of the living."

53

Seeing From Afar

Back when I was a cub newspaper reporter, I looked into the strange case of Philip Jordan, a teacher and minister in his mid-twenties from Spencer, New York, who'd been forced out when locals accused him of witchcraft. Come to learn he was a "psychic" and had been demonstrating his "ESP" in class. I don't know where it came from, but this fellow had *something* that was out of the ordinary. The first thing he did was tell me to hide anything I wanted anywhere in his apartment as he waited a block away with a colleague of mine who was on guard against cheating. This was in 1975—long before tiny digital cameras. I hid my college ring in a kitchen cabinet, completely out of view in a cup of tea bags. Then I went outside and waved them back up the street.

Jordan re-entered, closed his eyes for a moment, then went for the cabinet, finding the ring in less than a minute. Later, we set up a test in which the mayor of another town, Charles Leahy, in Whitney Point, was asked to hide his staple remover anywhere in that town and see if Phil could find it.

He did. On Sunday, June 15, 1975. In eight minutes. It was near a natural-gas tank behind a building. The only reason it took so long: he first went to another gas tank.

That made news because it was witnessed by politicians and reporters. I brought in a local hypnotist, to make sure this fellow wasn't using legerdemain or mesmerizing us.

Jordan, who was also a minister, called it "clairvoyance" and if that wasn't enough to ponder, he sat us around a heavy wooden card table and on multiple occasions (including with a magician present) caused it to rise up eerily on one leg as we lightly held our hands on top and strange rappings issued from the wood. When you tried to press down, the table would spring back up like a beach ball pressed into the surface of a lake.

Eventually I took Phil to Kent State University's Smith Hall of Physics, where a scientist who was interested in these things (because of his research with Uri Geller), Dr. Wilbur Franklin, set up tests and also filmed the psychic doing what Phil did best: cause a wooden card table to rise inexplicably, despite short-sleeved shirts and constant monitoring for subtle muscle pressure, magnets, hooks, or anything remotely indicating chicanery. One of the witnesses, a fellow reporter who initially had been skeptical, asked: "Is this a who or a what?" at the end of a session—a good question, especially in light of the fact that though a minister, Jordan practiced trance mediumship, which the Old Testament forbids, and a neighbor told me about hearing strange knocks and bangs in the psychic's home when he was away and the neighbor was checking on it.

I wrote about him for the Binghamton *Sun-Bulletin* on April 7, 1975, in an article that stood as the longest in that newspaper's 153-year history.

A Morse code in the supernatural? Or just . . . creepy? When he took deep breaths, the clicks sped up, soon turning into knocks. Parapsychologists swear there's also a phenomenon called "remote viewing," the *nom du jour* for clairvoyance, whereby a person can "see" at a distance, describing the surroundings of a person—what the remote person is seeing.

Can the mind actually travel any place it wants? And if so, is this not . . . occult?

There is no question that strange as it sounds, both the C.I.A. and K.G.B. have likewise experimented with it, in the hopes, obviously, of achieving another level of espionage. In fact, the Kent State lab had connections with one such ongoing project at Stanford Research Institute (funded largely by the Defense Department's Advanced Research Project Agency. No one questions that involvement, though at the time it was classified material).

So it was that Phil Jordan and others could find a hidden object. What about a *person*?

On my very last day in Binghamton, disaster struck. The five-year-old son of Don Kennedy, an associate professor who had assisted me in the research, threw a temper tantrum and got lost after wandering away from a campsite. It goes without saying that the parents panicked. It was near Empire Lake west of Binghamton, and a search party was immediately organized by a detective named Dave Retsicker from the Tioga County sheriff's office as sirens alerted the area to an emergency.

This was early afternoon on a Sunday. By nightfall, the weather had drawn down poorly. A thunderstorm erupted— to the further horror of the parents. All searches had to be called off.

At that point, cops decided to wait until morning.

Having a kid lost is one of the worst feelings on the planet. With night falling, and few other options, Don had the presence of mind to call Jordan to see if he could help, and Phil began "zooming" in on the child.

Right away, he later told television interviewer named Nancy Grace, Phil felt the boy was alive "because I could see him lying down with his head resting on his arm, as if he were sleeping under a tree." The assumption by now—the fear—was that the boy had drowned. He had been in his bathing suit after all, when the family set out on a picnic. If he wasn't already in the lake, exposure would get to him . . .

But Phil "saw" him alive and taking out a piece of paper, sketched what he saw when he closed his eyes. There were three overturned boats, he informed police, and across from that a building and also a pile of stones nearby, as if something were about to be constructed.

Jordan had never been to the lake.

But Detective Retsicker had—and was immediately astonished. The building was actually a wall tent, and the boats, placed upside-down, were next to it, exactly as Jordan had indicated on a map.

By this time at least two hundred searchers had spent more than twelve hours trying to locate the boy, before calling it off due to that storm. Jordan took less than an hour, leading them right to Tommy, who was dirty, wet, and cold, but very much alive. At the hospital the boy was found only to have some minor cuts and scrapes. It *seemed* like a good fruit, but . . .

"Man, what a story," remarked Grace, to her live national audience.

Like everyone, I was floored when I heard about it. Everyone knew by the hysteria and involvement of police there was no chance of fraud. Occult? A "gift"? A deception? A combination? I can't totally answer that. I do think, no matter how good it seems, one must leave psychics alone (*2 Corinthians* 11:14).

And so our research, which had started long before with Phil finding objects like my college ring in a tea container, and progressed onto remote viewing, ended, many months later, quite a while after we last had touch with Phil, in a mysterious little miracle . . . though not "little" to Don, wife Mary, and a boy named Tom.

54

Living Dinosaurs

Are there living dinosaurs?

The short answer is "maybe."

It's the longer answer, however, that's intriguing . . .

In the late 1980s I traveled to Africa for a book devoted to paleoanthropology and the search for the first modern *homo sapiens* and with help from the famous Leakey family connected with a guide for the grueling trip over raw savanna to a remote fossil site in western Tanzania. As we made our way past Ngorongoro Crater, I wondered at the range of wildlife, the wild lions, the gamboling giraffes, foraging monkeys, a troop of baboons, more flamingos than one could count, hippos, elephants—a rhino taking a dust bath.

Let's stop here on the elephants and hippos—largest animals in Africa, correct?

Not if you believe countless native accounts to the west, in the Republic of Congo, where veldt gives way to dense jungle—1,500 miles of it—and a creature they call *mokèlé mbèmbé* (the "animal that stops rivers").

Translation: dinosaur.

And no: not the size of those in the far past. Rather, relict ones about the girth, give or take a few hundred pounds, of forest elephants.

But, they say . . . far more ferocious—which is why you don't see hippos and elephants where *mokèlé mbèmbé* is reported.

Could a remnant of Jurassic Park really exist in our own time, or might it at least until recent decades? And why, if so, is it seen so rarely—frustrating virtually all Westerners who journey there in search of it?

Sort of a reptile. About fifteen feet in length—by some accounts up to seventy. A relatively small head—though still at least the size of a rhino's. A massive frilled tail. A Loch Ness-like neck.

Would it be that hard for an aquatic animal the size of a school bus to hide in dense, dangerous terrain, jungle that's eighty percent unexplored—an animal that ventures from Lake Tele or the stillwaters of Likouala Swamp only to nibble on liana leaves?

Natives are insistent. Shown a picture book of animals, they look in wonder at a bear and say, *No, we don't have* that *here*! or at a lion and say, *No—not here in the jungle; only on the savanna.* But when investigators turn the page to an illustration of a brontosaurus: bingo. (*Fishermen have seen that!* to paraphrase translations . . .).

Those who support the notion argue that if an "extinct" fish like the coelacanth—which co-existed with dinosaurs—still exists (as we now know they do), might the same not be true of a few sauropods? Is not God capable of a creature such as these? Or . . . do we take note that the region is steeped in dark magic? For the creature is widely considered as mystical—perhaps lending insight into how so many creatures of various types, especially lake monsters, have been and still are reported, yet not a shred of physical evidence is exhibited. In 1555, an archbishop from Sweden, Olaus Magnus, compiled a survey of zoology and described marine animals "of vast magnitude, namely two hundred feet long, and moreover twenty feet thick" that hid in shore-line caves and, when they came out, devoured all they saw—including, it seems, the occasional unfortunate proximate sailor. (Curiosity has its price!) In 1028 A.D. a Christian, Saint Olaf, is said to have killed a sea serpent in Valldal, Norway.

In the following centuries, captains and other observers spoke of aquatic reptiles with snake-like bodies such that rose in "humps" at the surface and slithered down like a roller coaster—or had long necks that poked into view like a plesiosaur from the Mesozoic.

And not all were ancient history: I spoke to a man, Robert Frew, who with wife and four friends caught sight of what they were sure was a plesiosaur on Memorial Day, 1982, along the eastern shore of Maryland. It was around seven in the evening that peering across the Chesapeake with binoculars, Frew spotted a thirty-foot creature—hardly the birds, frolicking swimmers, and sailboats he expected . . . at first discerned as a dark object in shallow water but, as he focused through binoculars, and then a camcorder, showed its size and shape: hoselike with the girth of an adult human thigh. He and others watched as the slithering, undulating black creature make its way near swimmers in five feet of water—littoral, diving and resurfacing, with most of the sunbathers oblivious.

Some called it "Chessie." Similar "creatures" were cited along the tip of northeastern Massachusetts and in Lake Champlain. During a visit there in 1993, I asked the first person I saw on the New York side if she had ever seen anything unusual in the water (here there is the legend of "Champie"), and with no hesitation she launched into the description of a sauric head that once poked out of the often smooth water near a bridge. There are at least three hundred lakes in North America alone with monster legends. But here it becomes peculiar: while bringing to mind an aquatic dinosaur or other beast, such "monsters" are often seen at spots of ritual, such as in North Dakota, at Devil's Lake—where Indians spoke of *mni wak'áŋ chante*, meaning "water spirit." One notes that back in Scotland at the River Ness, another Christian named Columba did battle with a serpent—prayer battle—causing the enormous "water beast" or leviathan to flee for *its* life (circa 565 A.D.).

Could such creatures really exist in the modern world—and in lakes that, while deep, should not allow, for a large animal to hide? Some hypothesize existence of undiscovered subterranean channels that connect lakes with each other and oceans.

In the Amazon, according to one explorer with whom I spoke, Milt Marcy, there are reports of a miniature *Tyrannosaurus rex*, leaving us with the choice of either labeling it fantasy generated by movies (like *Jurassic Park*) or something from the deep reaches of yesteryear.

Marcy put me in touch with a missionary named John Mortimer who told me of a forty-five-foot snake he personally witnessed after it was killed as well as an elusive reptilian that supposedly haunts Lake Vufao and surrounding bodies of water but is spotted only once or twice a year—one native so terrified with his close encounter that he vomited for three days (fearing the "creature" had cursed him; in Africa too are those who believe the relicts to be phantoms).

"The fellow was paddling across the lake," said Mortimer. "It was at dusk. All of a sudden this alligator-like thing raised its head, which was massive, above the water and did like this *roar*. The mouth was higher than the canoe, and this native felt he was being sucked toward it. It has a skull like an alligator but more prehistoric, with pointed ears and maybe forty-five or fifty feet in length."

The longest alligator ever reported in the U.S. was about half that.

In the remote highlands of New Guinea, where Marcy led a small expedition in 2015, and where missionaries have long claimed to spot the winged dinosaur called pterodactyls, he and a companion observed one (he told me) on their sixth day there (after a strenuous journey from America to Australia with several stops and helicopter rides in between). "We had set up an observatory at the top of a village," Milt said. "I was up in the observatory and decided to go down for lunch to our bunkhouse and heard all the locals, who were pointing to the sky, yelling, *'Bird, big bird, big bird!'* They were helping us to find this creature. I forgot I had a camera and told [my companion] Pete to get his but the sun was bright and he couldn't focus, didn't know how to properly use the viewer—it was a brand new camera. I was looking up at the sky and it was riding a thermal, flying in wide circles, hardly flapping its wings, circling and going up. I could see the bumps on its wings and just a slight indication of a head and the shape of the wings—sort of like a c-shape toward the chest and then swooping back, just like a pterosaur. We watched the thing for several minutes. We figured it was pretty big—fifteen or twenty feet, at least—because we could still see it as it flew into the clouds and when we got back and enlarged [the otherwise blurred shots], you could see the bumps, very different than a hawk or eagle."

Was it true they swooped over the ocean for fish before returning to lofty caves?

Milt claimed that in 1965, missionaries had managed to kill one and feed the whole village.

In at least one instance, the missionary nearly became dinner.

At least that seemed the case when Harriet Sconce, whose family had long spotted the reptiles winging high above, had a close encounter while navigating a harrowing mountain path. Suddenly, she said, one of the winged creatures was flying alongside, eyeing her as it circled closer.

Books on prehistory tell us what we need to know: a narrow head and beak full of teeth.

What of those who claim the "bird" has been seen elsewhere—including in Oregon (big-foot territory)—and at night is . . . bioluminescent?

Here we get back to that partition of strangeness that separates reality from fantasy, observation from hallucination, the physical from what may be (when there is the voodoo beat) a specter.

55

Ghosts Aloft

Air travel has its share of chilling stories. There was the young flight attendant whose family persuaded her to retire after the Lockerbie tragedy. It seems her mother had dreamed she would die in an airplane disaster.

The young woman became an accountant, and after years of climbing the ladder, was hired by a firm in New York. Her office was in the World Trade Center, and despite the precognition, she perished on 9/11.

There is the curious story of a Virgin Atlantic flight attendant who went to prepare crew beds. Many don't realize that pilots and attendants often sleep during transcontinental flights in tiny quarters accessed by a hidden little stairwell that lead to a compartment above first class.

As the flight attendant opened the stair house door and looked, she was startled to encounter an elderly man who was sitting on the stairs. When the crew member challenged this fellow about his presence in a restricted area, he said, "Oh sorry, I am traveling with my wife." He provided the seat number. "She will be worried about me. Can you tell her I am okay?"

The man then excused himself and went into the pilot's lavatory.

The attendant sought out the wife, who was in the seat the stranger said she'd be. But she was shocked at what the attendant was relating to her. And showed them a photo of her husband—who in fact was onboard, but could not possibly have been in the cabin. He was in a coffin in the hold, explained the almost speechless woman, on the way to burial; recently deceased.

True?

Some can be substantiated.

Years ago I met a flight attendant named Beverly Raposa who related the remarkable account of how she'd survived a famous plane crash in the Florida Everglades.

It had happened a few days after Christmas in 1972 as the airliner she was on, Eastern Airlines Flight 401, was approaching Miami International Airport. An error caused the passenger jet to quickly descend—so quickly that it crashed into the snake-ridden, gator-infested swamp. One of the other attendants, Mercy Ruiz, had a foreboding that something was going to happen, but not Beverly.

"Stop saying that," she had told Mercy when she kept repeating her fear.

It was all the more unnerving because weeks before, a devoutly religious woman Beverly knew predicted she'd be in a crash and advised her on protection . . .

Flight 401 flew south over coastal Virginia and then on to Wilmington, North Carolina, thereafter over water. A computer-stored flight plan would bring the great white Whisperliner inland over West Palm Beach, and onward south to "a long, dense galaxy of lights glittering on a north-south axis between two black voids, the Atlantic Ocean and the Everglades," as an account phrased it. Except for Mercy's anxiety, it had been an uneventful flight as the airliners drew within miles of its destination.

Welcome to sunny Miami . . . the temperature's in the low seventies, and it's a beautiful night out here . . .

As the plane approached, however, a maintenance manager in the seat behind the captain peered out a side window and observed that the plane was crossing the Palmetto Expressway—a major highway just west of the airport. It was then that he and others in the cockpit became aware of a problem: a light that indicates whether the nose landing gear is down was not illuminated. The pilot chose to take the plane back up and circle until they were sure they had the nose wheels.

The cause was a defective light, they speculated, and took turns trying to fix it. The plane was set to autopilot while the first officer tried to see if he could get the bulb to work. That failing, he sent the maintenance manager, Donald Repo, to the avionics bay under the cockpit where there was an optical device through which the landing gear could be observed directly. When Repo couldn't line it up, one of the pilots tried to help, and in all the commotion, the autopilot yoke was bumped—and accidentally shut off!

The plane lost altitude and was never able to regain it. Its left wingtip hit first, then the left engine and landing gear.

There were 176 on board. Of those, 101 ended up in the morgue.

It was an odd number, in that the jet was a Lockheed L-1011 TriStar. "Seventy-five of us made it," said Beverly. "I have the federal report, which said that crash was not survivable. None of us should have made it out. Seventy-five miracles that came out of the swamp that night." Beverly felt that a religious medal she had taken with her, on that prescient woman's advice, had saved her.

But the crash was only the beginning of strangeness.

The Lockheed was only a year old, and so its undamaged parts were sent around for use on other jets. The problem: soon, those aboard the other flights—most of whom had no idea their plane had parts from Flight 401—began to report uncanny happenings. On one flight a crew member noticed a spot that was peculiarly cold, and as she cleaned the galley spotted a reflection in one of the oven doors—someone standing behind her in flight regalia. When she peered over her shoulder, no one was there . . . but when her eyes slid back to the galley oven . . . there he was once more in the reflection.

Was it the pilot, Bob Loft, or Repo, the engineer, neither of whom had survived?

Others, too, claimed to have witnessed apparitions, and shown photographs, identified the two men.

Unsettled souls, some call them: attached to a traumatic place or event . . . or perhaps entrusted to prevent similar mishaps.

Guardians? Souls that are earthbound? Jesus Himself mentioned the term "ghost" (*Luke* 24:39, NIV).

Pilots, flight officers, even a vice president of Eastern saw and spoke to a captain they thought was piloting their flights—before realizing it was the deceased Loft.

When, just before a flight, the captain and two attendants encountered Loft—watching him vanish—so unnerved were they that the flight was canceled.

Most startling: a flight engineer who was part way through the routine pre-flight inspection when Repo materialized next to him. "You don't need to worry about the pre-flight," said the apparitional figure. "I've already done it"! Or so are the claims.

On yet another flight, a flight attendant named Faye Merryweather saw Repo's face in the oven of a Tri-Star 318 and dashed off to fetch two colleagues, one of whom had known Repo and instantly identified him. All three claimed the deceased engineer said, "Watch out for a fire on this airplane." And sure enough, the jet subsequently developed engine trouble and the last leg of its trip had to be canceled.

A group that monitors such claims notes that the sightings were all reported to the Flight Safety Foundation, which decided that "the reports were given by experienced and trustworthy pilots and crew. We consider them significant. The appearance of the dead flight engineer . . . was confirmed by the flight engineer."

Eastern refused to confirm the sightings—but quietly removed all Flight–401 parts from its other crafts.

56

The Doll That Texts

You may recall a classic episode of the Sixties television show *The Twilight Zone* in which a puppet eerily comes to life, a living, spooky entity that, in the end, kills its master.

No Howdy Doody.

Fortunately, just fiction . . . correct?

Not quite. Surprisingly, there are claims of the same in real life, the inanimate turning *animate*, particularly childhood dolls that take on lives of their own. It would be a laughing matter but for testimonies. These come from staid, sedate types, including museum curators I've spoken to—reports of dolls that move of their own volition.

You've perhaps seen them in movies. But real life is a different matter altogether. There was a famous Raggedy Ann doll called "Annabelle" thought to be inhabited by an evil spirit. The activity, we are told, began slowly. "The doll mysteriously seemed to move about the house, relatively small movements at first, such as a change in position, but as time passed the movement became more noticeable," the story reads. "Donna and Angie (her roommate) would come home to find the doll in a completely different room. Sometimes the doll would be found with legs crossed, arms folded, other times it would be found upright, standing on its feet. Donna sometimes left the doll on the couch before leaving for work, and would return to find the doll back in her room on the bed- with the door closed."

Soon, pieces of parchment began appearing in the home, with messages on them, such as: "Help Us!"

Haunted? Cursed? Proof of the power of suggestion?

Forty inches tall, stuffed with wood wool, and dressed like a sailor, a doll known as Robert is a rather plain-faced, bug-eyed specimen at Fort East Martello Museum in Florida. Manufactured by the same company that made the "Teddy bear" (in honor of Theodore Roosevelt), "Robert" once belonged to an artist named Eugene Otto. "Robert" and Gene were best buddies growing up. "Ostensibly a little boy in a sailor suit, his careworn face is only vaguely human," noted one scribe. "His nub of a nose looks like a pair of pinholes. He is covered in brown nicks, like scars. His eyes are beady and black. He wears a malevolent smirk. Clasped in his lap he's holding his own toy, a dog with garish, popping eyes and a too-big tongue lolling crazily out of its mouth."

That isn't what unnerves people. It's Robert's attitude. Staffers swear the doll doesn't like being moved—causing a stir anytime they rotate it through exhibits—and numerous visitors attest that the doll has turned its head to follow them as they were passing it.

Such strange behavior was noted by those who encountered Robert after Gene's death. Seems the doll was placed in an attic, after which tenants reported inexplicable footsteps up there. On one occasion a plumber fixing a pipe heard a giggle and turned to find that the doll had scooted across the room.

It was also known to walk past windows and dash from one room to another.

One can imagine seeing this from the outside! (Rumor was Gene practiced voodoo.)

When the doll was placed in a formal public exhibit, electronic devices failed in his presence. The curator, Dr. Cori Convertito, told me thousands come each year to see the doll but are warned not to take a photo of Robert without his "permission." Seems Robert is camera shy. Many send the museum letters attributing accidents, illness, divorce, deaths in the families, and even arrests to that unmannerliness. Yes, *Twilight Zone* material.

In a bridal storefront in Chihuahua, Mexico, is a mannequin called "La Pascualita" that (sober people insist) moves on a regular basis—changing poses and more inexplicably, expressions.

Uncannily lifelike, the mannequin resembles the original owner's young daughter—who died tragically before her own wedding.

Some insist that the mannequin resembles a human (down to the fingernails, veins, and thin hairs) because that's what it is—*the embalmed body of the owners' deceased daughter!*

Does one not expect Rod Serling to step from around the corner?

In 1968, a peculiar doll was found in a well-worn trunk in the attic of an old Victorian house in Upstate New York. The only other item—save for newspapers—was a yellowed piece of paper on which was printed the *Lord's Prayer.*

The doll was added to a doll collection they had and named "Charley." As in other cases, it seemed fine at first, then seemed to move from spot to spot. That was one thing; it was quite another to learn, as the family that "adopted" Charley did, the doll was speaking to their four-year-old daughter in the middle of the night. They put it down to a child's imagination. They never witnessed anything themselves. But their kids were terrified. Finally, the parents drew the line when the youngest child was found covered with scratches the kids said had come from Charley. Wisely, the doll was returned to the attic, though more wise it would have been to burn it.

At British Columbia's Quesnel and District Museum, another doll named "Mandy," if not quite as dangerous as

"Robert," is equally mischievous. After Mandy was given to the institution, employees reported strange footsteps and complained that pencils, pens, and other offices supplies disappeared in a paranormal pattern. When they glanced at Mandy, what they saw, they said—with no mirth—was a "sinister smile" that seemed to say, *I did it*. And once when photographs were taken, the next morning a laboratory that developed them was found in mysterious and total disarray.

Call it the poltergeist doll. Just don't call it on the phone! The current curator told me that just before starting work there, she had bought a new smartphone. Virtually no one knew the number. Yet somehow, as she rolled into town, a text appeared on the cell, greeting her. *From whom?* There was a jumble of hashtags and keystrokes (as if someone was randomly stabbing a keyboard). *What?* Indecipherable, were the letters and symbols, but for the signoff: "X Mandy."

57

When A Daughter . . . Wasn't

What if someone walked into your life claiming to be a grand duchess? Or more accurately, if a teenager, dragged half-conscious from a canal, claimed royal lineage from the famous Romanovs? You might react in the same way others did: disdain at such a wild assertion.

But that's what happened on February 17, 1920, when a young woman, the Grand Russian Duchess Anastasia, who'd fled during the Bolshevik revolution, was found in Berlin, Germany, in a bedraggled state.

A lot was at stake—and there had been no shortage of those who lay claim to the title—impostors all, cranks and con artists, lusting after a missing duchess's inheritance, for her claim was huge: estates in Germany and cash amounting to $4 billion.

While the czar himself was famously executed, the family had been spared and whisked to a secret location—so secret that there was no sign of anyone emerging from it, if alive anyone was. Now here was a girl who upon rescue was presented to a hospital, with papers proclaiming her appellation to be "Anna Tschaikovski." But that was subterfuge. As she regained strength, Anna insisted her actual name was Anastasia and proffered an incredibly detailed account of how she had managed to escape the revolutionaries. As she told her mesmerized rescuers, she had been taken with her family for execution in a cellar at Sverdlovsk but somehow, though wounded, and mistaken for dead, later regained consciousness in a peasant's cart, hidden there by two brothers and two women who had been Bolshevik guards but wanted no part of the carnage. As it was soon explained, they had whisked Anastasia off when they noticed that she was still breathing.

Out of Russia had Anastasia been spirited, eventually to marry one of the brothers—surname Tschaikovski—who, unfortunately, was soon after recognized in Romania and shot as a deserter, causing Anastasia such mental anguish that she had attempted to end her own life . . . in that canal.

Her knowledge of intricate family matters convinced many who listened that despite her mental state she indeed was entitled to the fortune. A cousin of the czar soon identified her, as did the czarina's sister, Princess Irene of Prussia. For Anna knew things no impostor could, and there was even physiological evidence: bunions on her feet matched those of the czar's daughter, as did a scar on her shoulder from a cauterized mole recorded in Russian medical records. It even got down to a minuscule scar on a finger she said was injured when a car door was slammed on it, and a former lady-in-waiting confirmed the occurrence.

Still, a court ruled against her—depriving her of the money and casting her as a mystery to this day.

Yet more mysterious was the disappearance of little Pauline Picard, a French girl who went missing in 1922 from her family's farm in Brittany.

She was but two years of age, was Pauline, when she vanished from her home in Goas Al Ludu. The suspicion was she'd been abducted by gypsies—ferried off with no trace. All seemed bleak. A parent's worst nightmare. A thorough police search had yielded nothing. Scores of locals joined in the hunt. The first forty-eight hours of such a disappearance is considered critical; by three weeks, hope is normally gone. But then . . . word came from Cherbourg, several hundred miles away, of a girl who matched her description, and when her mom saw a photo, immediately identified it as Pauline, with a sigh of relief heard around the world. A French paper, *Le Matin*, reported on May 8 that Mrs. Picard simply but definitively said, "That's my daughter!" Her siblings and neighbors agreed joyously.

But as one commentator noted, "The story got stranger and stranger as events unfolded and it was in fact her potential recovery that turned the entire investigation and search completely on its head." As they drove to retrieve her, the mystery remained of how she had found her way at such a distance, and the oddities piled up when they were reunited, for Pauline seemed strangely aloof from her parents. Shy. Fearful. She *looked* like Pauline, but certainly wasn't behaving like her!

Had she been brainwashed?

More mysterious still: the girl did not respond in her local dialect. She spoke with another accent.

Just trauma?

A celebrated case this was—making headlines as far away as New York. But within days, the Picards began to think the unthinkable: that a mistake had been made and that despite a fantastic resemblance, *this was not their daughter!*

The strange was about to morph into the bizarre. As they mulled over her identity, a local farmer came by, asked if they really thought it was Pauline, and then blurted, "God help me, I am guilty!" before running off—laughing hysterically. He was later committed to an asylum . . . from which he never emerged . . .

From bizarre it went to flat-out disturbing when another farmer happened across the body of a young, decapitated two-year-old—brutally disfigured. When police took the Picards to the scene, the body was not identifiable but the clothes, neatly folded beside the body—black-and-white checkered dress, navy blue jacket, black tights—matched precisely what Pauline had been wearing the day she had disappeared. The problem: gendarmes had searched this same location weeks before, finding nothing, and now causing them to wonder if the body had only recently been planted there. Strangest of all: the skull was too large to be that of such a toddler. In fact, it wasn't even a female skull—but that of a fully adult male. So now there was not only a kidnapped girl but also a murdered man!

Was the perpetrator that "insane" farmer who had run off, proclaiming guilt? Was it he who killed not only Pauline but the unidentified male? Where was her head—and where was *his* body? No missing man had been reported . . .

And how could the Picards have erred so badly in the mistaken identification of another child?

That child was placed in an orphanage, while the grieving Picards spent the rest of their days pondering the fate of their daughter . . .

The strange doppelgänger from Cherbourg?

Fate known. Lost to the pages of history . . .

58

The Miracle That Made a President

Of the hidden gems in U.S. history, one involving President Andrew Jackson may stand alone.

Did a miracle cause him to win the signature battle that won a war and propelled him to the White House?

Quick background: In 1727 a convent of Ursuline nuns from France was established in New Orleans, where they set about educating the children of European colonists as well as local slaves and Indians. They were the first nuns to arrive in what is now the United States, and they established the oldest school for girls in America.

In 1800, when Louisiana was ceded back to France, the good Ursulines were afraid the horrors of the French Revolution would spread to America. The territory had been bouncing between English, French, and American hands, and the nuns, knowing what had happened to their fellow sisters in Europe, certainly didn't want to see the French take permanent control. The Pope himself, Pius VII, would soon be under house arrest in Rome, a captive of Napoleon.

Most of the nuns fled to Cuba, but seven remained, and when Louisiana passed into control of the United States, they earnestly sought protection from the government. The response from President Thomas Jefferson is still kept at the convent. "I have received, holy sisters, the letter you have written me wherein you express anxiety for the property vested in your institutions by the former government of Louisiana," penned Jefferson. "The principles of the United

States Constitution and government of the United States are a sure guarantee to you that it will be preserved to you sacred and inviolate, and that your institution will be permitted to govern itself according to its own voluntary rules, without interference from civil authorities. Be assured it will meet all the protection which my office can give it . . ."

It was a largely unknown, historic statement, but it didn't quite end the Ursulines' worries. There were other problems. They were short-staffed. The work was overwhelming. And things grew desperate when a mainstay of the community, Mother Saint Xavier Farjon, died in 1810. That caused them to write another mother superior back in France and ask for her help.

The bishop predictably said no—she could not go to America. He told her only the Pope could grant such permission. The leader of the nuns knew that would take a miracle, but she prayed to Jesus before a statue of the Virgin Mary and quite quickly—startlingly so—permission was granted. A new title was created: "Our Lady of Prompt Succor." And a special statue under that name was carved and sent to America, where it took its place on Chartres Street at a convent in the French Quarter.

Nearly immediately, two momentous events occurred.

The first was in 1812, when a terrible fire erupted in New Orleans, devastating the French Quarter. Propelled by the wind, it was heading, at one point, directly for the convent.

That was when the nuns placed a small statue of the "Prompt Succor" on a window facing the fire and began to implore help.

It was said that the wind shifted instantly, driving the blaze away.

The Ursuline convent was one of the very few structures spared destruction.

Three years later . . . yet more trouble haunted New Orleans during the war between the Americans and British. By this time Louisiana was part of the United States, but England was looking to confiscate the former territory. The British arrived near the city on the plains of Chalmette to square off against Jackson, already famous as a general.

By all appearances, there was no way the Americans could win. The Brits had 15,000 troops and hundreds of battleships. The American force: 6,000. It looked like certain doom.

The night of January 7, 1815, the sisters prayed through the night, weeping before the statue and imploring help from Jesus. On the morning of January 8 the vicar general joined them. Prayers were said in special earnest, for all in the chapel could hear the thunder of cannons.

But during Mass, a courier suddenly rushed in. He had news—very, very unlikely news. He explained that the British had marched against Jackson with infantry and one rifle unit in two columns at five a.m., under cover of darkness and fog. Their strategy had been to first attack a twenty-gun battery, reducing American military power. Final orders had been given, and a canal had been dug to enable assistance from more than forty boats. The Americans were badly outmanned. But that's when bad luck for the British started. First, their canal collapsed, causing a delay for one of the units as soldiers dragged the boats through muck. The other unit proceeded with a frontal assault. But here too was a problem—a devastating one at that. As they neared the main enemy line, the fog had suddenly lifted, exposing them to withering fire.

The British had been defeated, confused by a mysterious fog that had caused them to wander onto a swamp in full view of waiting Americans, who fired on them from unseen positions.

About 1,550 British were killed or wounded, while the Americans, though outnumbered nearly three to one, suffered just a dozen or so fatalities and less than fifty missing or wounded.

"The result seemed miraculous," reported the New Orleans *Picayune.* "It was a remarkable victory, and it can never fail to hold an illustrious place in our national history."

Henceforth, citizens would not identify themselves by state but as Americans.

As one scholar notes: "Met by steady fire from the American lines, the British inexplicably fell into confusion. Then followed disorder, slaughter and rout of such a nature and magnitude that natural explanations alone cannot account for the disaster."

General Jackson, a Presbyterian, went in person to thank the sisters. Would he ever have become president without this signature defeat of the enemy? "By the Blessing of Heaven, directing the valor of the troops under my command, one of the most brilliant victories in the annals of war was obtained," he proclaimed to his troops, describing the victory, in a letter to the vicar, as a "signal interposition of Heaven." Alexis de Tocqueville later wrote that Jackson "was raised to the Presidency, and has been maintained there, solely by the recollection of a victory which he gained, twenty years ago, under the walls of New Orleans."

59

Dreams That Save Lives

Can nighttime visions be miraculous? Can they . . . save a life?

A dream to Joseph saved the Infant Jesus.

From personal experience, I likewise will testify that the answer is: yes.

In 1988, I had a particularly vivid dream in which I was standing at the desk in a room I used in my parents' home in Niagara Falls, having moved back there for a while after leaving Manhattan. In the dream, I was standing at that desk when suddenly there was smoke billowing into the adjacent bedroom—thick, swift, and about to blanket the second floor. It went from about hip level up, allowing for escape through a layer of clear air beneath it.

So lucid was this dream that the next day I called Marine Midland Bank to see about a night-deposit box for backup discs and critical documents . . .

A week later, a real fire burst forth on that floor of their house. I rushed upstairs when I heard the crackling, then dashed to my desk to call 911 and look for our dog. As I stood there on the phone in the bedroom, at the desk, I watched—this time in *real* time—as smoke filled that adjoining room just as in the dream. But because I had "seen" this before, there was no panic, knowing—from the dream—that if I crouched beneath the layer of hot, sooty smoke, I could easily get out (although the heat did singe my hair).

True, most dreams are from nowhere. Disjointed. Frequently they're regurgitations of the subconscious—especially fears. But exceptions? The "Battle Hymn of the Republic," one of the most famous patriotic songs in history, was written one night in autumn of 1861 when, rising in the dark, words simply arrived as a poem to Julia Ward Howe, who wrote as fast as her hands could move . . . before dozing back off. The next morning she was amazed at what was on the paper—a haunting, inspiring set of stanzas about the United States, which at the time was in the throes of the Civil War. Soon after, when the words were set to music, they caused no less than Abraham Lincoln to burst into tears. ("I wonder if I really wrote it," reflected Howe later. "I feel I did not . . . I was just an instrument . . . It really wrote itself!")

Likewise did Paul McCartney of the Beatles say the song "Yesterday" came to him in a dream (at first he called it "Scrambled Eggs"!). As we have seen, John Lennon felt he was more a spirit channeler than a songwriter—pretty good, though, at taking dictation. The iconic song "Stairway To Heaven" arrived with instant mystery to its composers.

"I Can't Get No Satisfaction" was another hit received at night.

(Where did *that* come from?)

Light and dark intermingle in dreams, leaving us to ferret it out.

And science?

The chemical composition for benzene was discovered when a chemist named August Kekulé had a dream of snakes swallowing each other—basically, what turned out to be the compound's structure. It was in a dream that Nobel laureate James Watson saw a spiral staircase that led him to decipher the structure of DNA.

In the literary world, Robert Louis Stevenson dreamt the plot to *Dr. Jekyll and Mr. Hyde*. Some things, it's obvious, come in nightmares.

(The same was true of *Frankenstein*.)

The sewing machine was seen by Elias Howe in night-time evanescence.

So it is that we ignore dreams at our own peril—as apparently was the case with the treacherous Roman emperor Caligula, who set aside a premonition of death and was slain the next day. New York attorney Isaac Frauenthal may have been saved by two dreams he had of a sinking ship, one of them before and the second occurring when he boarded that ship called *Titanic*. In the dream he had heard a collision, and so knew there was trouble—and what to do—when the real thing happened.

There was the woman who recalled words uttered in a subconscious mutter by her grandmother, who at the time was recovering from surgery in a Baltimore hospital, drifting into and out of consciousness.

It happened back in 1944 in Maryland to the grandmother while her two sons, Harry and James, were abroad fighting in the war, one in England, one in New Guinea. "She prayed for their safe return morning, noon and night, even while she was fighting her own battles," recalled her granddaughter. "Grandpop was flipping through the newspaper that day, skimming the war headlines, when Grandmom suddenly sat up in bed, her eyes wild. 'Sweetheart, what's wrong?' asked Grandpop, taking her hand.

"Duck, James!" bellowed the woman, and with those words, and no more, she fell back on her pillow, fast asleep on the hospital bed.

When the older woman awoke . . . she recalled nothing about it.

But weeks later, there came a letter postmarked from the U.S. Army with her grandson's meticulous script on the envelope. Her daughter tore it open.

"Dearest Mom and Pop, the strangest thing has happened," the letter began—going on to explain that his unit had been on high alert after reports of enemy troops nearby and he had been preparing his equipment for the nighttime attack when out of nowhere and everywhere he heard a woman's voice piercing the silence of the jungle, clear as a bell. Urgently he had bent his neck.

"Duck James!"

Just then a bullet had whizzed past his head, skimming the top of his helmet. It would have been different had he not crooked his head.

A life was saved—all thanks to words that came out of nowhere and everywhere.

60

A 'Bermuda Triangle'— in New England

When it comes to strange places, many are the sites that seem to sit on extra-dimensional "vortices" through which other times and spaces, other realities, decussate and interact. When they overlap, there are bizarre sightings. Might they be purgatorial or damned souls, taking visible form? Beyond count are the Bermuda Triangles and Devil's Seas and Sedonas. One might wonder why it is that besides "Nessie," Loch Ness is known for phantom cats and a human-like "insect"—or that Australia has a creature with long back legs, leathery skin, and the face of an anteater.

Near Roswell, New Mexico—so famous for "aliens"—is also . . . bigfoot.

Not far away, at the nation's largest Indian reservation—which sprawls across more than seventeen million acres in northern New Mexico, Arizona, and southern Utah—a Navajo Ranger assigned a special unit to investigate such incidents told me of a hotspot called "Satan's Butte" (about 120 miles northeast of Flagstaff, where "orbs" fly from and into the peak of a mountain). The name tells us what we need to know . . .

The same is true of the so-called Bridgewater Triangle in southeastern Massachusetts between Abington, Freeport, and Rehoboth, at points just thirty miles south of Boston.

Here one encounters the whole panoply: orbs, poltergeists, Indian curses, bigfoot, animal mutilations, UFO sightings, missing time, strange disappearances, and even pterodactyls—to grant us a hint of how it all dovetails into . . . unreality. A boulder called the Dighton rock is there, at a bay, with markings some say may date to the ancient Phoenicians. Others say it is just scrawl left by Native Americans, who called a swamp there the "Place Where the Spirits Dwell."

"Devil's Swamp," is what British settlers of the Colonial era more crustily named it.

In 1934, it's said, a boy named Aldie who disappeared there turned up a day later, with no memory of what had transpired. Others have never returned.

Did thick peat overlay a gravitational vortex?

Or is it just ground zero for more hokum—a forest for no more than . . . fraught imaginations?

The same question can be posed for "crop circles"—those inexplicable formations of stomped-down wheat, corn, or other vegetation that occur in patterns—often intricate ones—in arcane settings.

In England such formations, usually constituted by large geometric shapes, have characteristics that, when not obvious fraud, often are attributed to wind, dew, fungi, gravity—any known force of nature. Even shifts in the earth's magnetism. In some cases crops brittle to the touch have been pressed to the ground, however, with no breakage, or a configuration is found whereby one layer of grain is pressed down one way—clockwise—and the layer underneath counter-clockwise.

How is that done by fraud?

Is there a message?

Old English lore claimed it was "weather magicians" who created wheat-flattening, design-savvy storms: In 1678 a newspaper referred to one as the handiwork of a "mowing demon," the article ("Strange News Out of Hartford-shire") illustrated with the woodcut of a horned creature using a scythe to form a concentric pattern . . .

In western Australia aboriginal cave paintings of an ovoid object above circular ground formations was dated to 3000 B.C.

The patterns have appeared at Stonehenge and Silbury Hill, ancient burial grounds revered by occult Druids and formed of stones in perfect circles.

The mysterious megaliths of Stonehenge set the stage for an amazing disappearance in August, 1971, when a group of hippies decided to pitch tents in the center of the circle and spend the night. At about two a.m. a severe thunderstorm swept over Salisbury Plain, its brilliant bolts striking trees and even the megaliths themselves. "Two witnesses—a farmer and a policeman—said that the stones of the ancient monument lit up with an eerie blue light that was so intense they had to avert their eyes," asserts a website I found. "They heard screams from the campers and the two witnesses rushed to the scene expecting to find injured—or even dead—campers. To their surprise, they found no one. All that remained within the circle of stones were several smoldering tent pegs and the drowned remains of a campfire. The hippies themselves were gone without a trace."

The stones: do they memorialize an ancient "crop" circle?

What we know is that the formations have appeared in dozens of countries with patterns that confound the credulous. Or is it more than that? As in cases of cattle mutilation—which have been reported in conjunction with crop circles—there are luminous orbs, bigfoot, and, as in Flatland, West Virginia, a creature with glowing eyes.

Timeless, are the circles. And again, it seems . . . transmundane?

Were (and are) extraterrestrials leaving an enigmatic record, trying to communicate with each other—or with us?

In Minnesota more than forty circles materialized overnight in a field, along with a mutilated calf: tongue and jaw removed, as if by an adept surgeon. Intense magnetism recorded.

In Tasmania a loud prolonged roar was heard during December 1973 and the following day . . . a formation discovered.

Do the circles harbor binary language from aliens, or demons? A 150-foot indentation in a barley field in Wiltshire, England—which is the world's hotspot for crop circles—was deciphered as bearing a code for the first ten digits of *pi* (3.141592654).

If you believe one scientist educated at Cal Tech, formations with eight-point stars precede (as one did before 9/11) major disasters.

Inexplicable—or simply ingenious?

Two Englishmen named Doug Bower and David Chorley created a number of them with a board they held by rope, stepping on it as they pressed down on a field and fooling half the town. Others have fooled half the world— creating beautiful and intricate designs with rope, poles, and planks in shorter periods of time than initially imagined as plausible.

But such a technique: less likely in cases such as Milk Hill in Wiltshire in 2001, where a massive conglomeration of 409 circles, across eight hundred square feet, all in neat order, formed a pattern called the "double triskelion" with perfect interlocking spirals that appeared overnight.

And also in cases where the knots and joints of wheat have burnlike marks, as if energy had surged through them.

How is it, one might query, that wheat is pressed and stalks bent in such a way as to give formations the sense of motion—and three dimensions?

This has happened.

Mysteries there are, whether our eyes are wide open or . . . wide shut.

Are we meant, in the current era, to solve them?

Are we meant to be curious?

Or, if not trickery, are they best left alone, transcending science?

61

The Stranger in New Orleans

In 1986, while writing a book on pollution, I paid a visit to New Orleans and while there stayed with a physician who, along with her husband, was active in efforts to expose such dangers. They threw a little barbecue so I could meet others of like interest and one was Dr. Victor Alexander, a Harvard graduate who'd served as a senior medical officer at the federal Occupational Safety and Health Administration in Washington before moving to Louisiana—where he raised a loud alarm over pollution from the oil industry (coeds at one college complained of their nylons disintegrating) and where, in a bizarre turn of events, he was arrested and later convicted of a *local bank robbery.*

Needless to say, a doctor and former high-ranking medical officer holding up a bank—one near his office, no less—is bizarre. At the barbecue, he showed me photographs taken by bank security cameras, pictures he argued were of a man who bore striking similarities—a bit corpulent and round of face, with a dark beard—but was not him. He argued that it had been a frame-up (thus proximity to his office), an industry's attempt to halt his crusade against their pollution and particularly the dangers of its key product, ethanol.

There was no question that the oil and chemical industries in the state controlled politics and dealt severely with critics, especially physicians. Those who publicly warned of health effects were subject to government audits, and when it came to bucking Big Oil, Dr. Alexander was the most active doctor. He published articles about brain cancer, miscarriages, and other maladies—not at all to the liking of corporate executives who controlled many local and state politicians, including, during one period of my research, the governor.

Harassment was an open secret among medical experts, who naturally shied away from such research . . .

Not so Dr. Alexander—until, in May of 1985, he was apprehended by federal agents for the $2,600 holdup of the Central Savings and Loan Association at 710 Canal Street.

There were a number of mysterious details about that bank, starting with the fact that it was robbed four times in a three-month period, including the crime for which Dr. Alexander was arrested.

Two of the robberies occurred within just two days of each other.

Was something being staged?

The money was another issue. At the time Dr. Alexander was making at least what would be $230,000 a year in current value, exhibited no evidence of any sort of drug habit, and had no problem posting a $500,000 bail—yet somehow needed a couple thousand dollars so badly he kept hitting a bank that was on the same street as his office, risking his entire career. Police decided that he'd done it to finance cavorts at a local strip club . . .

Desperately trying to show me that he was innocent, Dr. Alexander showed me a grainy security camera photograph of the bank robber, who bore those highly distinct similarities, not just weight but with brunette hair and beard—but who, Dr. Alexander argued, had clearly different facial profile, as well as differently sized fingers. The testimony of identity experts (willing to show it was two different men) had not been allowed into the court. And so Dr. Alexander— a national star when it came to toxicology, and one who presented free workshops explaining hazards in the petro-chemical workplace—was ready for several years in prison.

We agreed to meet again at a pancake place near the airport when I returned to New Orleans following a trip to Texas. I had flown in from New York, and was heading back. It was a Sunday morning. A few minutes early, I sat in a chair facing the door so I could spot Dr. Alexander. I still couldn't decide if he was telling the truth.

Shortly after a waitress dropped off a menu, I saw him enter: stout, dark-haired, though dressed in a very debonair fashion—sporting a black suit. That seemed odd. It was a Sunday. I had no doubt it was Dr. Alexander, and waved to gather his attention.

There was no response. The man in the suit sat down and looked around nervously, glancing back and forth toward me when he noticed I was looking his way. Gently I waved once more, watching him. When he saw I was focused on him, he grew so edgy that—before ordering—he abruptly set down his menu, rose, nudged back his chair, and beat a path for the door, exiting the restaurant and leaving me totally confused. *Why'd he leave? Why had Dr. Alexander not recognized me?*

A minute or two later, the restaurant door opened and a man who looked very similar, but was casually dressed, entered and immediately noticed me, smiling as he quickly made his way and sat down at my table, a sheaf of docu-ments and photographs in his hands. It was Dr. Alexander, but in colorful weekend attire. Except for the clothes, he could have been the other man's twin. I asked what happened, if he had just been there and left—and he replied with a befuddled look. *What?* Lest he think I was crazy, I dropped the matter and we went about business—his argu-ment that he was the victim of a frame-up.

I never did figure it out. Did Dr. Alexander have a split personality? Or might he have set it up so that I was confused—first with him in one attire, then another—duping me into believing there was a double? There was no evidence of that, and it would have been very difficult to have changed that quickly. But then *who* was his dead ringer? Was it the *real* bank robber: by a tremendous quirk in synchronicity, had he happened into the restaurant that morning and then, growing nervous because I was looking his way, and guilt-ridden, took off? I was so desperate to explain it to myself that I even wondered if it had been an angel—taking the form of his *doppelganger* to show me the truth of the matter.

That's what I wondered, and likely always will.

62

A Village of Miracles

It's the village of wonders. There are those who have seen visions of Jesus and other celestial beings—eyes open. There was the time the letters "*M-I-R* (Croatian for "peace") appeared like skywriting, witnessed by all the peasants who lived there. There are countless who have reported the sun spinning and throwing off splendiferous striations of color—multivariate stories because each year two-and-a-half million visit here.

There a "seer"—one of six—who developed a serious brain tumor—one that put her in a coma—but was told the precise date it would disappear, which it did.

Another time, she and a fellow visionary disappeared in one of the rough-hewn, stone-and-mortar hovels, her mother unable to find them, despite the small nature of the house and the fact that they had gone into a room with no windows, in a part of the abode with no back exit. When they reappeared, they insisted they'd been taken to the after-life—glimpsing Heaven (as well as its opposite).

It is in Bosnia-Hercegovina, and I was initially skeptical until I saw phenomena myself, including a star that kept splitting into three smaller lights, each a different color—white, blue, and red, the smaller one reuniting to form the original star and then going through the same routine again, as more than a dozen of us watched it with binoculars for fifteen minutes.

Called Medjugorje (for "between the hills," in mountainous karst-stone terrain), it is not a place to off-handedly dismiss, no matter one's religious affiliation. In fact, Orthodox, Catholics, Protestants, agnostics, and Muslims have all found it a powerful touch of . . . something beyond this earth, the initial events here authenticated by a formal Vatican commission that studied it from 2010 to 2014. Like Fatima, Lourdes, and Guadalupe, the Virgin appears here. On rare occasions, so—allegedly—has Jesus. Many years ago I was sent two photographs, one taken of several pilgrims on a "hill of apparitions," showing a normal bright panorama there (it was daylight), but the very next, taken moments later, displaying it as a night scene with the letters "C-H-R-I-S-T" in the sky. No one could explain it. The great Pentecostal leader David Johannes du Plessis visited out of curiosity and to the surprise of many declared it a great outpouring of the Holy Spirit. The fruits—joy, peace, and closeness to God (*Matthew* 7:15-20)—are the opposite of the fear and confusion engendered by dark wonders of the supernatural.

Celebrities from Loretta Young to former U.S. treasury secretary William Simon and football coach Don Shula have visited. I spoke with a former ambassador to the European Communities, Alfred Kingon, a practicing Jew, who was so taken by the happenings that he put together a summary for President Ronald Reagan and Mikhail Gorbachev, both of whom personally received and read what it had to say. For indications were that momentous prophecies have been relayed through the seers, "secrets" that put Catholics in mind of Fatimá. If there are devilish hotspots, might there not be the opposite: holy ones?

The confidential messages—ten of them, to be revealed, they claim, at some time in the future—have to do, it is hinted, with events that will come as warnings to the world, circumstances to do with their own personal lives, in Christianity-at-large, and—in the last three—unnerving "chastise-ments"—catastrophes—that, if one believes this, will impact the whole world.

No one knows if the six have received identical such messages (they have never discussed them among each other), but they are dead serious about them and have kept them secret since the early 1980s.

Most incredible is the claim of seer Mirjana Dragicevic Soldo that her secret prophecies were written on a strange "rolled-up scroll" or "parchment" given to her by the Virgin Mary in 1982. "I could only explain it as a mystery of God," asserted Mirjana, who describes the parchment as light in color, "between white and yellow"—perhaps, one might say, beige—but really, unlike any color or material—"not quite paper, not quite fabric," with the unusual property that, as she put it, can "wrinkle or bend" but "in no way can it break, even by fire."

"How did that happen?

"How," she wonders, "am I holding an object from Heaven?"

When she received it, Mirjana says, "I carefully unrolled it and found ten secrets written in a simple and elegant cursive handwriting. There were no decorations or illustrations on the parchment; each secret was described in simple clear words. The secrets were not numbered, but they appeared in order, one after another, with the first secret at the top and the tenth at the bottom, and included the dates of the future events."

Ten prophecies—written down?

By any standard, an extravagant claim. Yet it is backed up by the many who return with miraculous photos, accounts of luminous clouds, reports of healings, and stories about mysterious, angelic strangers. Small "crosses" seem to be all around town, formed by twigs or straw, or on stones, and many have witnessed crosses in the sky. Even Communists were dumbfounded, especially by a large hillside fire at the site of apparitions that left no scorch marks (*Exodus* 3:2).

Once, during civil war in Yugoslavia, Mirjana left the scroll in Sarajevo, but miraculously, U.N. soldiers who found it brought it back to her.

When Mirjana showed the "scroll" to a cousin and a friend, the cousin saw a sort of poem or prayer, while the other read something entirely different.

Only Mirjana sees the secrets on the parchment. And only, when the time comes, she claims, will she give it to a spiritual counselor who will be able to see the same. She told him the first "warning" will be a regional event that will be heard about around the world. It will be followed by two other warnings, and a miracle. "If people saw the first secret, as it was shown to me, everyone would most certainly be shaken enough to take a new and different look at themselves and everything around them," she intimated to her spiritual director. "I believe that if everyone knew about these same things, each one of these people would be shocked to their senses and would view our world in a completely different light."

It's not the end of the world, she says, but incredible upcoming developments that, as Ambassador Kingon speculated, "will change the planet."

When will the events occur?

Some of the ten, says the seer (who was born in 1965), in her lifetime. She's not certain she'll be witness to all of them.

Strange, Strangest. How is anyone supposed to believe this? If I hadn't seen what I had there during repeated visits, I would never consider such a thing—and that's what I am doing, considering it, while remembering those words from J. D. Haldane: *"The universe is not only stranger than we imagine, but stranger than we can imagine . . ."*

63

The Mystery Man Near Chattanooga

Uncanny is the word for what Barry Hoare, of Cairns in Queensland, Australia, witnessed.

It went beyond remnant dinosaurs.

"In 1963 my wife and I went to work as lay-missionaries in the Vicariate of Wewak in Papua New Guinea," Hoare wrote me. "We were posted to a mission station at Roma in the Sepik River Are. On many weekends my wife and I would walk to nearby mission stations to visit with other missionaries.

"On one particular weekend we walked to a mission at Ulupu some four-and-a-half hours into the hills to visit [a friend]. We had lunch with father, listened to some of his stories, and spent the afternoon with him. As the afternoon wore on we were invited to stay the night but decided to walk home. We had a torch to help show the way as night progressed. Not long after leaving the mission station and walking downhill for some time we crossed a small river on our journey. Soon after crossing this river a very heavy thunderstorm came over, the sky darkened, and it began to pour heavy rain upon us. We stood in the pouring rain for a period of time; it was totally dark and I took the torch out of my haversack.

"With the pouring rain the torch gave a couple of flickers and the light went out—leaving us in the complete darkness and pouring rain. Wondering what was the best thing to do, returning was not an option because the small river would become a raging torrent. While pondering that, I suddenly noticed something burning on the top of a hill about a hundred and fifty meters in front of us—a very bright light in the darkness. We began walking toward it and while doing so the rain stopped. The light remained and we soon came across a native man holding a lighted 'boom-boom'—a palm branch from the coconut tree, which gives very good light and burns for maybe three or four minutes.

"He spoke to us in pigin English *'Yu pela go wer?'* ('Where are you two going?'). We answered that we were heading to the mission station of Roma. He then told us, in pigin, that he would take us on a short cut and we set off following him and the lighted palm branch into the jungle—up and down some hills and across some small creeks.

"Within what seemed a very short time we came out at the village of Saigisi about half an hour from home. The storm clouds had disappeared and it was now a moonlit sky. The whole journey that had previously taken four and a half hours was now completed in about an hour. It was really not until many years later that as I began to reflect on the ministry of angels that this whole episode came to mind. During our journey with the guide I cannot recall his ever changing the lighted boom-boom. I can still see him standing on that hill with the light in his hand beckoning us towards him. We felt no sense of fear being led off the road and into the bush of the jungle. There was wonderment at having completed so quickly the journey with him. What a wonderful God who sends His messengers to look after us!"

A four-minute torch lasting at least an hour—and burning in the rain!

Was it . . . an angel?

The most incredible such account I've heard involved a Christian chemist named Vincent Tan Ban Soon, who emigrated from Singapore. He was working in a laboratory late the night of March 25, 1993, this in Tennessee, and about 1:30 a.m., as he readied to leave, he happened to look out the door and spot a man standing next to his car, on the passenger side. It was a tough part of town, known for its crime. Fearing assault, Vincent grabbed a rod and, just in case, held it behind his back as he exited. He also gave thought to *chi-sao*, a form of martial arts he knew. As he opened the car door, he nervously asked the stranger if he needed something.

"Hi, Vincent," the fellow replied. Somehow, the stranger knew Tan's name.

"Do I know you?' asked Tan.

"Not really," said the man, who was dressed in jeans and a t-shirt, thirty to thirty-five years in age, with short, well-groomed hair.

"What is your name and who are you?" Tan summoned the courage to insist.

"I have the name of the secondary and primary school," replied the stranger cryptically.

Though Buddhist at the time, now evangelical, Tan had attended Saint Gabriel primary and secondary school in Singapore.

Continued this fellow: *"You don't need to use chi-sao on me."*

How could this stranger have read his thoughts! When Vincent asked him just that, the man cryptically replied, *"I know."* Then, in a different, more serious tone—an unforgettable one, referring to Jesus—the stranger said, *"He's coming very, very soon."* The man had had a normal American voice, said Tan, no accent, about six-feet-tall, very normal and casual except the sense of urgency, when he mentioned the Second Coming.

Soon? Jesus?

When Tan turned for a moment, the young fellow was no longer anywhere around.

Had that been the extent of it, I would have rationalized it in my head as a possible hoax played on Tan. A religious fanatic? . . .

There was, however, a second experience two days before Christmas that same year, in a way more astonishing.

This time it occurred on the way home from visiting a friend, when Vincent spotted a truck on the roadside—obvious car trouble. This was on Standifer Gap Road in Collegedale, about twenty miles from Chattanooga.

As Tan pondered whether he should risk stopping, he saw that it was an old man, maybe seventy-five, dressed in overalls—perhaps a farmer. He had a very old Ford truck. When Tan pulled over, the man explained that he needed a jump. His battery was dead. He was clean-shaven, perhaps 5'8", and a bit stout, with a full head of gray-white hair. Gray eyebrows. Normal nose—a bit pinched at the end.

Tan didn't think he had his jumper cables with him but remembered how he had recently gotten a car started by using a metal clothes hanger instead.

It turned out that Tan did have his cables and this fellow connected his end of the cables with abnormal speed despite using no flashlight in the pitch-dark night. It was cold and so they waited in Tan's own truck (he also owned a car) while the stranger's Ford was charging.

That was when the man asked if they could pray. *"God can work miracles, even start a car with coat hangers,"* he commented—somehow knowing about the incident!

His prayer: *"Most holy and powerful God in Heaven, we know You are coming very, very soon. Help us now in Your own time and way, in Jesus's Name. Amen."*

The stranger asked Tan if he believed the Lord was coming and when Vincent said yes, he repeated that it would be soon.

He also knew, somehow, that Tan had a King James Bible in the vehicle, and asked to use it (it was in the glove compartment), commenting that Bible study *"is like being in a big room with many candles that are lit."*

Again incredibly: Tan recently had had a dream about a room with many candles—but not all of them lit!

The old man also alluded to *Matthew* 24:36 and 42 (about not knowing the "hour," and therefore being watchful).

Lastly: the stranger referred to *Revelation* 3:11 ("Behold, I come quickly . . . ")

There was something in his voice that was extraordinarily powerful, recalled Tan.

After the Ford was charged, and before he left, the stranger said he was leaving a little token of appreciation. *"It will be enough to fill up your car tomorrow with gas,"* he intoned, again coyly.

Tan followed the man until they came upon a sharp curve, around which the Ford was suddenly no longer a part of the treeless landscape. "He had disappeared in front of my eyes!" Vincent told me.

The next morning, on the way to telling a friend what had happened, he decided to fill up his car. When he got to the pump he realized the tank was almost full. He filled it anyhow. It came to $2.34.

The next time Tan tidied up his truck, he found some money on the passenger side where the stranger had sat: a quarter, a nickel, four pennies, and two one-dollar bills . . . "exactly $2.34."

Notes

Chapter 1: The quotes on Closa come from a documentary by the Lester Sumrall Evangelistic Association (along with World Harvest) and an excerpt online of Sumrall's book, *Alien Entities: A Look Behind the Door to the Spiritual Realm.* The Orrick case is from Mysteriousuniverse.org. I also used trueghosttales.com and mysteriousunbiverse.org. The Lang account was said to have been first contrived by a fellow named Joe Mulhatten, a traveling salesman known for concocting stories and a competitor in tall-tales contests; but no one knows for sure; it may have simply come from a magazine writer who got it from the Bierce story; or, Bierce may have developed his story from the Lang events, which under a different name may have occurred in Illinois or Mississippi! Whatever the case, Lang supposedly is a piece of fiction (for a full account see anomaly.com). The accounts on Hoia Baciu come from Listverse.com ("10 Strange Mysteries From Around The World That Are Still Unsolved" by Estelle Thurtle), Lifedeathprizes.com, "Welcome To The World's Most Haunted Forest," by Natasha Wynarczyk; and Hoiabachiuforest.com. See also an account of a woman who vanished in Chicago, Miriam Golding, in *The World's Strangest Stories* (1983) selected by the editors of *Fate* Magazine.

Chapter 2: For Rendlesham see BBC, July 13, 2015, "Rendelsham Forest UFO Sighting: No Evidence Claim"; the London *Telegraph*, February 16, 2015, "Britain's Roswell: The Truth Behind the Rendlesham Forest Incident"; and last but not least, Nick Redfern's *The Most Mysterious Places on Earth*, for the paranormal accounts. Very valuable too: "The Full Report" on www.rendleshamforest.com.

Chapter 3: Certain of the details come from "Twelve terrible and creepy things that have happened at the Cecil Hotel," www.ranker.com; "The Disturbing, Gruesome Past of the Hotel

Cecil," in the January 30, 2014 edition of Australia's news.com; Wikipedia entries; and "'The water did have a funny taste': Body is found in water tank at 'cursed' Cecil Hotel," London *Independent*, February 21, 2013, I also used *Buzzfeed*. See also *Paranoia* Magazine, "Aleister Crowley, Elisa Lam, and Secrets of the Cecil Hotel," May 12, 2018.

Chapter 4: I have read many books and articles about Geller, interviewed scientists involved with him, and visited with the psychic himself. The details on the alleged teleportation from Manhattan to Ossining came in part from Jonathan Margolis's *The Secret Life of Uri Geller* (Osprey Publishing, 2013). The information on the CIA's release of documents comes from a number of news sources, particularly the London *Telegraph*, January 18, 2017. Geller participated in the agency's "Stargate" program concerning clairvoyance ("remote viewing"). During those experiments, he replicated pictures that were half a mile away. For other cases, see too my book, PK: A Report on Psychokinesis and for the Pansini boys *The PK Zone: A Cross-Cultural Review of Psychokinesis*, by Pamela Rae Heath, M.D. See also ww.urigeller.com.

Chapter 5: See *The New York Times*, December 20, 1897, "Wisconsin Mound Opened"; *The New York Times*, September 7, 1904, "Find Giant Indians' Bones"; *The New York Times*, February 11, 1902, "Giant Skeletons Found"; the Indianapolis *Journal*, unknown date, "Giants of Other Days: Recent Discoveries Near Serpent Mound, Ohio"; *The New York Times*, February 9, 1890, "A Race of Indian Giants"; *The New York Times*, September 8, 1871, "More Big Indians Found in Virginia"; the San Antonio *Express*, 1940, "Beach Giant's Skull Unearthed By WPA Workers Near Victoria"; the San Diego *Union*, 1947, "Trace of Giants Found in Desert"; *The New York Times*, May 25, 1882, "The Bones of a Giant Found"; *The New York Times*, August 10, 1880, "Two Very Tall Skeletons"; the Sauk Rapids *Sentinel*, December 18, 1868, "Reported Discovery of Huge Skeleton"; *The New York Times*, May 4, 1912, "Strange Skeletons Found"; and the website, "Secret History," January 20, 2013, "A giant mystery: 18 strange giant skeletons in Wisconsin: Sons of God; Men of renown." See also *Giants, Fallen Angels, and the Return of the Nephilim*, by Dr. Dennis G. Lindsay.

Chapter 6: The account of Thomas Burnett was on *Spirit Daily.com*, as were the articles about Maria Esperanza and her 911 prophecies. The account of the Vancouver woman came from *Strange But True* by Corrine Kenner and Craig Miller.

Chapter 7: I used *Newsweek*, "Did an Author from the 1800s Predict the Trumps, Russia, and America's Downfall?" July 31, 2017; *Politico*, "Trump Is the Star of These Bizarre Victorian Novels," October 7, 2017; Snopes; and Wikipedia.

Chapter 8: Much the data was culled from a website called "Unexplained Phenomena" (www.amasci.com: "The Weird Data Science Base of Electric People," May 2014); "Strange Podcasts," Episode six; the London Guardian, July 28, 2004, "It's Electrifying"; and *Strange Electrogmagnetic Dimsensions*, by Louis Proud. I also interviewed a scientist who studies such matters, as well as Mary Weigant.

Chapter 9: For James Dean's car, I used "The Curse of James Dean's 'Little Bastard,'" Jalopnik, December 31, 2008; the San Antonio *Express* (mysanantonio.com), September 30, 2015, "60 Years After James Dean's Death, 'Cursed Car' Mystery Continues"; and "James Dean Death Car," Snopes. For Archduke Ferdinand's car I used *Stranger Than Science* and "Curses! Archduke Ferdinand and His Astounding Death Car," *Smithsonian* Magazine, April 22, 2013.

Chapter 10: Most of these accounts come from our website, www.spiritdaily.com. The quote about the Swiss town is from an article by Jocelyn LeBlanc, "The Town That's Obsessed With the Number 11," www.mysteriousuniverse.org, February 24, 2019.

Chapter 11: I used, "The Bloody Benders, America's First Serial Killers," *Mental Floss*, November 14, 2013; "Bloody Benders,"

Wikipedia; "Deadly Hosts: Family robbed and murdered at least 11 at their small southeast Kansas inn," Topeka *Capital-Journal,* August 25, 2003; "Little House of Murder: the Bloody Benders," the Lineup, undated; "The Bloody Benders: Mass Murderers from the History of Kansas," by Troy Taylor; "The Six Most Terrifying Serial Killer Families in History," io9 Gizmodo, May 18, 2015. I also interviewed Don Richardson, a local history buff, and a woman who works in town at a bed-and-breakfast that has a small museum dedicated to the crime.

Chapter 12: For some of this, in addition to personal research, I used the websites *Oddee,* "Twenty Most Amazing Coincidences," May 2, 2007 and Listverse, "Top 15 Amazing Coincidences," November 12, 2007. See also *Beyond Coincidence* by Martin Plimmer and Brian King, and "Strange and Mysterious Coincidences That Actually Happened," in Unexplained Mysteries, January 21, 2018. Note that some relate the Kupcinet account as involving a letter to Hannin, not a phone call. I met Kupcinet when doing his radio show in 1980.

Chapter 13: For the phantom with no arm, see again Jonathan Margolis's *The Secret Life of Uri Geller.*

Chapter 14: Dr. Emoto's information is in part from his book, *The Hidden Messages in Water.*

Chapter 15: The Belmez faces account is from a number of sources, including "Historic Mysteries," October 2016, "Belmez Faces: Mystery of the People in the Floor." See also, "the Mystery of the Bélmez Faces," Cool Interesting Stuff blogsite, April 2, 2013. I reported on the Ukrainian phenomenon in my book *The Final Hour.* I also saw a strange formation in Hannibal, Missouri, at the Huck Finn cave: a clear image formed by erosion and rivulets of moisture that looked just like Mark Twain's face—startling not only to me but two employees I summoned; they had never noticed it before.

Chapter 16: For lightning, see "The World's Ten Biggest Lightning Hotspots," *Outside*, May 16, 2016; for the South Carolina man, an article in the London *Mail* on August 30, 2015 (untitled). For the team in the Congo, see BBC, "Lightning Kills Football Team," October 28, 1998. For ball lighting, see Wikipedia. The Alabama courthouse is from ExploreSouthernHistory.com, "The Face in the Window." The examples of images inflected by lightning come from *Lightning As 'Photographer,' Revisiting A Forgotten Phenomenon of Nature*, by Chidambaram Ramesh; for the various oddities, I used "Ten Bizarre Stories of Lightning Strikes" in *Oddee*, September 12, 2011. For Lake Maracaibo see BBC, August 10, 2015, "The Most Electrical Place On Earth." For ball lightning, I used Edwards' books along with Thoughtcompanyco, January, 16, 2016, "The Mystery of Ball Lightning."

Chapter 17: The main source here: Michael C. Luckman's book, *Alien Rock: The Rock'n'Roll Extraterrestrial Connection.*

Chapter 18: The report from *Pravda* on the cosmonauts is from the June 14, 2011, article, "Angels in Space Nothing But Top-Secret Hallucinations." The bog reporting a second "visit" was Tech Blog, December 26, 2012. I watched the CNN clip of an interview with Buzz Aldrin, on the "Larry King Show," August 4, 2007. The account of the cosmonauts seeing gigantic waves is from *Fate* Magazine, a 2014 article entitled, "Russian Cosmonauts and Their Sightings of UFOs and Other Strange Phenomena." The mass of water that vanished is from *Tekhnika-Molodezhi*, Issue 3, 1980. The pillar of water near Australia is from *NLO* magazine, 10/11, 1996.

Chapter 19: For the deepest hole, I used many sources, including, "Kola Superdeep Borehole," atlasobscura.com; "Seven of the Deepest Holes Mankind Ever Dug," *Popular Mechanics*, January 17, 2017; "The Deepest Hole In The World and What We've Learned From It," Youtube, SciShow, May 5, 2014; "What At the Bottom of the Deepest Hole On Earth," IFLScience!, November 3, 2015; "Drilling to the Mantle," *ZME Science*, December 15, 2015; "Welcome to the Deepest Hole on Earth," *Science Alert*, July 22,

2016; "You Won't Believe What Scientists Found When They Dug the Deepest Hole on Earth," *Ancient Code* (undated); and Wikipedia. For the European (Erdstall) tunnels, I used "Experts Baffled By Mysterious Underground Tunnels," *Der Spiegel,* July 22, 2011; "The Mystery Tunnels of Bavaria" (straightdope.com); WikiVisually and Wikipedia; "The Mystery Tunnels of Erdställe" (metafilter.com); "Stone Age Tunnels" (ghosttheory.com); "Going Underground: The Massive European network of Stone Age tunnels that weaves from Scotland to Turkey," London *Daily Mail,* August 8, 2011; "Ten Haunted Tunnels With Really Creepy Backstories" (Listverse.com); "The Medieval Mystery of Europe's 'Erdstall' Tunnels," zergnet.com; "We Still Don't Know Why" (atlasobscura.com); "Investigations Into the Unknown and Weird," Silentthrill.wordpress.com; "Unexplained massive European network of ancient tunnels," Youtube, December 13, 2016; "Why Are There Ancient Tunnels In Bavaria" (Neatorama.com); and "Tunnel Trek," Snopes. For the depth of Tahoe see Worthingtonjamie's Blog, "The Mysterious Depths of Lake Tahoe." For the Toronto tunnel see "Strange Encounters with Bizarre Tunnel-Dwelling Monsters," *Mysterious Universe,* January 28, 2018.

Chapter 20: I have owned an African Grey named Mikie for nearly fourteen years. The story of Alex comes from the London *Daily Mail* ("Alex, the parrot who learned to say 'I love you and mean it," October 13, 2013, which was an excerpt from Dr. Irene Pepperberg's book, *Alex and Me*; and I referred to *The New York Times* ("Alex, a Parrot Who Had a Way With Words, Dies") September 10, 2007. For the horses, I used Wikipedia as well as Edwards' *Strangest Of All* ("The Equine Wizards of Elberfeld"). For Jim Key see *Beautiful Jim Key* by Mim E. Rivas. I also interviewed Dr. Pepperberg of Harvard.

Chapter 21: My main sources were the paper by Dr. Paul Pearsall, Dr. Gary E. Schwartz, and Dr. Linda G. Russek, "Organ Transplants and Cellular Memories" in *Nexus* Magazine April-May 2005) and "Woman dies 21 years after heart-lung transplant that gave her a taste for beer," the Patriot-Ledger, August 9, 2009. I also drew from the London *Daily Mail*, "Art Transplant," March 21, 2006.

Chapter 22: For Hillary Clinton, I used Townhall, March 10, 2017, "Did A Siberian Mummy Curse Hillary Clinton In the 1990s? Some Russian Locals Think So," as well as other sources. For King Tut I used a site called UnMuseum, "Howard Carter and the Curse of Tut's Mummy"; also, I viewed the tomb artifacts in Cairo; LiveScience, "The Curse of King Tut: Fact and Fable," March 21, 2014; the *Guardian* article was July 23, 2014, "Digging up trouble: beware the curse of King Tutankhamun"; and Wikipedia. For the *Titanic* mummy, I used a site dedicated to the ship, www.titanicandco.com, along with Snopes and other sources such as the website *DW*, June 11, 2005, "Curse of the Iceman Linked to Scientist's Death." For the museum in Brazil, see CNN, September 3, 2018, "Brazil's National Museum engulfed by massive fire."

Chapter 23: My major source was *Sheppton: The Myth, Miracle, and Magic*, by Maxim W. Furek, though I also used newspaper accounts, including *East Union Township*, "Sheppton Folks Recall Mine Disaster"; and *Citizens Voice*, May 11, 2014, "Saint John XXIII's Second Miracle May Have Occurred at Sheppton Mining Disaster."

Chapter 24:   See, "Glowing Auras and 'Black Money': The Pentagon's Mysterious U.F.O. Program," *The New York Times*, December 16, 2017; "Ex-Navy pilot describes encounter with UFO off California," *The Washington Post*, December 19, 2017; the Pentagon's Secret Search for UFOs," *Politico*, December 16, 2017; "2 Navy Airmen and an Object That 'Accelerated Like Nothing I've Ever Seen," *The New York Times*, December 16, 2017; and *Thrillist Entertainment*, May 29, 2018, "Military Report Says UFOs May Have Communicated With A Massive Underwater Object." The quote on the alleged Collins Elite and others is from Nick Refern's *Final Events and the Secret Government Group on Demonic UFOs and the Afterlife*, to be read with healthy skepticism and cautious discernment.

Chapter 25: For savants, I used Listverse, "10 Fascinating People with Savant Syndrome," July 23, 2013, and Neatorama, "10 Most Fascinating Savants in the World," September 5, 2008. For Pichai see the *Economic Times*, "Google CEO Sundar Pichai Famous for His Phenomenal Memory," August 12, 2015. For "Benjamin Kyle" I used the *Orlando Sentinel*, "No Man's Land: Amnesia Stole His Identity for Eleven Years," September 22, 2015; and Wikipedia; for Nima Veiseh, BBC, "The blessing and curse of people who never forget," January 26, 2016, and Fox News 5, Washington, D.C., "Total Recall," May 17, 2016. For how a blind person can sometimes navigate, BBC, "The woman with a strange 'second sight,'" May 1, 2017; for seeing just one object at a time (the ultimate tunnel vision), see BBC, "Tunnel vision doesn't begin to describe this woman's sight," September 19, 2016. The blind folks who can tell colors: I interviewed a researcher working with this in the mid-1970s in the Buffalo, New York, area.

Chapter 26: For the tourists in France, see *Ultimum Mysterium: Beyond the Cutting Edge of Science*, by Anthony Burns; for the mountain climbers, *Unexplained Mysteries of the 20th Century*, by Janet and Colin Bord; the account on the Australian episode is from a website called "Weird Australia." Certain details on the two academicians in France are from an article, "The Mystery of the Versailles Time Slip," by Kathleen McGowan, on her website.

Chapter 27: For the Devon footprints, see the London *Times* of February 16, 1855, and the London *Daily Mail*, "Ancient mystery returns as 'Satan's hoofprints' are spotted in Devon back garden," March 13, 2009. The quote on Devon is from a website called "Mysterious Universe," July 23, 2017. See also Edwards' *Stranger Than Science* and Charles Fort's *Lo!* For the hoof marks in North Carolina, I used a website operated by North Carolina Historic Sites, "The Mysterious Hoofprints," and spoke to a librarian in the area, as well as a tourism official, unable to reach a fellow named Cutler who now owns the land and expressed an intention to open it up to the public, now that the land has been "logged out." Another source: NCPedia, "Devil's Horse's Hoof Print," 2006.

Chapter 28: For Clarita, I used Lester Frank Sumrall's book, *The True Story of Clarita Villanueva : A seventeen-year-old girl bitten by devils in Bilibid Prison, Manila, Philippines*; "Dracula Girl," an article in the Barrier Miner in Broken Hill, Australia, May 28, 1953; *The Argus*, May 21, 1953, "Dracula Victim Can Be 'Cured'"; the *Beaver Valley Times*, May 20, 1953, "Manila Mayor Confirms 'Spook' Attacks on Girl"; and an analysis by the aforementioned website, www.anomalies.com, as well as anomalyinfo.com.

Chapter 29: Much comes from Paul Blake Smith's seminal book, *MO41: The Bombshell Before Roswell*, as well as an interview with him. I also used online sources, such as MUFON Symposium Proceedings, by Ryan Wood ("the First Roswell: Evidence for a Crash Retrieval in Cape Girardeau Missouri in 1941"). The information on Kenneth Arnold's subsequent alleged sightings is from a website called "Hidden Experiences" ("Kenneth Arnold and UFO History," May 9, 2014).

Chapter 30: This is entirely my own personal research. I knew Maria Esperanza well—and never found any form of pretense or deception.

Chapter 31: Most of the information on the oil comes from Youtube ("The Supernatural Channel"); the Brunswick *News* (August 5, 2017, "Bible dripping with oil will visit area"); Hisnameisflowingoi.org, the website for the oil ministry); and from a personal visit to a church in Lake City, Florida, where it was on display in 2018.

Chapter 32: For Ya Chen and Terry Wallis, see *Oddee*, August 17, 2011, "Ten Unbelievable Coma Stories." See also a website called Everyday Health, "Waking Up: Famous Coma Survivors."

Chapter 33: See *Spirit Daily*, "Is it possession or psychological? Strange 'hysteria' brings question into sharp relief"; *The New York Times*, "What Happened to the Girls in Le Roy," March 7, 2012; *All Things Kenyan*, "Terror in the Kenyan Schools," December 26, 2015; Reuters, "School's End Clears Up New York's Students'

Mystery Twitching," June 23, 2012; and *Africa News Online*, "Ghosts Invade Kenyan Schools," July 19, 2000. I also used *Study in Kenya's* article headlined, "Bumula Girls closed after demons in the compound." For the government study, see the *Malawi Medical Journal*, "Episodes of mass hysteria in African schools: A study of literature," September 23, 2011.

Chapter 34: I visited Kibeho in 2010 and wrote the introduction for the first English book about it, simply titled *Kibeho: Rwanda— A Prophecy Fulfilled*, by Father Gabriel Maindron. I also relied heavily upon Immaculée Ilibagiza's excellent book (with Steve Erwin), *Our Lady of Kibeho: Mary Speaks To The World From The Heart of Africa*.

Chapter 35: For Devil's Hole I relied on my own research (I grew up there and was a reporter for the Niagara *Gazette*) along with an article in the Niagara *Reporter* and two articles on www.spirit-daily.com, "Blackout Another 'Pre-Warning Harking Back To Mysterious Similar Event in 1965" and "In Upstate New York Is 'Psychic Highway' With Astonishing History," undated. I also used, www.niagara frontier.com, "Devil's Hole and the Devil's Hole Massacre," excerpt from *Williams' Scenic and Historic Niagara*, 1925.

Chapter 36: The report in prions and military bases I took directly from the National Institute for Discovery Science research paper issued on December 30, 2003.

Chapter 37: For Ezekiel's "wheels," see Fort's *Lo!* and *The Book of the Damned*. For the Navy pilots, see *The New York Times*, December 16, 2017; "Ex-Navy pilot describes encounter with UFO off California."

Chapter 38: I have followed UFOs, since the mid-1960s, including weekly newsletters, serving as a background. It is astounding how little was known about Roswell until the 1990s. The Roswell incident was one of dozens of UFOs cases that year, albeit the only one with alleged crash material. The alleged

Boeche quote comes from Redfern's *Final Events* (previously cited). I have viewed numerous videos and read many books on alleged alien abduction, and interviewed Luigi Vendittelli, as well as Joe Jordan. For the parallels with the occult, see *Close Encounters of the Fourth Kind*, by C. D. B. Bryan.

Chapter 39: The quotes from John Lennon come from *People* Magazine, August 22, 1988, and an interview in Playboy (book form: Berkeley, 1982); for the spinning ball, see the website Atlas Obscura, "The Merchant Ball"; the information on Bishop Winstrup comes from CNN, "Sweden's mummified bishop: Buried in 1680 with hidden baby," June 23, 2015; and the London *Guardian*, "Scan of mummified body of Swedish bishop reveals baby hidden in coffin," June 21, 2015. For Sheffield Cathedral, the London *Mail* of June 13, 2013, "Mystery of the missing coffins: Who stole the remains of FIFTEEN members of aristocratic family from cathedral tomb?" The information on Christ Church in Barbados is from *Barbados Pocket Guide*. Calls to the parish were not successful. I also used: "The Mysterious Moving Coffins of the Chase Family Vault," September 16, 2016, in "The Chase Vault," 2017, *Atlas Obscura*, from Skeptoid Media; and "The Chase Family Vault: The Historical Tale That Haunts Barbados," November 16, 2016, www.historythings.com.

Chapter 40: For the "living fossil" accounts I used the website called *Anomalies*, which largely drew its information from *Stranger Than Science*, adding, however, as in the case of the Ottawa *Citizen*, some references. I also drew two snippets from a website called the Unmuseum (www.unmuseum.org, "Entombed animals"). For the quarry account, I used *Forbes* Magazine, October 31, 2015, "The Strange History Of The Myth Of Entombed Animals." Also: Wikipedia and ThoughCo.com, "Animals Sealed in Stone," May 9, 2017.

Chapter 41: See Linda Dunning *Lost Landscapes; Weird USA*, "The Highway To Hell"; The Witching Hour, "Hellhounds on the Devil's Highway," March 13, 2012; and *Overdrive*, "Highway Haunts," October 20, 2012. Also: *Real Ghosts, Restless Spirits, and*

Haunted Places, by Brad Steiger. See likewise, "The Unexplained Phenomenon of Highway 666," Haunted Places To Go.com. For Skinwalker Ranch, see *Wired*, "Inside Robert Bigelow's Decades-Long Obsession With UFOs," February 24, 2018, and Skinwalker-Ranch.org, as well as Wikipedia.

Chapter 42: Sources for mothman include the original police reports (themothman.wikia.com); National Public Radio, "Welcome To the 'TNT Area,' Home of Mothman," January 23, 2012; "The Official Website of Colin Andrews"; an article called "Convincing Stories of People Who Saw Mothman" on Ranker.com; an article entitled "The Return of Mothman" on a site called Ground Zero; a list of deceased and a description of unfortunate incidents on a page called "The Mothman Death List" by Loren Coleman; an article headlined "Four Alleged Mothman Sightings That Preceded Disasters" on www.theportalist.com, *American Monsters: A History of Monster Lore, Legends, and Sightings in America* by Linda S. Godfrey; *Crypto-zoology A to Z* by Loren Coleman and Jerome Clark; and "The Real Story of the Mothman Prophecies" on a site called www.ign.com. As for the TNT in Upstate New York: I studied this extensively both as a newspaper reporter investigating radioactive contamination and chemical threats there as well as a private citizen intrigued by reports of strange animals there. I will note that a friend of mine who found the place endlessly curious died in 1989 in a car crash returning from there. Barton Nunnelly's exhaustively researched book is *The Inhuminoids: Real Encounters with Beings That Can't Exist!* See also Wikipedia.

Chapter 43: Material comes from the biography, *Padre Pio: The True Story*, by Bernard Ruffin (who initially thought Padre Pio to be a hoax or worse), and a website called Padre Pio Devotions (www.padrepiodevotion.org). I also visited San Giovanni Rotundo twice.

Chapter 44: The book I referenced, by Vincent H. Gaddis, is *Mysterious Fires and Light: All the Latest Facts About the Weird and Amazing Events That Science Cannot Explain—or Deny*, was published by Dell in 1967. The article cited in *The New York Times* was headlined, "Canneto di Caronia Journal; Electricity Goes Wild. Did the Devil Make It Do It?" in the June 24, 2004, edition. A key source was the *Atavist* Magazine, "When the Devil Enters," November 21, 2016. I also used the BBC, "Sicilians fight 'Satanic' Fires," November 2, 2004; the *Ibi Times* "Italy: Mystery Fires in Sicily Village Blamed on Aliens," July 29, 2014; *World-NetDaily*, "Baffling 'demon' fires blamed on space aliens," October 27, 2007; Abovetopsecret.com, posted December 9, 2016; and the London *Times*, "Families flee Sicily's village of fire," July 29, 2014.

Chapter 45: The news story was from the London *Guardian*, "Morgellons: A hidden epidemic or mass hysteria," May 6, 2011. The details on the 17th century case come from a website called *Jezebel*, "Real Delusions of an Unreal Disease: A History of Morgellons," April 15, 1015. The scientific papers for analysis of the fibers include an online paper in *BMC Dermatology*, "Exploring the association between Morgellons disease and Lyme disease: identification of *Borrelia burgdorferi* in Morgellons disease patients," February 12, 2015; and "Morgellons disease: the search for a perpetrator," *Atlas of Science*, January 18, 2016. For the background on Plum Island, I relied, in part, on a news website for pet owners, TheDogPress.com, "Plum Island Lyme Disease" (July 2016); and "Tick Talk," a collaborative investigative reporting project conducted at the State University of New York at New Paltz. See also *The Long Island Press*, "Inside Plum Island: Mysteries, Myths and Monsters Explained," September 1, 2013.

Chapter 46: I used the Jim Parish newsletter; The Plymouth *Herald*, "Plymouth hum mystery solved—French scientist has found the cause," November 26, 2015; "Strange trumpet sounds heard from the sky," Youtube, November 13, 2016; the London *Guardian*, "The Windsor Hum: Where Is the Noise Plaguing A City of 210,000 Coming From?" June 7, 2016; the *Huffington Post*, "Weird Noise: Strange Sounds Popping Up In Different Parts Of Canada," January 16, 2012; WNEP-TV, News 16, "Mysterious

Boom in Luzerne County," January 1, 2015; "Nashoba Hill: The Hill That Roars," an article by Daniel V. Boudillion (www.bouldillian.com); "Strange Noises in Sky Strange Sounds Being Heard Apocalyptic Sounds Worldwide Explained 2016," Youtube, August 23, 2016; the *Huffington Post*, "Strange Sounds Heard In Terrace, British Columbia, May Be Connected To Worldwide Phenomenon," August 30,2013; CFTK, "Strange Sounds Heard All Over Terrace This Morning," August 29, 2013; and CTN News Saskatoon, "Strange Sounds Heard Over Saskatoon," November 11, 2013; and again the Huffington Post, "Are Strange Sounds Videos A Hoax?" April 9, 2012. For Loch Raven, see the Baltimore *Sun*, "'No place to run': Loch Raven Reservoir's forgotten UFO, 60 years later," October 22, 2018.

Chapter 47: Among the sources for lottery winner: *The Atlantic*, "A Treasury of Terribly Sad Stories of Lottery Winners," March 30, 2012; Syracuse.com, January 13, 2016, "Powerball jackpot: 13 unlucky lottery winners who were 'cursed' by the money"; among other resources, *Oddee* was used for Oak Island, "Nine Cursed Treasures," September 16, 2013. For Arthur Stilwell I primarily used Frank Edwards' *Stranger Than Science*.

Chapter 48: The account of the cabin attack is from *I Fought the Ape Men of Mount St. Helens, Washington*, by Fred Beck, 1967. Certain of the background information, as well as specifics concerning certain cases, such as the Lake Mack stone-throwing incident, in Ocala National Forest, come from the Bigfoot Field Research Organization. I spoke to the investigator from that organization, Dave Bakara, who now owns a museum called Expedition Bigfoot, in Florida, and who looked into the supposed Florida sighting, and I visited the location twice. I also consulted Kevin Smykal, who is in charge of BFRO investigations in the state.

Chapter 49: For the most folks have eaten, I used *Buzzfeed* as well as the Guinness Book of World Records. For Alexandrina I used the blog site of Glenn Dallaire, "Miracles of the Saints." For Prahlad: *Livescience*, May 10, 2010, "Indian Mystic Claims Not To Eat for 70 Years." BBC was a source for the Irishmen.

Chapter 50: I visited the Georgia Monuments, and also relied upon the granite company's literature, a phone call to the local government, online resources, and an article, "American Stonehenge: Monumental Instructions for the Post-Apocalypse," *Wired*, April 20, 2009.

Chapter 51: For the Peshtigo fire see my books, *Fear of Fire* and *Where the Cross Stands*. For ancient times, *The Atlantic Monthly*, "The Sky Is Falling," June of 2008; *The New York Times*, "Ancient Crash, Epic Wave," November 14, 2006; *Discover* Magazine, November 2007, "Did A Comet Cause the Great Flood?" November 15, 2007; see the blog site, People On Fire and an article posted there, "539 AD and 1014 AD . . . The Tsunamis From Hell," on April 11, 2016; and multiple scholarly papers such as Moe Mandelkehr's comprehensive papers include, "An Integrated Model for an Earthwide Event at 2300 BC, Part I: The Archeological Evidence," in S.I.S. Review, volume five; and two follow-up papers, "An Integrated Model for an Earthwide Event at 2300 B.C., Part II, the Climatological Evidence," in Chronology and Catastrophism Review and "An Integrated Model for an Earthwide Event at 2300 B.C., Part III, the Geological Evidence X. Natural Catastrophes During Bronze Age Civilizations" (Archaeopress, 1998). See also the work of Lars Franzen and Thomas B. Larsson in their paper "Landscape Analysis and stratigraphical and Geochemical investigations of Playa and Alluvial Fan Sediments in Tunisia and Raised Bog Deposits in Sweden" in the same valuable volume; British Archaeology, December 1997 issue, number 30, pages 6-7; and Courty and Weiss in "The Scenario of Environmental Degradation in the Tell Leilan Region, NE Syria, During the Late Third Millennium Abrupt Climate Change," in NATO ASI Series, volume I, 49. Third Millennium Abrupt Climate Change and Old World Collapse, edited by Weiss, along with N. Dalfes and G. Kulka (Springer-Verlag, Berlin: 1997). Some of the material on climate change comes from Moe Mandelkehr's paper "The Causal Source for the Climatic Changes," Chronology and Catastrophism Review, the 1999 issue. His quote on quakes is from "The Causal Source for the Geological Transients at 2300 B.C." in the same journal. For Egypt see Cyril Aldred's book The Egyptians (Thames and Hudson, 998). For the meteorite and comet in Greece see Comets, Popular Culture, and the Birth of Modern Cosmology by Sara Schechner Genuth (Princeton University Press 1997) and Comets by Donald K. Yeomans (John Wiley & Sons, 1991).

Chapter 52: The issue of *National Geographic* was January 6, 2006, "Hungry Ghosts" Keep Tourists From Tsunami-Hit Resorts"; the BBC report was on January 25, 2005, "Ghosts stalk Thai tsunami survivors"; for the other taxi accounts, see ABC News, January 14, 2005, "Thai tsunami trauma sparks foreign ghost sightings." For the tsunami in Japan see National Public Radio, "Tsunami's Ghosts Haunt Japanese Earthquake Survivors," March 16, 2014.

Chapter 53: This is largely from personal research. For the use of random event generators in ESP, see my piece, "Getting Serious About the Occult," in the October 1979 *Atlantic Monthly*. My book on psychic phenomena, which included chapters on Jordan, was as mentioned *PK: A Report on Psychokinesis*, released in 1976. There was also the cited newspaper article in the Binghamton *Sun-Bulletin* as well as from a transcript of the "Larry King Show," with guest host Nancy Grace, "Psychic Detectives," CNN, April 29, 2004. For Jordan finding the mayor's staple remover, see the Binghamton *Evening Press*, "Psychic Meets Test in Whitney Point," June 17, 1975.

Chapter 54: This is based on personal interviews as well as generic references and websites dedicated to cryptozoology. The quote from *National Geographic* was from the article, "Why Pterosaurs Were the Weirdest Wonders On Wings," November 2010.

Chapter 55: I met Beverly Raposa at one of my speaking engagements. I also consulted an article on a website called Ghosts and Ghouls, "Five Tales of Haunted Aircraft," June 25, 2012; another website called Flight, "Haunted Aircraft, Airports, and Museums" (undated); *News* from Australia (news.com.au), "Flight attendant reveals craziest plane 'ghost stories' she has heard," June 24, 2017; and Near-Death Experiences and the Afterlife, "Ghosts of Flight 401." The seminal book on this was *The Ghost of Flight 401*, by John G. Fuller.

Chapter 56: In addition to personal interviews, the accounts of strange dolls come largely from the internet news site *Buzzfeed*, "8 True Stories Of Cursed and Haunted Dolls," February 17, 2018. The account of Robert comes from the Key West Art and Historical Society, "Robert the Dolls." The quote on "Robert" is from *Atlas Obscura*, "The Story Behind the World's Most Terrifying doll," October 26, 2015. The quote on "Annabelle" is from the *Hindustan Times*, October 11, 2018. For "Charley," see "Charley the Haunted Doll," Atlas Obscura.

Chapter 57: The account of Anastasia comes from the book, *Strange Stories, Amazing Facts*, published by *Reader's Digest*, 1978. The Picard account comes from *The New York Times*, May 27, 1922, and the website for the Occult Museum, "Stranger Than Fiction: The Mysterious Disappearance of Little Pauline Picard," as well as the website for Historic Mysteries, "The Bizarre Story of Little Pauline Picard," May 1, 2017. See also a website called The Thread, www.ozy.com, "The Terrifying Disappearance of Little Pauline Picard," October 29, 2017.

Chapter 58: This comes from encyclopedias; the U.S. Center for Military History; as well as my visits to Ursuline, where I viewed Jefferson's letter; and my book, *Seven Days With Mary*. See also "Our Lady of Prompt Succor" by Marian T. Horvat on the website Tradition In Action.

Chapter 59: The first account—the fire—is a personal experience from 1989. For "Duck James!" see *Guideposts*, November 10, 2014, "Mysterious Voice That Sacred a Soldier." Other dreams come from internet lists.

Chapter 60: The quote on the Navajo reservation is from the *Huffington Post*, "Paranormal Files of the Navajo Rangers," December

6, 2017. My main source for historical information is the excellent compilation, *The Secret History of Crop Circles*, by Terry Wilson, a must-have reference for anyone pursuing this strange realm. See also, "The Crop Circle Mystery: A Closer Look," *Live Science*, June 9, 2017; "Ten of the Best Crop Circles Ever," *Collective Evolution*, June 29, 2013; "Reported Crop Circles for the State of Colorado," Independent Crop Circle Researchers' Association; and "Most complex crop circle ever discovered in British fields," the London *Telegraph*, June 17, 2008. I also referenced a BBC report, "Wiltshire's Wicked Witches," September 24, 2014. The website I quote is Phantoms and Monsters, June 16, 2012, "Stonehenge: Ancient Vortex?"

Chapter 61: The book I was working on was *The Toxic Cloud*, published by HarperCollins; Dr. Alexander is mention in Chapter 17; I also obtained a few details from a journal called *The Raging Pelican*, "Occupational Hazards: The Bizarre Case of Dr. Victor Alexander." My inclination: he was innocent.

Chapter 62: This information came from a tape recording made by Father Petar Ljubicic, spiritual director to Mirjana Soldo, that I had translated by a Croatian priest in Buffalo; details on the parchment come from a number of sources, most notably Mirjana's later book, *My Heart Will Triumph*, with Sean Bloomfield. Also, I interviewed Mirjana several times in Hercegovina. See also, for Ambassador Kingon, a more detailed account in my book, *The Day Will Come*.

Chapter 63: This information was from personal e-mails and an interview with Tan.

About the Author

Michael H. Brown is the author of twenty-eight books, including bestsellers *The Final Hour*, *The Other Side*, and *Laying Waste: The Poisoning of America*. His articles have appeared in publications such as *The Atlantic*, *Reader's Digest*, and *The New York Times Magazine*. He now specializes in spiritual books from a Christian perspective.